Business Rules and Information Systems

Business Rules and Information Systems

Aligning IT with Business Goals

Tony Morgan

✦Addison-Wesley

Boston • San Francisco • New York • Toronto • Montreal
London • Munich • Paris • Madrid • Capetown
Sydney • Tokyo • Singapore • Mexico City

The publisher offers discounts on this book when ordered in quantity for special sales. For more information, please contact:

Pearson Education Corporate Sales Division
201 W. 103rd Street
Indianapolis, IN 46290
(800) 428-5331

corpsales@pearsoned.com

Visit AW on the Web: www.aw.com/cseng/

Library of Congress Control Number: 2002101260

ISBN 0-201-74391-4
Text printed on recycled paper
1 2 3 4 5 6 7 8 9 10—CRS—0605040302
First printing, March 2002

Contents

List of Figures

Preface

Why this book

It seems that every week brings a new story about a software project or a system that's failed in some way. Quite often, the failures are so big that they make it to the national press. Most of the information given is anecdotal and circumstantial, but even a nontechnical observer might suspect that something is seriously wrong with the way we develop software systems.

My own view is that the core of the problem lies in the casual way we treat "the requirements": the statements that tell us what an information system is supposed to do. These statements are typically captured only in a rudimentary way, are poorly structured, and are linked to the software only by ideas in the heads of analysts and developers and so aren't open to examination or verification.

If we can return "the requirements" to a more prominent role in the process and use them to drive the subsequent development stages, we have the potential for a drastic reduction in the number of errors. Adding automation to this process can further reduce the opportunity for error and, as a bonus, also give big reductions in time and cost. We haven't been able to do this in the past, because there's been no clear strategy that we could adopt to drive things forward.

The idea of business rules, rooted in a business model, might provide part of the answer. But practical information on the topic is unexpectedly sparse, even though most of the basic ideas have been around for some time. Ideally, this book will help plug the gap.

The goals of this book

I wrote the book to pull together a load of separate strands and to show how they fit together to provide a coherent foundation for building information systems. In truth, very little in the book is completely new, and maybe that's a good thing. What we need is not so much new technology as a renewed focus on what's important.

The intention is not to convince you to use rules. You're already using them. In fact, if you're in a large organization, you probably have thousands of them. They guide the way your organization works, they make sure that you comply with legal and other regulations, and they are a source of competitive advantage or a barrier to success. But in most organizations, rules lead a shadowy existence. They may be enforced by your information systems, so that you're always directed toward the goals the business has adopted. But then again, the rules may not be so enforced.

You need to get an adequate level of control over your environment. I cannot know about your specific circumstances, but maybe the material in this book will help you to come up with some actions that put you in a better position to be a leader, not just a survivor, in your industry.

Although the information here is probably enough for you to develop your own complete set of tools and processes for building rule-centered systems, it's not really what I would recommend. Generally speaking, you should prefer a properly supported commercial product—if one exists—to a home-brewed tool. But all products have their little foibles, and before you fall into the arms of a particular vendor, you need to understand what you're gaining and what you're giving up. The information in this book should help you to ask the right questions before you make a commitment. You can also use the material in this book to help you to define any local "glue" that may be required to make your tool set stick together properly.

This book contains no information about particular commercial products or vendors. This comparatively new area for tool support is an immature technology, and is undergoing rapid change. Any descriptions of current tools would be out of date in a few months or even weeks. The best sources of information are the suppliers' Web pages, where you'll usually find product descriptions, white papers, and other supporting materials. Just search for terms like "business rule," pull out the sites that are on topic from the list returned, and build up your own set of favorites. You should also check out the Addison-Wesley Web site at www.aw.com/cseng/, where you'll find more information relating to this book.

Who should read this book

This book is aimed primarily at professionals working in the field of information technology (IT). If you have any involvement in the definition, creation, or management of an information system, you should be able to gain something of value from this book.

Analysts, responsible for capturing requirements and for specifying information systems, can find out more about producing logically complete definitions of the needs of the business. This includes understanding business models and their various constituents, knowing how to locate business rules, and determining how to express them in a form that maintains their true value.

Designers and developers, with responsibility for the implementation and testing of systems, can find practical examples of how business logic, expressed in the form of rules, can be conserved and taken forward into operational software. This also provides for two-way traceability between the worlds of specification and implementation.

Managers and strategists are obliged to take a higher-level view of the whole process. What they will find here are practical steps to help them to manage the intellectual property represented in a system, along with ideas for improving the development process in order to deliver information systems faster, cheaper, and, above all, to a level of quality that can far exceed current ad hoc methods.

How to use this book

Please don't treat this book as a set of edicts about what you should or should not do. It's meant to be a source of ideas that you can meld into your own approach to the needs of information systems in the twenty-first century.

The thing that resonates with me most strongly after engagements in a large number of IT environments is that they are different! Of course, there are similarities from place to place, but no one wants to be just the same as everyone else in their market sector. In fact, you can't really afford to be a "me too" player, who at best expects to survive, not to be a winner.

Using IT effectively requires you to balance out two different things.

- You need to be realistic about what technology can provide but also be prepared to take up new capabilities as they arise.
- You have to look for ways in which you can differentiate your operation by doing it faster, cheaper, or to a level of quality that the competition can't match.

The material in this book is aimed at providing you with the information you need to make crucial decisions in this area. I can't tell you how to run your business, but I can provide pointers to ideas that you may be able to use to lead your industry in the application of information technology.

The content falls into four main parts. Part I—A New Approach to Information Systems—sets the scene by suggesting how we could begin to approach information systems in a different way. Chapter 1 paints a picture of an alternative future that uses structured descriptions of a business to drive system development. Chapter 2 fills in some of the background on what we mean by structuring and managing knowledge about a business. This chapter introduces business models and the role they can play in meeting the demands of new business directions, such as e-commerce.

Although business rules have a particularly important part to play here, they are probably the least well documented of all the business model elements. Part II—Capturing Business Rules—therefore delves into rules in greater depth and provides some fairly detailed information that should help you to set up a sound framework for delivering logical business descriptions. Chapter 3 explains how to define business rules in a systematic way. Chapter 4 discusses how to identify business rules and pull them into a managed environment. Chapter 5 shows how the business logic that underlies the rules can be validated, providing assurance that the intentions of the business have been captured accurately so that later stages can proceed with confidence.

In Part III—Implementing Business Rules—we take a look at the other end of the process and consider realistic mechanisms for the implementation of information systems and business rules in particular. Chapter 6 reviews the kinds of technical architectures that dominate in most organizations and shows where rules can fit into the kinds of structure that are likely to be available. Chapter 7 goes into more detail on the various ways that business rules can be realized using readily available technology. Chapter 8 discusses ways of managing rules and models and the part they play in information system development.

Finally, Part IV—The Role of Business Rules—rounds things out by summarizing the current state of play. Chapter 9 shows how business rules build on long-standing ideas about structuring descriptions of interactions between people and between people and machines and points to some directions that this may take in the future. Chapter 10 gives a summary of the main characteristics of business rules and the value they can provide.

The Appendix summarizes the key elements of logic that need to be understood by anyone working with business rules. If you're entirely comfortable with the ideas of formal logic, you can skip this material, but you may want to dip into it if you feel the need for a refresher.

Most of all, I would be happy if this book encourages you to think about information systems in a different way. Let's focus on producing a logically complete description of what we want and let the machines take care of the details.

Acknowledgments

The core ideas in this book were forged in the heat of an extended Unisys R&D project called Columbus. Somewhat ahead of its time, this project was a rare attempt to explore the trade-offs between technical versus commercial and abstract versus pragmatic: to find a more systematic way of building information systems. Many colleagues at Unisys made valuable contributions, and much of the consensus that emerged from that hard-won experience is reflected in the pages that follow. In particular, Peter Barnsley, Joe Barrett, John Duplock, and Kelly Potter showed me how even the toughest problems can be overcome by the right blend of experience, technical know-how, and a sense of fun (and croissants).

While the book was taking shape, several of the ideas were further sharpened through discussion with partners in the SITE project at Brunel University. Sergio de Cesare, Mark Lycett, Valerie Martin, and Ray Paul all provided valuable insights that helped me to clarify some fuzzy areas and gave me a better understanding of the research context.

Dot Malson at Unisys and Peter Gordon at Addison-Wesley nursed the book through its development and generally kept the project on track throughout its extended gestation period. Their advice and encouragement made a daunting task seem realistic.

Two other influences deserve acknowledgment. The first is Ron Ross, who for many years has provided thoughtful leadership for the business rules community. His seminars on this subject are a model of clarity, and I highly recommend them to anyone interested in this field. The second is the late Bob Muller, who gently spurred many of his colleagues at SPL, SDL, and elsewhere to be more creative than they ever believed they could be.

Last, but certainly not least, thanks to Gwen, Eleanor, and Robert for putting up with all the stress and the strain that goes with writing—at least the way I do it!

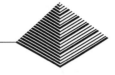

PART I

A NEW APPROACH TO INFORMATION SYSTEMS

1

The Problem

1.1 What this book is about

Like some other hot topics in information technology (IT), *business rule* is one of those terms that many people use but few can define. Over the past few years, we've seen the level of interest in business rules rising rapidly, which is a useful indicator that they might have some value in building modern information systems. It's now quite common to find books and articles on multitiered architectures advocating the use of business rules, or *business logic,* in a middle layer of processing, somewhere between the user interface and back-end servers.

In spite of this rush of enthusiasm, little hard information is to be found on business rules. Analysts, designers, developers, managers, and anyone else involved in creating systems must either rely on external consultants or commercial products or work out his or her own approach from first principles. With a few honorable exceptions, most published discussion of business rules is either vague or trivialized into a couple of lines of Visual Basic code.

The fact is that all organizations operate in accordance with a set of underlying principles—that's what "organization" means. Among other things, these principles define the "business logic" that governs the way in which the business conducts itself. There's scope for plenty of variation in the principles adopted by different businesses, even in the same sector, because of the need for differentiation in the market. However, there are also many points of similarity: some arising because of common external forces, such as legislation, and others because of common goals, such as profitability.

It's certainly true that businesses are not always fully aware of their own business logic. Often, many factors that crucially affect business operations are buried in office memoranda, informal local practices, "folklore," and so on. The aim is to replace all this with a set of clear statements that describes how the business intends to conduct itself.

1.1.1   Why should you care?

Powerful information systems ought to be able to stimulate new business ventures, so let's brainstorm a couple of possibilities. Here's an idea for a new kind of banking service.

- About 10 percent of accounts will be handled correctly, without errors.
- Most customers will be subject to unpredictable and unexpected bank charges after their accounts have been opened.
- Access to funds will be unpredictable and subject to arbitrary delays.
- A significant proportion of transactions will fail to be posted for the majority of accounts.
- At least 10 percent of accounts will just disappear, leaving those customers without funds.

Would you use this bank?

Here's another suggestion, this time for a new-style public transportation system.

- About 10 percent of journeys will arrive on time, with passengers charged the advertised fare.
- Most fares will be subject to arbitrary surcharges, which will be demanded after departure.
- Journey times will be unpredictable and subject to random delays after departure.
- The majority of journeys will stop short of their intended destinations.
- At least 10 percent of journeys will end in crashes.

Want to buy a ticket?

We would have grave doubts about the sanity of anyone who made these as serious suggestions. But here's how it really is in the strange world of information technology.

- About 10 percent of projects will complete on time and within the planned budgets.
- Most projects will suffer from unexpected cost increases after starting.
- Project durations will be unpredictable, and most projects will overrun.
- The majority of projects will fail to deliver their intended benefits.
- At least 10 percent of projects will be canceled before completion

The levels of performance accepted as normal in IT would be considered utterly appalling by the standards of any other mature industry. Even though many information systems are alive and well and doing a good job, their results have been achieved at a very high cost. We're continually bombarded with stories of software failure and spiraling costs that even make the nontechnical press. Here are some conservative estimates.

- Of the average IT budget, 10 percent is spent on projects that never deliver measurable benefits.
- Of the average IT budget, 25 percent is spent on rectifying errors in previously delivered software.

As a first approximation, and allowing for the fact that we will never be perfect, it seems reasonable to assume that at least a quarter of the total worldwide spend figure on IT goes to paying for various kinds of failure. The total worldwide annual spend figure on IT is about $1 trillion; on this basis, the cost of failure is around $250 billion every year! We can add to this the consequential losses suffered as a result of software failure—loss of trading opportunities, unproductive staff, falling investor confidence, and so on—which could turn out to be a similar order of magnitude.

It's clear that the total cost of our inability to produce software in a well-ordered way runs into hundreds of billions of dollars per year, and the figure is growing. Countless efforts have been made over the past 30 years or more to fix various parts of the process. Although these efforts may have helped to contain the problem, they obviously haven't solved it. This leaves a lingering suspicion that maybe it's the process itself that's fundamentally flawed.

Our current development culture puts a huge emphasis on programming, and the popular perception is that 90 percent of building an information system relies on the cleverness of the coders. Several Hollywood movies have perpetuated the myth by featuring teenaged hackers as their heroes.

As always, the reality is different. Many research projects have shown that the vast majority of software problems originates from specification error, not from the code as such. Putting it simply, the programmers are programming the wrong things, and no amount of cleverness in the coding can compensate.

Frustratingly, few people seem to care. The number of books published on programming is orders of magnitude greater than books on analysis and specification. We seem to just keep on doing the same things in the blind hope that it will come out right next time, but unless we address the root causes of the problems, there's no rational reason why it ever should.

The biggest problem of all is the industry mindset. We won't make real progress until we're brave enough to challenge some fixed ideas on "this is the way it's done." This means opening the door to new ways of thinking and being willing to reengineer the development process if there's a promising alternative.

1.1.2   What is a business rule?

Basically, a business rule is a compact statement about an aspect of a business. The rule can be expressed in terms that can be directly related to the business, using simple, unambiguous language that's accessible to all interested parties: business owner, business analyst, technical architect, and so on.

It's a constraint, in the sense that a business rule lays down what must or must not be the case. At any particular point, it should be possible to determine that the condition implied by the constraint is true in a logical sense; if not, remedial action is needed. This interpretation, which might be described as Boolean from a software perspective, is the main reason that the term *business logic* is so commonly used.

GUIDE (an IBM-oriented industry user group) produced a useful, quite widely quoted definition of a business rule: "a statement that defines or constrains some aspect of the business. It is intended to assert business structure or to control or influence the behavior of the business." This is as close as you're likely to get to a satisfactory short statement of what we mean by a business rule. Of course, one rule does not a business make, but this simple idea is a building block from which we can construct systems of surprising power.

Capturing the logic of an entire business would require probably many thousands of rules; a smaller subsystem, perhaps several hundred. Even so, the individual rules are small and relatively easy to understand, simplifying such tasks as discovery, definition, review, and maintenance.

All this may sound a bit daunting, but individual rule statements can be—and indeed ought to be—quite straightforward. The following examples give an idea of what you can expect. These are just isolated examples and aren't meant to demonstrate any particular business area, but they do show the size and complexity of rule we'll be dealing with.

R101   A valid inbound Contact must be associated with a specific Customer.

R102   A withdrawal from an account may be made only if the account balance is greater than zero.

R103   A Customer must be considered as high worth if at least one of the following is true:
—The Customer is a VIP,
—The Customer has a current balance of at least X,
—The Customer has held an account for more than Y years.

1.2   The way we build software

To understand the importance of business rules, we need to take a look at how we build information systems. Figure 1-1 shows a sketch of the system development process as it exists in most places today.

Of course, this is highly simplified and hides a lot of detail. For instance, deployment of the software also involves some form of testing to make sure that the installation has fully completed and that the new software is interacting correctly with other system elements. Nonetheless, even this high-level view is enough to point out some features that should worry us.

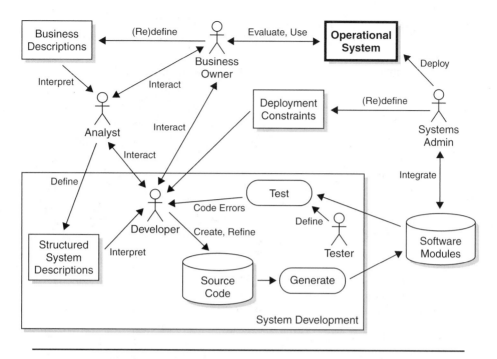

Figure 1-1   The current development process

- The business owner—the person who needs the software and is presumably paying for its development—is somewhat remote from the process. Once an initial description of the business need has been created, typically in the form of a requirements specification, involvement is limited to interaction through technical specialists, mainly because the materials generated and used in development are difficult to understand without special training and experience.

- The process contains an implicit acceptance of frailty. It's taken for granted that the code produced will contain errors and that a significant amount of testing may be necessary—perhaps up to a third of the project. Even worse, the testing has to be terminated when the number of errors has reached an acceptable level. Any changes to the software may introduce new errors, so the opportunities to improve quality by refining the process are limited. A certain likelihood of undetected residual problems always has to be accepted.

- The process relies a lot on descriptive material that has to be interpreted by people with the right kinds of skills to turn it into development products. Typically, analysts interpret the business requirements to produce a design document, and developers interpret the design document into the source code. This sequence introduces many possible places for misunderstandings that may not get detected until very late in the process.

- The process is very labor intensive. Almost every major step, apart from generation of the deployable software from the source code, is undertaken by manual effort. Not only that, the people involved require specialized skills, making them difficult to find and expensive to retain.

- The process is fairly slow. For a large system, moving from a requirements specification to operational software can take years. Some big software projects have been abandoned, at huge cost, because the needs of the organization were changing more quickly than the software could be developed. Even a small system can take weeks or months of development before it's delivered.

- There's little separation of concerns. For example, business needs and deployment constraints tend to be integrated only in the mind of the developer. The resulting source code often tangles these together in a way that's very difficult to unpick. This makes it difficult to do things that could be highly beneficial to the business, such as moving a working system to a newer technology base to take advantage of lower hardware and support costs.

We could go on, but the drift is probably already clear. Developing software is risky, slow, and expensive. This is especially relevant for e-commerce, for which a system may represent a one-time, make-or-break opportunity that simply *must* go live within a very limited time frame.

Why do we do it this way? The answer is the dead hand of history. In the earliest days of computing, the key step was creating the machine instructions that coordinated the activities of the various elements: arithmetic unit, primary and secondary storage, and so on. High-level languages provided a welcome abstraction away from many of the details and created the job of "computer programmer." Since then, many, many technical enhancements have been added, and various supporting specializations have emerged, but the craft skill of programming has remained central.

The codecentric view of life probably reached its zenith during the 1980s, when many organizations ploughed huge sums of money into software engineering environments, which were aimed mainly at increasing programmer productivity and reducing errors in released code. The 1990s started to see a shift in perspective, as people who were born during the early days of commercial computing began to make their presence felt in the workplace—some of them as business owners. Questions began to be raised, such as, Why is a page of C++ produced in the 1990s no more intelligible to the business than a page of assembly code from the 1950s?

Probably the biggest question of all is, Can we find a better way?

1.3   The vision

1.3.1   How could it be?

There has to be a better way. To find it, we need to start without any preconceived ideas about what software development should be or how to accommodate existing practices. Take a look at Figure 1-2.

What's changed? From this view, it's basically only the system development process. Improvements could also be made in such areas as systems administration, but that's part of a different story and would only be a distraction here. After all, someone has to look after the (server) farm!

As before, we're sticking to a high-level viewpoint and omitting a lot of detail. It's clear that the system development box has become a lot simpler, but why? The key step is automation of the craft skill of programming. After all, who better to write a set of machine instructions than another machine? To see how this might be practical, we need to follow the process in sequence.

First, the business owner describes his or her needs. This is similar to the start of the traditional process but with one crucial change. We provide the business owner with some means to *structure* the description: to organize the material—text, diagrams, tables, or whatever—in particular predefined ways.

Why structure? Because it allows us to use machine processing to analyze the descriptions. It would be nice if we could let the business owner ruminate on

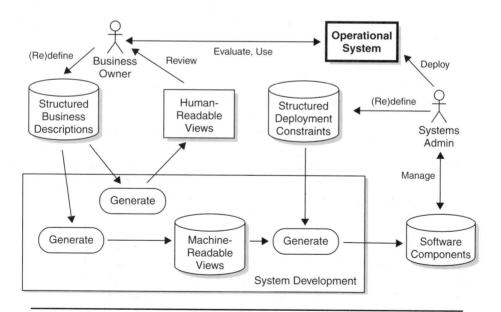

Figure 1-2   The way it could be

ambitions, goals, aims, objectives, and so on in a free-thinking kind of way and then get a machine to reorganize the resulting mess into a crisp definition of what that means in computing terms. If only. Perhaps a HAL—the computer from the movie *2001*—of the future will be able to decode the subtleties of human language with 100 percent reliability, but in the near term, we need to give the machine some clues about what it's looking at.

Once we have a structured description, what can we do with it? The most immediate need is to generate a human-readable view of the structure. This allows the business owner to rectify any misunderstandings or omissions before going further. It also provides a kind of contractual statement, with the development system effectively saying, "This is what I promise to implement."

Once the description at the business level is acceptable, things can move on. The next step is to generate an equivalent machine-readable view of the same description. This is really the key to the whole process. The human definer of the system and the machine implementer of the system are sharing the *same* description; they're just handling it in the way to which each is best suited.

Given the definition of what the business wants and a machine-readable set of deployment constraints—what machines? how connected? what operating system and version? . . .—there's no reason, in principle, why the construction of the code should not be completely automated.

This is important, so it's worth saying again. If we have a complete definition of the functionality required and a complete description of the processing environment, the creation of the software to do a specific job in a specific environment can be reduced to a mindless automated process. Not a simple one, that's for sure. A lot of internal structure may be hidden inside the innocent Generate box. Big programs, intermediate files, agendas, blackboards, processes, and decisions on thread management: You name it; it's going to be there. But the key point is that no technology barrier stands in the way.

One other point to get a grip on at the output end is the way that software is packaged up for deployment. No matter how hard we try, we just can't seem to stop development spilling over into operations. Did you ever buy an automobile that asks you to enter a code to define the brand of gas when you fill up? Did you ever buy a flashlight that needed a special 11.2-volt power cell, because that maximizes bulb efficiency? If you put a hard disk into a computer, do you care about the physical properties of disk coatings? Voice coil technology versus stepper motors? It's doubtful. More likely, you look at the type of interface, the physical form factor, the seek time, and other issues that are going to make a difference to your computer.

Sadly, in the software world, the demands of producers have triumphed over consumers. It's time to fight back. Software needs to be packaged for convenience of use, just like hardware. Anyone who has to operate a software utility should not have to worry about how the software got developed. It should be hermetically sealed—who cares about what's inside?—and provided with clearly labeled interfaces that can be used to join it up with other, similarly accommodating pieces of software.

This is already under way under the banner of component-based development (CBD), although progress is still hampered by disputes that spill over from the residue of programming. What's needed is a view that clearly separates how it was made from how it gets used. Once we achieve this goal, the job of rolling out any new software becomes much easier. It's more like upgrading the lighting or the power distribution. It still needs to be done right, but there aren't so many nasty surprises on the way.

1.3.2   Some implications

Before looking at the practicality of this vision, let's speculate on how it might change the way we do things. What would it mean if this really could be done?

Most obvious is the potential for a huge reduction in the time needed to develop a system, once the requirements have stabilized. What might have taken weeks or months could be done in minutes or hours. This might be partly offset by some additional time needed to structure the business description, but the net gain is still considerable.

Alongside this, there would be a shift in the staffing profile needed. Although a small increase in the number of analysts might be needed, very large reductions in the numbers of developers and testers would certainly be realized.

Software quality would improve. Most of the opportunities for human error would be eliminated by machine translation of structured specifications. Because the process is data driven, the generating software, as distinct from the generated software, would need to change only rarely. It's therefore much easier to stabilize the environment and to identify process improvements.

The efficiency of generated software would probably be lower than the equivalent written by a skilled programmer, although the history of optimizing compilers indicates that this could be reduced to a fairly small percentage. In any case, the cost of a hardware increment to bring performance up to the same level as cunningly crafted software would be trivial compared to the potential savings.

Finally, a number of knock-on effects would change the commercial landscape somewhat. For example, there would be little point in buying packaged application software. Much better to buy a set of structured specifications representing some specialized know-how—say, in accounting or human resources—and build that into your own software. That way, you avoid the compromises needed to accommodate a packaged view, you eliminate interfacing problems, and you can introduce wrinkles that your competitors don't have.

1.4   Is this really practical?

Because the advantages seem so compelling, why isn't everyone producing software this way already? It's pretty obvious that there must be some barrier to implementation. In fact, it's not one single thing.

The idea of creating code from a model has been around for a long time, but it has never made the breakthrough to being a mainstream activity. There are several reasons for this.

- Code generation has mostly been seen as subservient to manual programming: a convenience that a programmer might entertain to save some time and effort. The result is that techniques are small scale and casual, management happens only at a personal level, and there's little consistency about how or where it's applied.
- Current styles of models do not provide the richness of information that would be needed for larger-scale automation. At present, modeling tools and techniques support only the production of scraps of code, which require considerable extra work by a programmer before they're of any practical use.
- There's little agreement on how the needs of the business and the constraints imposed by a particular technical architecture could be expressed in a systematic way. In both cases, these need to have a well-defined structure that's easy for an automation tool to navigate.
- Generating a significant chunk of a system is much more difficult than most people think. It requires the application of a great deal of knowledge that's currently hidden away in the heads of IT specialists. Capturing this knowledge and applying it effectively are not trivial tasks.

There's no need to feel too depressed, though. All the pieces of the puzzle exist. No radical technology breakthrough is needed to make progress. But we do need to make wholesale changes to many parts of the development process, and that's difficult to achieve in a single jump.

A more realistic strategy is to "adopt, adapt, and improve"—in other words, *evolution* instead of *revolution*. By making incremental changes to the development process, you can gradually shift from the kind of traditional twentieth-century programming shop shown in Figure 1-1 toward the streamlined operation of Figure 1-2 that's needed for e-commerce in the twenty-first century. A sketch of such an intermediate stage is shown in Figure 1-3.

Again, this is a high-level view that omits a lot of detail. However, it shows several key places where we can start to make improvements along the right lines. Here are some things we can do immediately.

- Provide increasing structure in the description of the business needs. Generate feedback for the business owner from these descriptions, using formats that don't require deep technical knowledge.
- Improve structuring in the description of the computing environment. Where automated usage is not practical, try to hook these constraints to the business descriptions, so that they can be used together.
- Generate fragments of code from the enhanced business descriptions. As the structuring improves, so can the size and the scope of the code fragments.

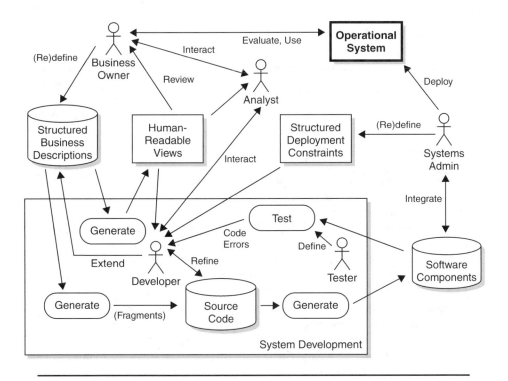

Figure 1-3 A practical way forward

- Focus program development on refinement and extension of generated code instead of its creation. Within limits, accept some degree of inefficiency in the resulting code.
- Package developed software in component form to simplify subsequent management and deployment. Focus on interfaces, and hide implementation details as much as possible.
- Raise the profile of process improvement so that it's recognized as a key activity. Use good people in this role, quantify and measure the process, and keep it under continual review.
- Reduce common system elements to templates that can be managed and reused. Increase levels of commonality by moving differentiators out into rules or rule sets.

Even though none of these steps is particularly controversial, it can still be difficult to know where to start. Is software componentization the same as object-oriented programming? How can the quality of the development process be measured? What exactly does a structured business description look like, anyway?

1.5   Moving forward

This book is an attempt to answer these questions and others of the same kind. No simple patch will magically transform the way you produce software. Progress will be required on many fronts, not the least of which is likely to be changing the organizational mindset to understand why it's even worth making the effort. But the prize at stake is a big one. Organizations that do evolve will have an increasing advantage over competitors that do not. In the extreme, commercial organizations that cling to craft practices will cease to exist.

Even if you're a long way from automating your software production, you can still gain a lot from this approach. Software development is notoriously risky, error prone, and expensive. The worldwide cost of rogue software probably runs into hundreds of billions of dollars per year. Improving software quality will repay the investment many times over, even in a craft programming shop.

Later chapters go into a lot more detail about the issues we've just covered. The intention is not to impose a particular framework but to explain how and why each element can be improved. Given enough information, you should be in a position to translate this into what makes sense in your own organization, whether it means internal development, the injection of external expertise, purchased packages or tools, or some combination of all these.

Before summarizing what we're going to deal with later, it's worth noting one thing that lies outside our scope: any coverage of interfacing, especially user interfaces. Instead, our main interest is centered on the core business functionality. In fact, as we'll see later, it's worth going to some trouble to make sure that these two things are definitely decoupled. For instance, it might be desirable to change the look of a Web site to reflect marketing initiatives or sales seasons, just as traditional stores might change their window displays. These changes can, and probably should, be made completely independently of the major business functions.

That's not to say that user interfaces are unimportant. On the contrary, they can have a big effect on the success of an e-commerce site. They're simply a different subject, and trying to include them in our present concerns would just be confusing. The business functionality we'll be defining could work with pretty much any kind of interface: browser, Win32 GUI (graphical user interface), even character-based green screens. The broad assumption built into the remainder of the book is that this is likely to be accomplished by using structured messages in an application-, vendor-, and technology-neutral format. If you need a more concrete picture, visualize some form of mark-up language, such as XML (eXtensible Markup Language), for the content, plus style sheets to define the graphical layout.

1.6   Where we stand

Before moving on to more detail, it's worth taking a moment to summarize the ideas we've covered so far.

- The low quality levels common in the software industry result in a huge burden of unnecessary cost. This hits companies in all sectors, not just specialist IT companies.
- Most problems arise during the initial analysis and specification stages of system development. The majority of problems can be traced back to the lack of a sufficiently clear definition of business requirements.
- Regardless of the extent to which we introduce automation into development, we can take some sensible actions right away.
  - State business needs in a form that is easy to understand for the business owner.
  - Structure these business descriptions so that they can be checked for coverage and consistency and can be navigated by automation tools.
  - Use these structured and logically consistent descriptions to drive the development process.

Before we get down to the detail of how we can capture the business logic in the form of rules, we need to understand how they fit into the bigger picture. The next chapter describes how we can go about producing a richly structured description of a business. It's time to look at business models.

2

Frameworks, Architectures, and Models

2.1 Needful abstractions

The future scenario painted in the previous chapter has some tempting features, but we obviously can't deliver on it right now. Unless you're working for a remarkably advanced organization, you'll likely need to put several things in place before the pieces of the puzzle start to join up properly.

One of the most important pieces—probably the single most important one—is the notion of describing the needs of the business in a richly structured form. Ultimately, this is how we will be able to provide sufficient grip for a machine to get hold of what's being described. But this is not just about wholesale automation; the same structured representation can also provide the basis for big improvements in quality and reductions in cost, even if the software is developed manually. The real prize is the ability to produce a complete, accurate, and detailed statement of the requirements for our information system. This will allow us to eliminate a large proportion of the problems that plague current software development, regardless of how we create the code.

The generic term that we'll use for this kind of structured description is a *business model*, although the term *enterprise model* is also used. The term business as used here includes governmental and not-for-profit organizations, which share the same commitment to operate in what we could call a businesslike way. In this chapter, we'll look at what's needed to create a model of this kind and the features that can provide hooks for subsequent stages of development. We'll start with a very high level view of what modeling is about and then zoom in to look at the various elements in more detail. The outer limits of what might be included in a model of this sort are defined by the bounds on the enterprise, as shown in Figure 2-1.

Because reality is complicated and messy, we need some abstractions that help us to see though the confusion and to impose some order on the chaos, and

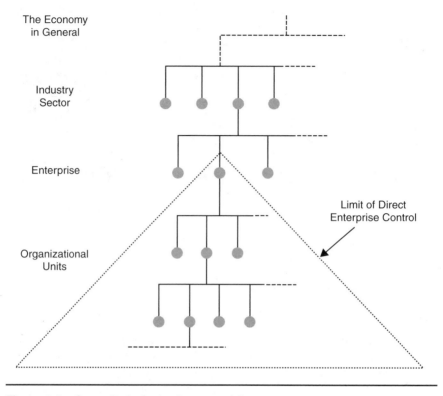

Figure 2-1   Scope limits for business model

we'll look at these in more detail shortly. The main motivation is, ultimately, to deliver an information system to support the business, but it's worth noting that these abstractions are useful for other purposes, including

- Defining how the business works, or should work, which is closely related to the aims of many organizations to acquire quality certification to ISO (International Organization for Standardization) 9000 or similar standards
- Identifying key business processes so that they can be tracked, measured, and improved as necessary
- Supporting the training of new staff on "the way we do things"
- Providing a common vocabulary for the various stakeholders in the business to discuss issues of common concern

Although quite a few candidates have been put forward as the right way to do business modeling, there's only tenuous agreement among them, and there's certainly no accepted industry standard. You're perfectly entitled to make up your own mind about what's useful for your particular situation. Here, we're not going to try to impose a particular one-size-fits-all view of what kinds of models you should produce. Instead, we'll try to clarify the issues involved, so that you'll be in a position to make sensible decisions to suit your own circumstances.

If you're intending to produce anything more than a trivial model, you're going to need some solid tool support. You can treat the information here as either a checklist of features to look for in a purchased tool or as an initial but negotiable set of requirements if you want to build your own.

It's easy to become disoriented by the variety of ideas floating around. Because most of them describe abstract things that have no tangible form, it's difficult to get a clear picture of what's being described.

For the purpose of this book, we'll take a simplified approach. At a high level, we'll focus on just three kinds of abstraction: frameworks, architectures, and models. Each of these terms has many overlapping shades of meaning, so we need to take just a little time to be clear about the way they're going to be interpreted here.

2.1.1   Frameworks

We'll start with frameworks because, conceptually, they should be considered first. It's only fairly recently that people have started to discuss such things explicitly, and many—perhaps most—organizations stumble into more detailed activities without having any clear framework in mind.

From our perspective, the purpose of a framework is to define the way in which we're going to describe the information system of an organization. "System" here does not necessarily mean just an automation system; we need to think about people too. A *framework*, in the sense that we're describing it, is a piece of virtual scaffolding that provides places to hang some less abstract notions that come later. You can't build a physical example of it, but you need its help to structure your progress into the unknown.

A framework will give you

- A checklist for the dimensions that you need to consider in modeling
- A context for understanding the relationships among various information system properties
- A consistent baseline vocabulary for communication within the organization

The best-known framework is probably the Framework for Enterprise Architecture, first described by John Zachman (1987) and usually just referred to as "the Zachman Framework." Zachman himself consistently and carefully explains that the framework is intended to be an aid to thinking and should not be taken as a detailed catalog of parts that can be bolted together directly to form an information system.

The distinctive feature is its arrangement of concerns in a two-dimensional grid. The rows of the grid represent different viewpoints, or perspectives, that can be taken when looking at an information system. The columns represent various aspects of the system, corresponding to the different kinds of questions that could be asked about it.

We'll start with the rows and the perspectives they cover. All perspectives are equally valid, and all can coexist. However, there's normally an evolution of ideas, and so the rows are arranged (downward) in an order that roughly corresponds to the sequence of their appearance during the growth of an information system. Table 2-1 describes the purpose of each row.

Table 2-1   Rows of the Zachman Framework

Row	Viewpoint (Perspective)	Typical Viewpoint of
1	Scope (contextual)	Planner
2	Enterprise model (conceptual)	Owner
3	System model (logical)	Designer
4	Technology model (physical)	Builder
5	Detailed representations	Subcontractor
6	Functioning enterprise	-

The columns (see Table 2-2) represent the various dimensions that need to be considered at each level of an information system. Again, these are not alternatives: All dimensions have to be taken into account to give an adequate all-round picture. The questions echo the well-known lines by Kipling from his poem "The Elephant's Child":

I keep six honest serving-men
(They taught me all I knew);
Their names are What and Why and When
And How and Where and Who.

Table 2-2   Columns of the Zachman Framework

Column	Aspect	Answers the Question
1	Data	What
2	Function	How
3	Network	Where
4	People	Who
5	Time	When
6	Motivation	Why

The row/column grid provides a set of coordinates, each of which represents a particular aspect as seen from a specific viewpoint. The cells at each intersection can be used to hold a description of the kind of element that's relevant. The examples suggested by Zachman for each cell are shown, slightly abbreviated, in Table 2-3.

Table 2-3 The Zachman Framework

	What	How	Where	Who	When	Why
Scope	List of things	List of processes	List of locations	List of organizations	List of events	List of goals
Enterprise Model	Semantic model	Business process	Business logistics	Workflow model	Master schedule	Business plan
System Model	Logical data model	Application architecture	Distributed system architecture	Human interface architecture	Processing structure	Business rule model
Technology Model	Physical data model	System design	Technology architecture	Presentation architecture	Control structure	Rule design
Detailed Representations	Data definition	Program	Network architecture	Security architecture	Timing definition	Rule specification
Functioning Enterprise	Data	Function	Network	Organization	Schedule	Strategy

Because the cell contents are only examples, we don't need to get too hung up on their precise interpretation. It's also worth repeating that this is a framework for thinking about information systems, not a decree that they be subdivided into exactly 36 boxes—or 30 if you leave out the Functioning Enterprise row. As an example, take the How and Who cells of the Enterprise Model viewpoint. It maybe wasn't so common in 1987, but business processes today are often implemented through automated workflow systems. Their separation in the framework is the result of an emphasis on different aspects—in this case, how things happen versus who does things; it's not meant to imply that these features must always be forcibly separated into different packages, models, tools, or any other kind of compartment. A key point to be aware of is that joining cells together can result in overlooking a particular aspect or a viewpoint, and you need to be sure that the use of a common tool, notation, or other device does not cause an important facet to be neglected.

Many other frameworks exist, but they usually highlight a particular row or column—or even just a cell—with the claim that this is the truly important way of thinking about information systems. The Zachman Framework is preferred by many people because it encourages a balanced picture and offers the kind of rich structure that we need for more sophisticated development approaches. It's sometimes criticized for not being sufficiently prescriptive, but that's not what it sets out to do. To take the next step, we need to make some decisions about particular choices of architecture.

2.1.2 Architectures

The use of the word *architecture* in computing has been inspired by some similarities between the planning, design, and construction of buildings and their equivalents in information systems. Practitioners in the built environment tend to frown on this crossfertilization. In fact, they're right, although maybe not for their original reasons. The computing usage tends to lump together things that are separated more clearly in the world of bricks and mortar. It's too late, though; the computing usage has already made it into dictionary definitions!

Generally speaking, you can expect an architecture in the computing sense to cover two main things:

- Definitions of the various kinds of building blocks available
- Rules that govern how these can be put together to make a more complex artifact

As we'll see, several kinds of architectures are possible, each with its own set of parts and construction rules. *Architecture* is such a comfortable term that there's a danger of overusing it; for instance, no less than seven examples are mentioned in the Zachman Framework. You should also be warned that the term often arouses strong passions, as well as heated debate about whether something should be described as an architecture. We'll try to be frugal with the word and also define a fairly limited interpretation.

If you look at the blue-sky vision presented in the previous chapter from a very high level vantage point, you can see that it views the development of an information system as relying on two key inputs:

1. A structured description of what the business wants to do

2. A definition of the technology that's to be used to achieve this

And it produces two main outputs:

3. A set of human-readable views of the business definition

4. Specific software components, or modules, that together realize an appropriate information system

For the moment, we'll put (3) to one side, because changing it does not fundamentally affect the information system in the way that a change to (1), (2), or (4) would. In old-fashioned terminology, (3) is simply a set of reports. Changing their format might affect the visibility of some part of a system definition—and, hence, indirectly influence whether the system covers the right things—but would not directly alter what the system does.

The remaining three areas are the ones we're going to define in terms of architectures. Let's start with a brief definition of each.

- *Business architecture* is a way of describing businesses and what they do or intend to do in the future. The building blocks available represent various aspects of the business. No single aspect is the most important; all are necessary to give a balanced picture of what a business is all about. We can use the business architecture to produce business models: descriptions of specific businesses, couched in a consistent and well-defined vocabulary. The business architecture corresponds reasonably to the Conceptual viewpoint in the Zachman Framework, although the terminology is not necessarily the same.

- *Technical architecture* defines the technology building blocks that can be used to create specific information systems. As in the business case, the architecture does not represent an individual situation; rather, a wide variety of systems could be built from the generic capabilities described. If worthwhile, you can gain extra flexibility by expressing the technical architecture at more than one level. For example, your generic database technology might be relational, with your specific product choice being Oracle or SQL Server. The technical architecture corresponds roughly to the Logical viewpoint in the Zachman Framework.

- *Component architecture* describes the technology output from the development process: the nuts and bolts of the modular units that are deployed to realize an organization's information needs. This architecture describes how independently released elements can be managed and composed together to make a working system. It's obviously highly dependent on choices made in framing the technical architecture. The component architecture corresponds very crudely to the Physical viewpoint in the Zachman Framework.

It's worth emphasizing that these three architectures are not different levels of description, in the sense that lower levels are more detailed expansions of higher levels. Each of the architectures describes something different, and the relationships among them are complex and nontrivial.

One thing that complicates these definitions is that various concerns are not always well separated in the real world. For example, it would be nice if we could define information systems in terms of functional components without worrying about the technology used to build them. In practice, functionality and technology can become horribly confused. For example, Enterprise JavaBeans—functional components—are totally dependent on the choice of one particular programming language.

The preceding definitions effectively cover rows 2, 3, and 4 of the Zachman Framework, albeit with slightly differing terminology. For our purposes, it's not necessary to define architectures corresponding to the other rows of the framework. Row 1 consists of comparatively unstructured statements about what should be considered as in or out of scope. This will influence what gets put into a business model. For example, should we consider the whole organization? Or just the subsidiary in Brazil? Or just the manufacturing division? The scope will tell us, but somehow "architecture" doesn't seem to be an appropriate word. Similarly, row 5 contains detailed technology artifacts that already have well-established names: data definition, program, and so on. Row 6 is the functioning enterprise itself and so can't really be thought of as an architecture.

You may feel the urge to use the A-word more than three times. For example, you may want to define security architecture as part of your technical architecture.

That's fine: All we're saying here is that "separation of concerns" should be your guideline, and you'll have a minimum of three concerns.

In the remainder of this chapter, we focus on the business architecture and how we can go about building business models. We cover the technical and component architectures, though in less detail, later in the book, when we discuss realizations.

2.1.3 Models

Why model? The rationale behind business modeling is very much tied up with the area usually described as *requirements analysis*. The objective is to find a definition of what the business wants to do, with the crucial word being *what*. A good statement of requirements avoids prejudging technology issues. A bad statement of requirements drags in Windows or Java or other ideas about how a supporting information system should work. This is bad because it makes technology the master, rather than the servant, of the business.

Let's look at a couple of reasons for wanting to separate *what* from *how:*

- *Business agility.* It's an increasingly competitive world out there. New market entrants, new products, and new ways of doing business make flexibility essential, not just nice to have. The last thing a business needs is for its freedom for action to be artificially limited by previous choices of technology. To succeed, or even just to survive, businesses need to be able to change in ways, and at times, determined by business drivers, not by their IT systems.
- *Technology freedom.* The other side of the coin is being able to change the technology without impacting the business. Sadly, many businesses today are locked into particular choices of hardware or software because they're needed to support crucial business activities. Being obliged to maintain a data center full of antiques while your competitors are all using the new Wizzo Quantum computers is unlikely to prove much of a business advantage.

Of course, a model is not reality but rather a simplification of it. Part of the skill in modeling is in deciding what you should leave out. A model is an excellent means of pinning down the *scope* of your intentions. Sometimes, the term *enterprise model* is used, but this can be misleading because it implies that you have to model absolutely everything. Not so. You can model as much or as little of your business as makes sense. If you're defining a business model as a step toward building an information system, there's a clear implication that the things in your model have been included because, ultimately, they're going to be useful as part of the system definition. If you don't think they will be useful, you can leave them out.

In some cases, a clear picture of the present business is needed as a baseline. In most cases, a view of a possible future business situation is needed to define a goal to work toward. We can call these the *as-is* and *to-be* views of the situation. The requirement for the system is defined by the difference between the two. Obviously, if you're defining a brand new system, you won't have an *as-is* model, so the *to-be* model will represent your entire requirement. If you already have something in place, you can play with alternative *to-be* models to understand their implications before you choose a specific path to go down.

Structure and notations   Clearly, the kind of business model we're thinking about is going to contain a great deal of internal structure. It's probably not very profitable to look at the detail involved, because this will be wrapped up in the design of a repository, which in turn will be geared up to support one or more tools. The Object Management Group (OMG) has given some thought to how we might describe such structures in a nonproprietary way. If you're interested, look for more information on the Meta Object Facility (MOF) and XML Metadata Interchange (XMI) at www.omg.org.

For our purposes, it's more useful to describe models in terms of human-readable notations. These are the sorts of things we would expect to see as views on the underlying model structure. Whatever we use has to cope with two crucial issues.

- We can't use just a single kind of description to capture everything about a business. One reason for the limited success of earlier approaches is that they attempted to force everything into a limited mode of expression, with definitions based exclusively on business processes probably being the most common. We'll want to talk about business processes, for sure, but other features don't sit naturally in a process description, and we need to find a comfortable home for them.
- The description has to follow a delicate line between sufficiently expressive and precise to fully capture the intended meaning on the one hand and being accessible to a mixed audience on the other. If it's to be of real value, the model must be usable by both business practitioners and technologists. For example, natural language is fairly accessible but has too many quirks to be relied on for precision. At the other end of the scale lie semimathematical notations that offer precision but are usable only by a few specialists. Neither extreme delivers what we want.

Over the years, a variety of notational styles have been proposed, but recently most attention has been concentrated on the Unified Modeling Language (UML). Dozens of books describe UML, so here we'll consider only the features that are most relevant to business modeling.

Just to be absolutely clear, you don't *have* to adopt UML. If you prefer something else that does the same job, fine. However, if you don't have any commitment elsewhere, the widespread support for UML makes it a fairly safe choice as a baseline.

At first glance, "bare" UML does not look all that promising. In its present incarnation, it's aimed more at supporting software development and has few features that relate directly to business modeling. However, UML can be bootstrapped in at least two ways, individually or in combination, to provide the features we need. The first approach is to take advantage of the extensibility features of UML. Typically, this involves the definition of additional stereotypes to provide new primitive entities related directly to business concerns. The second approach involves using plain UML to model the things that it can't describe directly. That's right, we can model some of the elements of the model!

Throughout the remainder of the book, we'll make use of a number of UML features to illustrate various points. If you've never come across UML, now's the time to get reading (see, for example, Booch, Rumbaugh, and Jacobsen 1999; Eriksson and Penker 2000). Given its widespread acceptance, some degree of familiarity with UML is becoming essential for anyone involved with information systems, and we'll discuss some ways of using it in business modeling shortly.

Introducing modeling in your organization   Business modeling could play a crucial role in the development of your information systems, but it probably won't happen unless you make it happen. If you look around your own organization as it is at present and take in reported experiences from elsewhere, you're likely to see a consistent story.

- Business requirements are poorly defined or bypassed by IT staff in a hurry to get down to the "real" work of writing the code.
- Information systems are developed on a per project basis, so successive projects frequently find themselves going over ground that's already been covered by another team.
- Business owners want to hedge their bets by avoiding definitive answers to questions that would pin them down to a particular set of intentions.
- There's a considerable history of failed projects, system downtime, and extensive rework and repair, but the people involved don't want to talk about it openly.

Maybe these facts are connected! The main obstacle may well turn out to be a fairly unyielding mindset about how systems should be developed. Leaving out cosmetic changes in technology, you'll probably find that the overall development process has not seriously changed for many years. If you introduce a systematic approach to business modeling, you at least have an opportunity to see things in a different light.

Here are a few things you could consider.

- Collect some figures to show the real cost of information systems failure in your organization. Include resources expended on projects that were canceled, software that failed to provide the expected business benefits, the effort required to fix problems in supposedly working systems and the consequential costs of lost customers to the business, due to reduced investor confidence, regulatory fines, lost business opportunities, and so on.
- Decide what to model. Producing one giant model for the whole organization is usually unrealistic. Decide how you are going to partition concerns

into several models and how you're going to handle the overlap among them. You'll need to think about such things as version control—How do changes happen?—and ownership—Who has the right to change a model? Approve a model? This will allow you to start in a small but controlled way and build up gradually as experience is gained.

- Force the issue by refusing to start development until the business intentions are clear and agreed. If there are pragmatic reasons for going forward before this can be achieved, isolate the risk—for example, by partitioning the model into "agreed" and "unresolved" areas. The model should provide the business with a clinical view of what is or is not being covered and so should eliminate a great many potential misunderstandings.

- Plan to maintain models over an extended period. At present, this is rarely done. Resources tend to be assigned on a project basis, and even if a model is produced, it's usually no one's job to look after it once the project has ended. In the long run, maintaining a model will provide a faster and cheaper ramp-up for any new projects in the area. It will also support other kinds of activity, such as a drive toward improved quality management across the whole organization.

2.2   Case study: a sample business architecture

2.2.1   Overview

To make some of these abstractions clearer, we'll look at an example of business architecture and drill down into the kinds of details that you'll have to think about as you build your own models. A high-level view of the architecture is given in Figure 2-2.

   This pretty much covers the concerns of row 2 of the Zachman Framework, with a couple of caveats. First, some aspects are represented by more than one block in this architecture because its designers wanted to emphasize particular issues. In particular, *who* has been expanded to clarify the difference between *actors* and *roles,* and *why* is answered by both *rules* and *intentions.* Second, *where* is defined in terms of organizational boundaries, not geographical locations. This is a deliberate choice, made to decouple the definition of the business from short-term office shuffles. It's a decision that the designers might want to revisit if physical geography becomes important to how the business works. This might be the case, for example, if a manufacturing plant is moved to an overseas location.

   The designers of the architecture could have considered other aspects. One example would be the explicit recognition of the resources required to carry out the business—machinery, logistics, raw material, and so on. This might be useful if the model serves other purposes, such as business planning. In this case, the designers have decided to focus only on those aspects directly related to information systems.

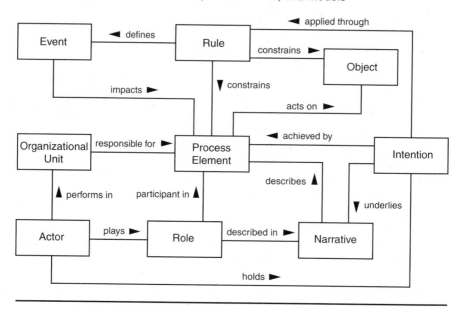

Figure 2-2   Example business architecture

Something that's not brought out in Figure 2-2 is that all the elements shown at this level can also have a finer-grained internal structure. For example, organizations are usually described hierarchically, so an organizational unit will break down into lower-level units, which in turn may have a further breakdown. At the level of architectural definition, the links among the elements are conceptual and represent an aggregation of many links at many levels that will exist in a particular model that conforms to this architecture.

In the following sections, we'll take in more detail on each of the blocks shown in the architecture diagram and discuss some of the modeling issues involved. The notation will follow the UML style; so, for example, names are created by removing spaces between words and capitalizing at word boundaries.

2.2.2   Business objects

Business objects are all the things that the business has to deal with. It's difficult to find a better natural term than *thing* as the highest-level expression that's common across all the diverse collection of———well———*things* that concern a typical business, which is perhaps why we need to introduce an artificial term.

Let's say straight away that the term *business object* is far from ideal. First, it implies that we're concerned only about object-oriented (OO) systems. This is not the case; we'll want to describe things of interest to a business long before we even think about what kind of implementation route might be appropriate. Second, the term introduces confusion about whether we are talking about a particular kind of thing or a specific thing of that kind—for example "an invoice" versus "the invoice dated December 11 to J. Jones." Most times, the use of *business object* indicates a *type* of object, not a specific instance. Third many businesspeople instinctively feel that the word *object* should refer to something with a physical existence and are a little uncomfortable about an intangible, such as *customer desire,* being called an object.

In spite of these problems, the term *business object* is in pretty widespread use. Some attempts have been made to clean up the neighborhood by introducing such terms as *business type,* but they never seem to stick. In this section, we'll use *business object* in an informal way but try to be precise wherever it's necessary.

Defining business objects comes down to three main things.

1. What kinds of objects should we concern ourselves with? The range of possibilities is huge, so we must be able to decide what things are relevant to a business model. Two filters come into play here. First, is this candidate *thing* really best described as a business object, or should it be treated in another way? Second, even if it is a plausible object, is it something we need be concerned about?

2. How much do we need to say about a particular kind of object? Again, some kind of filtering will be needed so that the amount of information we have about an object is just right: not too little—or we won't have an adequate description—and not too much—or we'll be wasting time on information that has no value.

3. How do different kinds of objects relate to one another? This involves understanding several features of relationships. One is multiplicity; for instance, a mother can give birth to one or more children, but a child has exactly one mother. Another is composition; for instance, a car is composed of engine, gearbox, wheels, body panels, and so on. Yet another is containment; for instance, a box of chocolates might contain walnut whirls, strawberry crèmes, raisin sundaes, and other goodies. And there are still more features of relationships, which we won't go into here.

Defining a set of business objects has one especially important consequence. By implication, it also defines the information that we might expect to find stored in an automation system, usually on a long-term, or *persistent,* basis. Although the business model does not directly model an automation system, the business objects and their relationships provide an excellent baseline for the eventual database design. Therefore, the way that business objects are usually shown in a business model has strong similarities to the way that a logical database design might be defined in some form of entity-relationship model.

The UML definition includes a ready-made diagram type that's ideal for modeling business objects: the class diagram. Even the terminology is better;

class is a more accurate description of what we're talking about. There's also a UML object diagram, but that tends to be used less in practice. As well as modeling business objects, class diagrams are also useful for defining how to represent business aspects that are not covered by the standard UML features.

Classes   Each kind of business object, or class in UML, is represented by a box on the class diagram. The box is subdivided vertically into several compartments. The first identifies the name of the class. The next contains a list of the things that we want to say about objects of this kind. Following object-oriented practice, these are called *attributes*, but they're sometimes also referred to as *properties* of the object type or class. The lower compartments of the class box come more into play during the design stages and so can be ignored in the business model.

Quite a common situation is to find "families" of business objects that obviously belong together. This is often a clue to the need to consider one class as being a special example of another—or, the other way round, as one class being a more general example of another. A convenient UML representation for generalization/specialization relationships of this sort looks like an open-headed arrow pointing toward the more general class. Figure 2-3 shows a generic class with some attributes, together with a couple of subclasses.

In this diagram, the Party class represents an external entity that is—or has been or might be—involved in a business relationship, such as a customer, a supplier, a business partner, or something equivalent. There's an obvious need to hold some information about such parties, represented simplistically in Figure 2-3 by name, address and telephoneNumber. This simple class diagram also shows two special cases of Party: Individual and Organization. Both of these are valid legal entities, able to take part in a business relationship. Anything about either of these

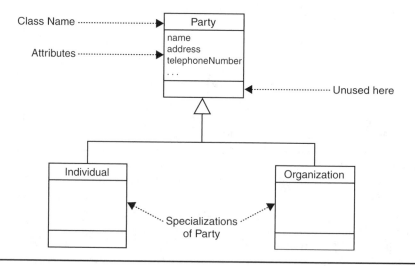

Figure 2-3   Class diagram with specializations

that is different from the more generic Party can be shown in its own class box. In this case, the diagram shows that the two entities have nothing extra, implying that we're currently defining just the standard Party information for both of them.

Intangible objects, such as "customer desires," are treated as though they are real. This elevation of an abstract to a concrete form is sometimes called *reification*. Reified business objects are treated in exactly the same way as any other kind of object.

Associations Associations between classes are shown on the diagram as lines connecting the class boxes. The ends of the lines are marked to show the *multiplicity:* how many of the relevant class can take part in the association, sometimes also known as the *cardinality*. The most common markings are summarized in Table 2-4.

Table 2-4 Multiplicity markings in UML

Marking	Meaning
0..*	Any number, including none
*	Same as above
0..1	None or one
1..*	At least one
1	Exactly one

Figure 2-4 shows a simple example of two associated classes. The multiplicity labels show that an Account object can be associated with any number of Entry objects—including none—but an Entry object is always associated with exactly one Account.

It's sometimes also useful to give the association—the line joining the two classes—a meaningful name as a reminder to explain why the classes are associated. There's no point in doing this just to add something like "is associated with," which is already obvious from the line joining the classes. Naming the association is worth doing only if it adds value; otherwise, it just clutters the diagram.

Another commonly used feature is giving a specific name to an *end* of the association, as opposed to the whole association. This is done to clarify the role

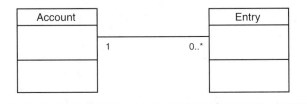

Figure 2-4 Multiplicity labeling

that the adjacent class plays in the relationship, so, not surprisingly, it's known as a *role name*. Again, there's no point in adding a role name unless it provides extra value. By default, UML assumes that the role name on the end of an association is the same as the name of the class at that end of the association but starting with a lowercase letter.

Classes versus attributes   A natural tendency is to think of an attribute as something intrinsically smaller than a class, but that's just an artifact of the analysis. From the point of view of a particular class, the other classes that it's associated with could be thought of as somewhat complex attributes. Equivalently, its attributes could be thought of as very simple associated classes.

To give a concrete example, imagine that we are setting up an online e-bank. One of the products we want to offer is a loan account. A likely first step in the analysis of this might be to define a Loan business object to contain the information related to a specific loan. This would probably include the start and end dates for the loan, the interest rate, an association with a Party object—the recipient of the loan—and a few other things, as shown in Figure 2-5.

We'll focus on the *interestRate* attribute. The initial analysis has identified the need to hold the interest rate applicable to the loan. This would be a percentage figure that can be used for such tasks as calculating repayments. Different kinds of loans may have different interest rates, so the Loan class looks like a good home for this attribute.

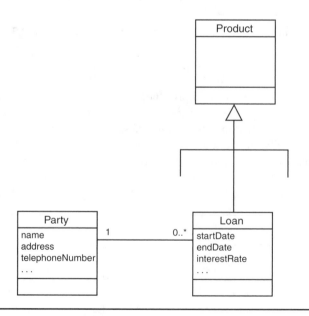

Figure 2-5   Simple loan model

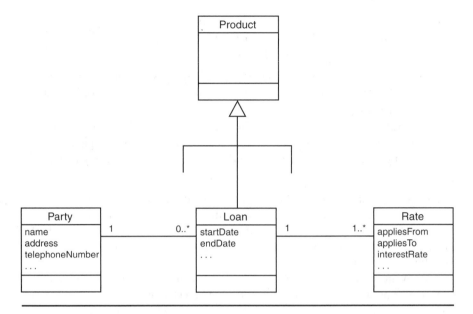

Figure 2-6   More complex loan model

Later, though, it might turn out that a rate is more complicated than we first thought. We might need to allow for loans that have a variable rate, such as 2 percent above base rate. But how do we know which rate was applicable at any given time? The likely answer is to promote the rate attribute to be a Rate class, as shown in Figure 2-6.

Now, we can hold not only the percentage value of the loan, but also all kinds of other information about the rate, such as the dates between which it was current. A Loan business object could be associated with one or more Rate objects. When this model is realized in an information system, we can imagine that a piece of software will figure out the right Rate object to use in a particular calculation, but that's going further than we need to at present.

State   Another useful notion that applies to some objects is the idea of *state*. You can think of state as an adjective that's applied to an object as a shorthand way to indicate a specific set of conditions that should be true at a particular point in time. At some moments in its life, an object will transition from one state to another in recognition of a changed situation or an external stimulus. State can also apply to other model elements, such as business processes.

A customer order in an e-commerce system is a good example of the kind of object that exhibits multiple states. At various points, the order might be received, accepted or rejected, packed, shipped, and so on. These conditions can be thought of as the states of an order, and it should be possible to define not only them but also the circumstances that cause a transition from one state to another. Knowing the state of an object is useful because we can

- Limit future actions to those that are suitable to the situation. For example, in our e-commerce system, it would not be appropriate to pack an order that has been rejected.
- Infer values that may not be explicitly stated. For example, if the acceptance of an order in our e-commerce system is dependent on advance payment, knowing that the state is "accepted" allows us to infer that the payment has been received.

It's convenient to show state in a diagrammatic form, usually with a box to represent state and an arrowed line to show the possible transitions. The lines can be annotated to show the conditions under which the transitions can occur. UML includes a notation for state diagrams. Figure 2-7 shows a simple example of the possible states for a bank account.

We want to avoid getting bogged down in detail, but it's worth noting that a common technique is to keep the current value of a state variable in an attribute of the object concerned, and so we would expect to see it on the class diagram. What's special about attributes defining state is that they exhibit a controlled, and often nontrivial, evolution through a limited set of values.

Less commonly, it may be useful to have more than one state variable for an object, if it can be described by multiple adjectives that vary independently. For example, we could conceivably want to identify the status of a member of an Internet shopping club in different ways, as shown in Figure 2-8.

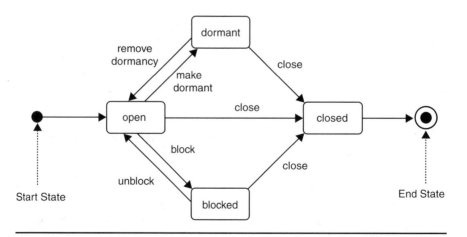

Figure 2-7   Bank account states

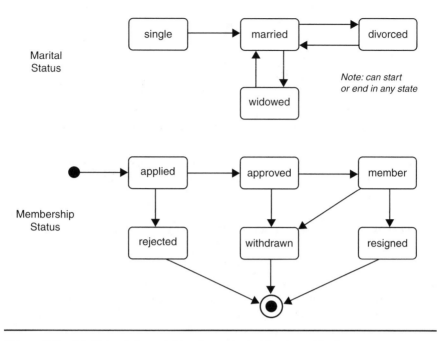

Figure 2-8   Multiple state variables for a single Member object

2.2.3   Business process elements

If you dip into a company and ask a non-IT person to describe how the business works, he or she will most likely immediately describe a business process. A *business process* is a sequence of activities aimed at producing something of value to the business. The individual explaining the business may not be aware of the complete process and so may be describing a process fragment, but even that will still have all the same hallmarks; a subprocess is a process too! The terminology varies a little from place to place, but most business processes display a similar set of features. Here are some of the most common ones.

- They have at least one start point and at least one end point, which can be clearly identified, recognized, and described in business terms.
- They can be broken down into a set of tasks or subactivities. A particular low-level task may appear in more than one business process.
- Many instances, or *enactments,* of a given business process may be active at the same time, and each could be in a different state of completion.
- A process has an objective—or goal or purpose; the activities are defined to achieve that objective.

- A process requires resources in order to meet its objective. The resources may take several forms but particularly will include people and technology elements, such as processing, storage, and communications.

- The enactment of a business process occupies a time interval that may be quite significant, perhaps measured in weeks or months.

- A process often spans several organizational units, each of which delivers some value to the process. This may mean that no one person is in charge of the whole process.

- Process instances can be impacted by external events, or happenings that aren't a result of the process itself. The impact may cause the process to react in various ways, such as pause, change direction, or cancel all work done up to the event.

- There's a natural ordering of the activities in a process because of internal dependencies. For instance, activity B might need something provided by activity A, so it's obvious that A has to happen before B.

- A process handles one or more *things,* which could be physical objects or pieces of information. These are usually transformed or augmented during the process and handed on from one stage to another. There will be at least one input and at least one output.

A typical example of a business process is the handling of a loan application by a bank. Over a period of days or weeks, the initial application form might be passed through several departments of the bank, acquiring additional information that gets attached on the way. A first step might be to register the application and make details available to other activities. This might be followed by a check on the worthiness of the applicant, with the option of terminating the process if the person doesn't measure up. If it's a secured loan, it may be necessary to value the security being offered. Eventually, if all goes well, the funds will be released and the applicant advised. The process can be impacted by externally triggered events, such as a change in interest rates enforced by the central bank or withdrawal by the applicant.

Over a period from roughly the late 1980s to the late 1990s, businesses were advised to make radical changes to their accepted activities, and the phrase *business process reengineering* (BPR) came into vogue. As with many such fashions, marketing pressures quickly overwhelmed the grains of sense in the original concepts, and BPR came to be overused. In spite of all the fads and fancies, the plain fact is that a good understanding of "what the business does" is fundamental to the proper management and development of any organization. Our interest here is in the context of an information system that automates some or all the process activities. Other uses, which we won't go into, include planning organizational changes, reducing cycle times, and improving the quality of the organization's products or services.

Business processes of the sort we're considering here are very much a poor relation in the official UML world. In fact, some UML protagonists argue that business processes exist only as a side effect of a series of elementary operations. For example, the *UML Version 1.3 User Guide* (Booch, Rumbaugh, and Jacobsen 1998) provides no information on business processes, the word *process* being used solely for an instance of a software unit running on a particular processor. Going into denial like this is a shame because it forces would-be users to invent their own ways of describing business processes, thus undermining the standardization that's one of the UML's biggest attractions.

To get a better handle on how we might be able to model a business process, we'll first take a look at how they are commonly described. Several approaches exist, but they're not mutually exclusive. Each provides a different kind of view into a business process, and so they all can be, and usually are, used together.

Process hierarchy   The first type of description provides a structured breakdown of the tasks involved in the process. This is usually in the form of a hierarchy, so it's often referred to as a process hierarchy diagram. At the top of the hierarchy is the name of the business process, such as *secure loan application*. Below that are the major chunks of activity that the process involves: register applicant, check credit status, and so on. The breakdown continues until it reaches a level that provides sufficient detail. Figure 2-9 summarizes the general idea.

How do we know what level of detail is sufficient? There are no absolutes here; it's a matter of judgment. The bottom is reached when no purpose would be served by going deeper. For instance, checking credit status might involve a telephone call to a credit agency; making the call involves picking up the phone; picking up the phone involves tensing the muscles of the upper arm; and so on. You

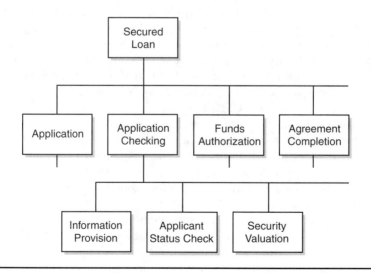

Figure 2-9   Process hierarchy diagram

probably get the picture. At some point, the granularity of the description is sufficient to provide all the details needed, and no further breakdown is necessary.

Some organizations like to fix the number of levels and have special names for each level; other organizations allow any number and simply refer to activities at all levels below the top with a generic name, such as subprocess. It's useful to have a name for the lowest level; one that's in fairly common use is "elementary business process"—elementary in the sense that it doesn't subdivide any further.

A handy indicator of when the elementary level has been reached is given in the mantra *one person, one place, one time*. This shouldn't be taken too literally, but it does get across the idea that a subprocess

- Requires a close focus that would be difficult to share across a group
- Can't easily be split into physically separated pieces
- Normally goes from start to finish without interruption

Elementary business processes are good places to link descriptions that are naturally process oriented to other parts of the business model. Another reason for distinguishing them is that they are also good candidates for reuse in other business processes.

Process flow   The other type of process description in common use is a flow diagram. Activities, at some level, are shown in boxes and are connected by directed lines to show their sequencing. The direction of the flow usually goes from left to right and/or from top to bottom. Special symbols are used to identify branching, or joining, points in the flow to allow for alternative paths and parallel activities. Figure 2-10 shows a typical process flow diagram.

Different levels of process, as identified in the process hierarchy diagram, are usually shown with separate flow diagrams for each level. Obviously, at the most detailed level, the boxes on the flow diagram will represent elementary business processes. There's scope here for some fancy tool support, such as clicking on an intermediate-level activity to show its lower-level, more detailed, breakdown.

Flow diagrams are a powerful means of communicating the essence of a business process. They are easy to understand and to create, requiring minimal or no training on the part of the user. UML provides a notation style, called *activity diagrams,* that are well suited to process flow descriptions.

The popularity of flow diagrams has made them a natural candidate for automation, and they provide the essential underpinning for software products that go under the general name of workflow. A typical workflow tool includes a flow designer and automates the transfer of information from one stage to another, using the flow lines laid down.

Quite a few other methodologies and notations, such as role-activity diagrams (RADs), are built around business processes, but we don't have space to consider them here. You may want to include these in your model, but you should be wary of proprietary approaches that may mortgage your future flexibility against some attractive but short-term benefit.

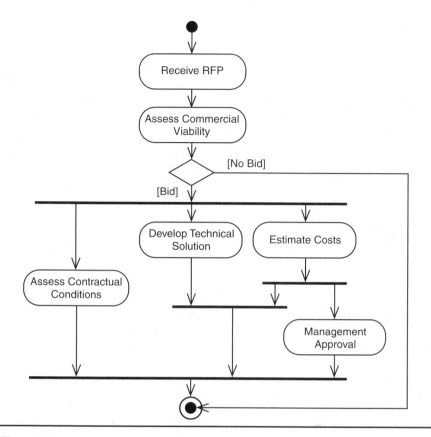

Figure 2-10   Process flow diagram

2.2.4   Narratives

A business narrative is a description of a fragment of business life. It's a walk-through of a situation that the business expects to encounter during its operations. These situations may be very common, enacted perhaps hundreds of times a day in many locations, such as a customer purchase in a retail store. Other situations, such as the need to cope with a natural disaster, may be expected to happen rarely, if at all.

The kind of business narrative that's most common these days is the *use case* view defined in UML, and we'll look at some details shortly. Other examples of narratives are the *business stories* used in Extreme Programming and the *knowl-edge elicitation protocols* used in the capture of heuristic knowledge from experts.

The common feature of all narratives is that they describe the way in which the business is expected to operate in the given situation. Here's an example of a very simple unstructured business narrative.

A customer enters a branch of the bank and joins a queue for a free teller. On reaching the counter, the customer requests a cash withdrawal from his or her account. The teller asks the customer for the account number and the withdrawal amount and enters this information into the system. The teller also requests some form of identification to authenticate the customer. If authentication is satisfactory and if sufficient funds are available in the account, the teller confirms the withdrawal to the system and hands the customer the cash.

You can probably spot several ways in which this narrative could be improved and several questions it leaves unanswered, such as, what if the customer doesn't have identification? Or, What happens if the customer has insufficient funds? However, even this simple level of description helps to paint a picture of what goes on in the business—obviously, a bank in this case.

Whatever style you end up with, there will be trade-off decisions to be made, and, as usual, there is no single answer that will be right for everyone. Let's start by establishing a few principles.

Purpose   The most important thing to get clear is the *purpose* of the narrative. At the start of a business analysis project or phase it's useful to make this an explicit statement, so that all team members carry away the same intention. The main purpose of a narrative is usually to describe the interactions between some agents and an amorphous thing called "the system." This doesn't necessarily imply an automated information system, although most of this undifferentiated lump will, ultimately, be resolved into various parts of a computer-based system. The agents involved might be part of the business, such as front-office sales staff, or might be external to the business, such as customers, and can be either human or machine.

From this it follows that the main functions of a narrative are to define a boundary around a system and to describe a set of interactions taking place across that boundary. And that's about all it should do. You may need to be ruthless in pruning excess detail and helpful explanatory text that would otherwise bloat the narrative. More temptations to be avoided are describing interactions in terms of their interfaces and guessing at the internal details of the system. The narrative should be about *what* happens in the business, not *how* it is achieved.

Structure   Although it's perfectly possible to produce unstructured stream-of-consciousness narratives, they're greatly improved by the addition of structure. Structuring the narrative in a standardized way offers the following benefits.

- It's easier for a human reader to locate points of interest, instead of wading through solid blocks of text.
- Possible errors, such as unfinished branches, show up more clearly and are therefore easier to eliminate.
- Sophisticated tools can make use of the structuring, increasing the degree of automation that can be applied.

The main challenge lies in finding the right balance between rigorous structuring and readability. A high degree of structure is of doubtful value if it makes the narrative unreadable for normal business users. A more complex approach to structuring, made easier by good tool support, is to provide multiple levels of description. Among other things, this opens the possibility of separate but linked human- and machine-readable versions of the same narrative, each of which can be optimized for its respective uses.

Any nontrivial narrative will raise the issue of alternative courses, or different sequences of actions that may or may not be taken, depending on local circumstances. The preceding simple narrative shows a couple of examples where this may arise. A customer wanting to make a withdrawal may or may not have sufficient balance and may or may not have acceptable proof of identity. Two main ways of structuring narratives to reflect this are to

- Follow each branch and subbranch as it is encountered in the description
- Produce a separate description for each outcome

The second of these approaches may sound like a lot more work, but this isn't necessarily the case. Our withdrawal example has four possible branches but only two possible outcomes, as shown in Table 2-5.

Table 2-5   Possible cash withdrawal outcomes

ID	Balance	Outcome
Acceptable	Adequate	Allowed
Not acceptable	Adequate	Refused
Acceptable	Not adequate	Refused
Not acceptable	Not adequate	Refused

In most realistic situations, the total number of possible branches multiplies alarmingly, but the possible outcomes remain at a reasonable level. Use cases in UML tend toward the second approach, with the most common path through the use case being described in detail and other scenarios being added if relevant.

The various ways of showing structure can be used individually or in combination. Methods include the following.

- Paragraph numbering can be used to identify major steps in the narrative and to associate groups of actions or branch points.
- Interactions can be clarified by using a table with separate columns for agent and system, with actions being recorded in the appropriate column. The focus switches from one column to another as the flow progresses down the table.
- Indentation of text can be used to indicate different levels of description or possible changes in the course of events.

As ever, the overriding principle governing the choice is the need to keep the narrative accessible to nontechnical readers. For example, technical presentations, such as wrapping actions within a pseudocode structure or using IF-THEN-ELSE constructs to indicate alternative paths, are not recommended, because they're unfriendly to business users.

Style   Because a business user with little or no training must be able to pick up a business narrative and understand it, writing style is important. Readability is the key concern, closely followed by consistency. Here are some guidelines on style; you may have some additional in-house standards to follow.

- Sentences in the narrative should use the active voice rather than the passive voice. For example:

    The account holder's ID is checked by the customer service agent.

  would be better as

    The customer service agent checks the account holder's ID.

- Insist that analysts check references to other model elements to ensure that a particular element is always denoted in exactly the same way. A reference to "customer" might mean the same as "account holder" but we can't really be sure. "Account number," "account-number" and "accountNumber" might be equally understandable to a human being, but there's always the possibility of confusion, and they certainly look different to a machine. Apart from reducing ambiguity, consistency of usage will allow you to use simple text searching as a reasonably reliable way of locating cross-references.

- Consider applying special markings or formatting in the text to identify words or phrases that have a special meaning. For instance, you might decide to place the names of agents inside angle brackets— <customer service agent> — or format the names of business objects in italics—*account*. You'll need to make sure that the style you adopt doesn't impede the readability of the narrative. There's no recognized industry standard for this: As long as you're clear and consistent, you can set your own conventions.

Size   One thing you should think about before you start is your preferred size for the individual narratives. Together, your collection of narratives will define the external scope of your system in terms of the services it provides to various agents. However, this could be accomplished anywhere along a spectrum that ranges from a few large narratives to many small ones. Here are some general guidelines.

- Whatever structure you adopt, keep the size of each individual narrative down to a few pages: five at the absolute maximum. This will pay off by simplifying reviews and making it easier to spot repeated patterns of activity that you can generalize later. If you're struggling with ten- to fifteen-page narratives, you've either given the narratives too wide a scope or included too much detail.

- Stop each narrative at the first break point that would seem natural to the agent(s) involved. Indicators to these points are often when the action is taken up by a new set of agents, when the action is transferred to a new location, or when there is likely to be a pause or a delay before the action can resume.

UML also defines two kinds of relationships between use cases. Common behavior can be put into one use case that other use cases can *include*. Behavior that's a variant or an addition to the norm can be put into a use case that will *extend* the normal, or base, use case.

Use case diagrams provide a way of showing a related set of actors and use cases. Actors—whether human or not—are conventionally represented by stick figures and use cases by ellipses, both marked with the relevant names. The relationship between an actor and a use case is shown by a solid line joining them. Figure 2-11, a typical use case diagram, shows two actors and three use cases. Unfortunately, books on UML tend to give an inflated view of the importance of use case diagrams. In practice, the amount of information they add is usually minimal.

A business process and a UML use case have some superficial similarities: They both deal with a sequence of activities, perhaps including alternative paths; they both have inputs and outputs; they both require resources; and so on. However, they also have some significant differences.

- A use case is normally oriented around a specific actor, the principal actor. Business processes usually span organizational groups and so, inevitably, incorporate the perspectives of multiple actors.
- Therefore, business processes tend to be bigger than use cases; that is, business processes generally include a greater number of activities of a given size.
- Use cases are written from the viewpoint of an actor outside the system. Not surprisingly, business processes tend to be described from the business's internal point of view.

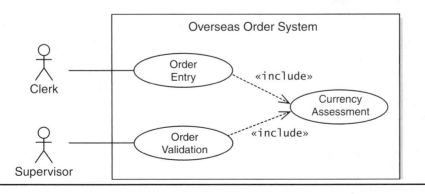

Figure 2-11   Use case diagram

- Business processes commonly have a hierarchical breakdown into subprocesses. Use cases do not decompose into sub–use cases, except in a very limited way through <<include>> and <<extend>> relationships, which in any case should be used sparingly because they impair readability.
- The activity flow in a business process is usually described in terms of a flow diagram that can be automated quite directly: for instance, using a workflow tool. The flow description of a use case is mainly textual and has no direct implementation.

The exact format of a use case is open to debate, and you'll find plenty of suggestions in various books and articles. In practice, the choice is likely to be constrained by whatever tool you're using. The main thing you should try to avoid is treating the whole use case just as a lump of text. Generally speaking, the more structure and regularity you can introduce, the better.

Tool support   Most analysis and modeling tools support some form of business narrative, typically use cases. Unfortunately, the support often consists of little more than a text editor. In an ideal world, tools would interoperate among the various views of the model, so that cross-references are maintained automatically. For example, references to business objects in a narrative should link to a definition of the object. Apart from helping the analyst during the construction of the narrative, this would enforce consistency, so that the same object would always be referenced in the same way.

If you're stuck with a tool that does little more than accept narrative text, you'll need to impose your own local practices. This involves a little more work initially but greatly improves the maintainability of the model in the longer term. The main things to highlight are the structure of the narrative and cross-references to other model elements.

2.2.5   Business events

A business event is a happening that has an impact on the business; the most interesting ones originate externally. There's no standard definition of what should be considered as an event: It's entirely up to the business to decide what counts. It's useful to identify potential events because this allows the business to plan ahead and to identify the action to be taken if a particular event happens. On the other hand, it's important not to attempt to recognize too many different kinds of events because of the effort required to define them and to track them. Most organizations will therefore want to take a pragmatic view and carefully select the kinds of events on which they're prepared to invest time and effort.

If we take a bank as an example, we can imagine the kinds of events that might or might not be noteworthy. Table 2-6 gives some examples.

Table 2-6   Example events and actions

Event	Special Actions Needed to Update Information System
Takeover bid received from competitor	None in the short term; perhaps plenty in the longer term, but too many unknowns to be able to plan in advance
Main data center devastated by earthquake	No *information* change; disaster recovery plans put into effect to restore normal business activities
Change to interest rates imposed by central bank	Important: Need to reflect this change into current products and agreements
Bank customer changes address	Important: Need to update customer records to reflect relationship and to maintain contact
Relaunch of long-term investment product	Marginal: As long as the product is properly represented in the system, advertising campaigns, and so on, may come and go
Customer withdraws small amount from ATM	Marginal: Probably just a routine activity that requires no special attention
New head of central bank appointed by government	Not relevant: *Identity* of appointee has no impact; any changes of policy will appear as other events
Customer's parrot dies	Condolences offered by sympathetic Customer Service Agent, but parrot unlikely to figure in bank database

As the bank examples show, for an event to be considered important, it's not so much a question of its being big or small but rather something that requires a preplanned response, probably changing information that's held along the way. At some point along a scale of importance, the owner of an information system will decide that it's worth explicitly identifying particular kinds of events. Events on the "not relevant" side of that line won't need to be recognized as such by the information system. Events on the other side of the line will trigger activity and, usually, will also be logged so that a historical record is maintained.

It's convenient to treat an event as having zero duration because it's something that either does or does not happen. One way of thinking about an event is as the boundary between a *before* state and an *after* state. From this point of view, it's clear that it's the *states* that have measurable durations, not the boundary between them. A consequence of this way of thinking is that a business event can't be interrupted, halted, paused, or anything else that suggests that it can be broken down. Looked at as an entity, an event is atomic: It either does or does not exist, and there is no way that you could end up with something that's a partial event.

The crucial feature of an event is that it defines a point at which a particular set of circumstances becomes recognized. The situation might be something that's easy to define or might be the combination of several conditions coexisting. The classification of situations into events can become quite complex. As we'll see in more detail later, business rules provide an excellent way of managing this sort of complexity.

ECA rules   Several attempts have been made to realize event-based processing, typically in the form of event-condition-action (ECA) structures, sometimes also called ECA rules. These have a general form that looks like:

- E: Recognize the onset of an event. The event classification defines the rules required.
- C: Use the rules to determine the conditions that apply and hence the actions required.
- A: Carry out the appropriate actions.

Jumping ahead to possible realizations of information systems, it's worth noting that structures of this kind are popular in the active-database community. For now, though, we're going to stick with the business focus and try to understand the value of events in purely business terms.

The main problem from this perspective is that ECA rules tend to mix together the *what* and the *how;* they blur the distinction between specification and realization. We've already stressed that it's a good idea to keep these apart so that we avoid prematurely constraining the implementation and don't put arbitrary limits on the future reuse of analysis patterns.

Using ECA rules as a means of realization usually means finding ways of making important points in the information processing look like events, so that they can be picked up by the ECA framework. In some cases, this results in the meaning of *event* being bent toward a situation that's governed by technology—"new message enters queue"—rather than business—"customer application received".

You're not going to miss out on anything by deferring the realization issues. In fact, waiting until the business features have been defined will probably give a clearer idea of what and how to implement. The line we'll take here is therefore a little different from the ECA approach. The following points summarize the features of business, as opposed to ECA, events to underline the differences.

- The definition of what constitutes an event is best described in terms of rules, so there's no separate definition of events and conditions.
- Business events always arise from outside the information system; they are never simply a step in normal processing.
- It follows that events are not synchronized with the actions of the information system; we have to allow for their happening at any point.
- By definition, recognizing an event has business value; otherwise, it wouldn't be considered an event, so it's worth creating an audit trail of their onset and impact.

Using events with UML The main effect of a business event is to start, stop, or change the direction of one or more business processes or activities. The way in which they're modeled is therefore tied up with decisions about how to model processes. Like business processes, business events are not recognized explicitly in UML, so it's a matter of adopting a pragmatic approach.

At the very least, events can be identified as business objects, or classes, which will allow them to be handled in the same way as other kinds of objects. Events often cluster into families of types and subtypes, and the UML generalization feature is a natural and convenient way of showing this.

Events will have various properties, depending on what the business decides is relevant. These properties may be defined as attributes, or links to other parts of the model. At the highest level, these attributes are likely to include at least the following:

- Event name: a short, snappy title for the event
- Event category: a reference to a locally defined event taxonomy
- Description: a brief textual description of what the event is about
- Recognition rules: how to identify an event of this sort
- Potential impact: the processes/activities that might be affected by the event
- Impact rules: how to decide what to do about an event of this sort

In addition, each instance of each particular sort of event will have its own associated attributes, including at least the following:

- Time identified: the time, including date, when the event was first recognized as such
- Actual impact: the impact decision that was made

These elements can be elaborated as needed. For instance, if human interaction is needed to classify an event, it might be useful to record two different timestamps: the time that the event input was first received and the time that it was eventually classified by the operator. There's probably no need to make explicit associations between events and other "business object" classes; these will be effectively built into the links that are required to the associated business rules and business processes (see Figure 2-2).

There's also an indirect link with use cases. However, whereas a use case describes parts of processes, an event tends to be the thing that triggers a process, ends it, or directs it into an alternative scenario. In a business model, this can be handled directly, by including associations between events and use cases, or indirectly, as in our sample architecture, by linking use case to process and process to event.

2.2.6 Actors and roles

People play an important part in any information system by providing many of its inputs and by consuming most of its outputs. Because the system we're modeling represents a business—or perhaps a part of one—we may also want the model to include people who are part of the process. The reason is that we need to have a properly joined-up view of how the business is supposed to work. Later, when we draw up the boundaries of the automation system, the people will all be external to it, by definition, but we must be aware that this boundary is likely to change over time.

The word *actor* is commonly used as the generic term for any agent interacting with a system. An actor can represent a person, an organization, or a machine resource. At the level of a business model, there's a real advantage in not discriminating, because the reality may change as the business evolves.

Actors have their starring role in UML as participants in use cases. In fact, a use case can be defined as a view of a system from the perspective of a principal actor. On diagrams, actors are conventionally shown as stick figures, but this doesn't necessarily imply that they are human. The word *actor* can be a tad misleading, and we'll look at some of the subtleties shortly. In the meantime, we'll take a look at handling actors in the UML sense.

You'll certainly need to identify actors by name and probably keep a short description with each. It's quite likely that you'll find the same actors appearing in a number of business scenarios, and it's helpful to maintain this information in an *actor catalog* so that you use the actor names consistently and don't reinvent actors that you've already defined. If your tool doesn't provide this feature, it's easy enough to implement with an ordinary word processor.

The usual specialization/generalization mechanisms can also be applied to actors, so it's possible to have specialized actors that inherit the characteristics of more general actors. A UML diagram showing a generalization relationship between actors sometimes disorients business users because it appears to invert the more familiar organization chart layout. Figure 2-12 shows both perspectives.

The reason for the difference is, of course, that the diagrams are intended to show different things. The actor generalization shows that, in this case, a supervisor can be considered to be a kind of clerk. In other words, a supervisor can do everything that a clerk can do and presumably extra things as well. Similarly, a manager could fill the role of a supervisor or a clerk. Being at the top of the diagram does not indicate rank or seniority, as it does in the more traditional organization chart. It's not unknown for emotions to become engaged during analysis owing to misunderstandings about this, so it's probably worth your while to take a little extra care with the definitions.

The word *actor* is used in UML to make a distinction between a specific individual and the part that person plays in the use case. For instance, if we wanted to describe a business activity involving an *order-entry clerk*, that's the term we would use, not *Arch Stanton,* the person who happens to be employed as an order-entry clerk. The definition in UML is that an actor represents a coherent set of roles.

This sows the seeds of potential confusion because the UML intention is subtly different from the more familiar theatrical usage of the term. If you think of

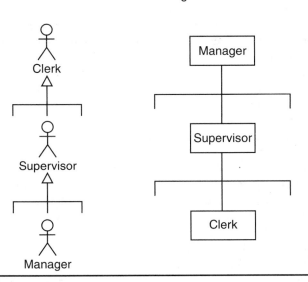

Figure 2-12   Two kinds of actor hierarchy

a movie script as being just a particular style of business narrative, it's the name of the character that appears in the script, not the name of the person playing the character. We would expect the script to describe the role of Luke Skywalker, not the actor Mark Hamill. In contrast, the name of an actor in UML is more descriptive of the role that's being played rather than the person playing it.

Putting this into a business context, think about the two columns in Table 2-7. Clearly, it's possible for a person with a particular job title to have more than one role. Some roles may tend be more associated with a particular job title; for instance, the Sponsor role in the table is more likely to be associated with a Manager than either of the other two job titles shown. But this cannot be relied on. For example, a consultant could equally well be a Team Leader, and an Analyst could be a Reviewer.

Table 2-7   Jobs and roles

Job Title	Role
Consultant	Reviewer of document X
Analyst	Team Leader on project Y
Manager	Sponsor of system Z

We can see from this that it's a mistake to equate actor names with job titles. The inevitable evolution of the organization will cause positions and the job titles that go with them to be merged, split, reassigned, and changed in various other ways. It's also likely that an individual may temporarily take over the tasks of someone else to cover for short-term sickness, training, vacations, and so on.

We certainly want to preserve the flexibility to reassign roles to job titles to meet the ever-changing needs of the business. The designers of this business architecture have therefore decided to model the distinction between them by separating actor—the kind of person involved—from role—the part(s) that the person may be playing at a particular time. In fact, this use of the word *actor* is closer to the thespian idea of actors who specialize in a limited range of parts, such as leading man, villain, or femme fatale, so the intended meaning is more like *actor type*.

Is this sort of elaboration necessary? Do you really care about the niceties of whether you're describing a job or a role or an actor? Ultimately, it's your choice. The designers of this business architecture wanted to make some distinctions that were important to them; those distinctions may not be important to you. If you just want to follow the UML usage, that's fine. If you want to refine the people part of your model in much more detail, that's fine too: It's your model!

The actor/role debate is a good example of why we can't claim any particular business architecture to be the right one. You can certainly look at other ideas about how a business should be modeled, but at the end of the day, you will need to take responsibility for your own particular situation.

2.2.7 Business intentions

Intentionality is probably the most slippery of all the concepts involved in business modeling. It's the aspect most closely related to the *why* of information systems. It's the underpinning that should allow us to answer questions about our system.

- Why do we need to include this feature?
- Why do we constrain values in this way?
- Why are we building the system in the first place?

One thing that makes it difficult to pin down is the vocabulary, which is not only varied and diffuse but also highly dependent on interpretation. A generic all-purpose answer to such questions could be phrased something like:

> "The *[rationale, motivation, purpose, reason, incentive, explanation]* is that we have a specific *[intention, goal, aim, objective, end, target, ambition, aspiration, desire, mission]* to realize, taking into account that we also have particular *[charges, undertakings, duties, responsibilities, liabilities, obligations, requirements]* that have to be met."

One interpretation of such terms as *goal* and *target* is that they define a particular objective that has to be reached: for instance, hitting a sales target that's been set.

In this case, the interest is in the attainment of the objective; once it has been reached, it can be ticked as done and it's time for celebration.

Another interpretation is quite common in business but subtly different: not just achieving but also *maintaining* a given state of affairs. For instance, a reasonable business goal might be to keep the average length of time taken by credit customers to pay their bills to within 45 days. It's perfectly possible for a goal of this sort to be unachieved, at least for a while. Ideally, though, if all is working well in the business, the underachievement will be identified and measures put into effect to bring the situation back into line.

Goals of this sort figure strongly in quality management. If you're in an organization that's gone through certification to ISO 9000 or equivalent, your company manual will probably contain quite a few examples of similar steady-state objectives. You'll certainly find clear descriptions of the practices to be followed to ensure that the business operates in the desired way. You should find some statements of core business values, perhaps in the form of a mission statement. You may find an explicit measure identified that can be used to track business performance. What your quality manual probably won't do is spell out the rationale that links a particular activity to a business intention.

Another problem with pinning down intentionality is that a lot of people dismiss things like mission statements as corporate gobbledegook: something to pay lip service to but nothing to take seriously. And in many cases, they are quite right. Bad mission statements are produced for all kinds of ulterior motives: to paper over political cracks within the organization, to impress investors, to deflect criticism, to get a tick in the box during a QA (quality assurance) assessment, and many other poor reasons. It's perhaps not surprising that there's a certain amount of cynicism about such things.

But does that have to be the case? In spite of all of the negative associations, is there something of value here that's important to hold on to? Of course, the answer is yes. Imagine a large organization—a major bank, say—that did not have any core values or objectives beyond *be profitable*. Pretty soon, the reception area would house a pizza parlor, the IT department would be building systems for rivals, the fifth floor would house an Internet betting operation, and so on. It would not take too long before the bank ceased to exist as a recognizable entity.

So what is the glue that makes an organization hang together? What is it that makes betting on the horses a bad thing for a bank to do? Or makes offering pizza in the reception area something that's worth considering? It all comes down to core values: what makes the business what it is and not a different kind of business.

Companies incorporated with limited liability are obliged to define the nature of their business in their articles of association (or equivalent). In earlier times, this provided potential investors with some guidance on what the company was about. Nowadays, these legal statements are worded so as to allow the organization to do just about anything it could conceivably want. The real signposts are more likely to be found in analyst briefings, keynote speeches, press days, and the like.

At the topmost level, the number of intentions is likely to be quite small. Unfortunately, it doesn't stop there. Each intention carries with it a number of

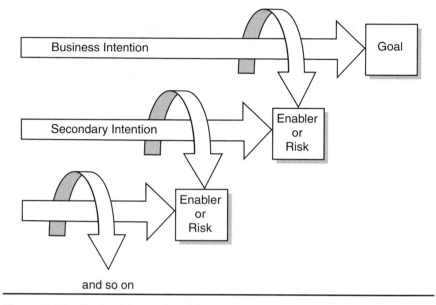

Figure 2-13　Goals, risks, and enablers

implications. First, some *enablers* may be required. These lower-level factors need to be in place in order for the higher-level intention to be achievable. Second, an intention may introduce risks, which must be addressed to make sure they don't threaten the achievement of an intention. As Figure 2-13 shows, both of these elements can be resolved by expressing new intentions at a lower level.

But these intentions have their own implications, creating a need for additional intentions, and so on. To prevent the cascade of intentions from becoming a flood, a commonsense filter has to be applied. The breakdown stops on reaching enablers that are so mundane that they don't need mentioning or risks that are so small that the business need make no special provision to counter them.

Intentions, risks, and enablers are good examples of abstract notions that can be reified into business objects. Figure 2-14 shows a recursive model construct that would support an intentional hierarchy of this sort. Obviously, this could be

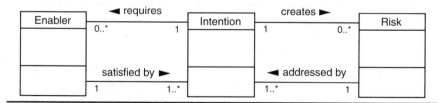

Figure 2-14　Intention hierarchy as UML classes

enhanced in various ways. For example, it might be useful to base risk assessment on quantitative estimates of both financial impact and percentage probability. As with other model elements, it's up to you to decide how far you need to go.

2.2.8   Organizational units

Internally, businesses like to define themselves by how they are organized. This usually takes the form of a hierarchical breakdown, in which smaller units form parts of larger units, the largest unit being the business itself.

This pattern was established in the earliest days of modern business and provided an effective way to create orderly operations, using a largely uneducated work force. Medium to large business in the nineteenth century invariably had quite deep hierarchies, with a strict pecking order from the lowest to the highest levels. In the latter part of the twentieth century, this model began to be questioned, as emphasis shifted from the use of materials, capital, and labor to the knowledge-based economy of today. However, all companies of any significant size still require some kind of organizational structure to provide a matrix for their day-to-day operations, and the obvious starting point is a hierarchy.

Defining the structure of an organization has several plausible approaches. Common examples are to subdivide the organization by

- Function: marketing, finance, manufacturing
- Geography: eastern region, central region, western region
- Competence: products, fixed-price projects, time-and-material projects
- Product line: mil-spec, industrial, consumer

Of course, these categories aren't mutually exclusive, so you're likely to find a combination used in practice: for example, corporate headquarters—finance, legal, public relations—plus a manufacturing division plus regional marketing operations.

An organizational unit is the closest thing we have in this architecture to a place where things happen. If the organizational breakdown is defined geographically, this might indeed correspond to a specific physical location. More often, though, the need for organizational flexibility means that it's treated as a virtual place that could be physically located and relocated anywhere the business needs it.

Whichever way the organization is subdivided, a unit at any level contains a group of people carrying out a defined set of activities. The involvement of the people is usually described in terms of the roles performed, not the individuals performing them. Within a unit, there's an association between one or more roles and one or more activities, which, at the lowest levels, correspond to elementary business processes. One way of thinking about an organizational unit is that it provides a named boundary around a set of links between specific roles and process elements.

Deciding on the best grouping is something that managers agonize over, because there's no single answer that's right for every situation and that applies for all time. The traditional approach has been to cluster on the basis of roles, so that people with similar or closely related competencies are colocated in the organizational matrix. The downside of this approach is that it creates the right conditions for an us-versus-them culture to spring up. Such groups often focus inward, optimizing their own area but often to the detriment of the organization as a whole.

More recently, the emphasis has shifted to process-oriented groupings to improve end-to-end control over chains of activities. Extending this same line of thought, many organizations are now also including external agents, such as customers and suppliers, in the definition of their processes. Whatever line your own business follows, this is fertile ground for business process reengineering, and you're going to need to be responsive to change.

We've already met activity diagrams in the context of business processes, where they're commonly used to show sequences of activities. Activity diagrams are also often used for the secondary purpose of identifying which organizational units are associated with which activities. This is done by using "swim lanes" that divide the diagram into parallel strips, each strip being labeled with the name of a related organizational unit. The boxes representing activities are still joined together to represent their sequential dependencies, but they're put into the swim lane corresponding to where, in an organizational sense, they are carried out.

For the modeler, the organizational units themselves are more examples of things that require explicit representation. The hierarchical organizational structure can be captured by UML classes, using recursive relationships on an OrganizationalUnit class, so that a unit at one level can contain other lower-level units. Subclassing can be used if appropriate to show specializations. These classes also provide a convenient link between other classes representing roles and process elements, increasing the coherence of the business model structure.

2.2.9 Business rules

Business rules are one of the most important pieces of the puzzle. They are contained in every information system that's ever been built but for a long time have been implicit, hidden behind the fabric of other elements. Only fairly recently has the value of an explicit representation been recognized and business rules become first-class citizens in their own right.

In the business architecture, rules provide an excellent means of encapsulating knowledge about the intentions of the business. This knowledge can then be applied to define and to control other entities. There's a lot more to say about business rules, and now that we've seen the business context, we can get down to describing them in depth.

The following chapters provide the details of how business rules can be defined, validated, managed, and used to bridge between specification and realization. The key point to take away from this chapter is that rules can't stand in isolation but need to be rooted in a rich representation that captures the many facets of a business that are needed to provide a balanced picture.

2.3   What does a complete model look like?

One reasonable question to ask is, How big should a business model be? The short answer is, As big as necessary. The business architecture we've discussed gives some examples of the kinds of elements you'll need. The number required of each will depend on the scope of your model and the level of detail you want to include. Figure 2-15 gives an idea of the sort of scope you could expect, with the upper end of the range corresponding to a reasonably complete model of a medium- to large-scale business.

The diagram shows that a large model will generally have tens or hundreds of each kind of element, except for rules, which may range into the thousands, owing to the relatively fine granularity of rules compared to other elements. Fortunately, rules commonly group into clusters that can be treated as units in their own right. We'll see more of this in later chapters.

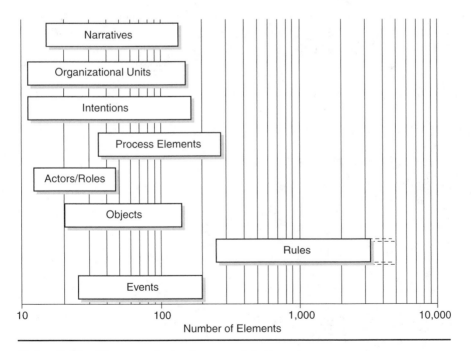

Figure 2-15   Size range for business model elements

2.4   Modeling summary

To have any hope of building an information system that meets business require-ments, you will need a clear idea of what they are. In this book, we're using the word *model* to describe a multifaceted information structure that's used to capture the requirements. It does this by describing how the business intends to operate. The description covers several interlocking viewpoints, each of which highlights a particular aspect of "the way we do business."

There's no absolute definition of what goes to make up a model. You will have to make choices about the kinds of things that are important in your situation and the extent of the model(s) that you feel comfortable about creating and main-taining.

The true defining characteristic of a business model is that it should be built entirely from business terminology. This may sound obvious, but it's surprising just how easy it is for technical features to creep in. Two good reasons for exclud-ing technology from a business model are that

- We want to avoid being saddled with premature decisions on what may or may not be the most appropriate technology.
- We want the model to be understandable by businesspeople, with a mini-mum of training.

The second of these reasons allows debate about the scope and the direction of the business to be concluded before technology is considered, so that subsequent development can proceed from a reasonably clear and stable baseline.

PART II

CAPTURING BUSINESS RULES

3

Defining Business Rules

3.1   Rule statements

In this chapter, we concentrate on what a business rule looks like. This begs the question of how we find rules in the first place, but that's the subject of the next chapter. On balance, it's probably better to start with a description of what to look for rather than how to find it.

3.1.1   Business rule characteristics

Broadly speaking, business rules are constraints: They define conditions that must hold true in specified situations. Sometimes called invariants, business rules are not descriptions of a process or processing. Rather, they define the conditions under which a process is carried out or the new conditions that will exist after a process has been completed. (The word *process* is used here in the general sense.)

Putting this another way, business rules define *what* must be the case rather than *how* it comes to be. A set of rules that define pre- and postconditions can act as a specification for a process, without constraining the mechanisms through which the preconditions are transformed into the postconditions.

Business rule statements in the business model define the desired logic of the business. They describe a state of affairs that the business wants to exist—in fact, what the business demands. If they were to be expressed as Boolean functions, business rules would always return a value of true; otherwise, they would be pretty useless as a definition of the desired logic. From a logical business rule perspective, there are no exceptions; there are only rules. A supposed exception to a business rule is simply another business rule.

You should not confuse this with what happens after the rule has been implemented. During processing, conditions may exist that would result in false if the business rule were to be evaluated. The whole point of the business rule approach is that it identifies the conditions that need to be detected and the corrective action that's required to restore the system to a state in which "true" always prevails. Typically, these are inside transactions, which we'll consider in more detail in a later chapter. Once a transaction has reached a stable state—has completed or aborted—it must not leave the system in a condition that contravenes any business rule.

The job of the business analyst is to specify a series of clear statements about the logic underlying a business. The emphasis on clarity is crucial. The business rule statements must be in a form that the business owner can immediately accept as valid or reject as invalid. If you are an analyst, this is your job. A retreat into "technospeak" is an admission of failure. It's no good complaining that the businesspeople don't understand first-order predicate calculus or whatever you may think is particularly cool from a technology perspective. The fact that they already operate the business without using anything more than simple natural-language statements is a strong proof that esoteric notations, technical languages, and so on, are not essential.

More than two thousand years of experience have shown that it's perfectly possible to make clear, logical statements using nothing more than ordinary words: in English, French, Chinese, German, Japanese, Spanish. The language doesn't matter as long as the logic is clear. To be sure that what you're saying is really sensible, it's useful to break a description of a complex system down into a set of small, manageable units, like logical propositions. If you're not sure what this means, the appendix gives an overview of how to form and to manipulate logical statements.

On its own, one business rule statement may not look very impressive. It may say something about the business that seems trite, obvious, and hardly worth the trouble. Don't worry; this is a good thing. If it seems obvious, you've cracked the most difficult problem: making the business logic understandable.

The real power comes from two directions:

- The ability to make business-level statements that can be translated in a fairly direct way to become part of an operational system
- The combined effect of relatively large numbers of simple statements, so that together, the whole has an impact that's greater than the sum of the individual parts.

The starting point for all this is nothing more than a series of simple statements about the business. There's nothing technical or difficult to understand here. What we're trying to do is so simple, it seems patently obvious. The strange thing is that so many organizations become diverted by other concerns, especially political ones, that they forget the obvious and get diverted onto side issues.

Let's start with a simple list of the characteristics that we would like to see in business rule statements. These universal characteristics apply across any language, tool, application domain, or any other sort of division. We're looking for business rule statements that are

- Atomic: can't be broken down any further without losing information
- Unambiguous: have only one, obvious, interpretation
- Compact: typically, a single short sentence
- Consistent: together, they provide a unified and coherent description
- Compatible: use the same terms as the rest of the business model

In the following sections of this chapter, we'll see how to put together statements that fit with this agenda.

3.1.2 Business aspects

At a high level, business rules could be classified under one or more concerns, such as the following:

- Reducing risks to the business or minimizing their impact
- Improving customer service
- Making the most efficient use of corporate resources
- Controlling or managing the flow of work

However, knowing this does not necessarily help with identifying the rules in the first place. At a finer level of detail, rules are commonly associated with various aspects of the business; Table 3-1 summarizes a few of the most common ones. We'll look at the process of rule discovery in more detail in the next chapter.

Table 3-1 Some uses of rules

Aspect	Examples
Consistency of information	Dates, modes of address, corporate styles, and so on that should be treated in the same way throughout the organization
Entity relationships	Relationships that must be enforced between entities relevant to the business, perhaps under certain conditions; for example, a Party must have at least one Contact Point
Identification of situations	Recognition of common business situations, allowing standardized, predictable, and well-managed responses to be made
Data integrity	Default values, algorithms for computation, checks on correctness of values, and other means of ensuring the correctness of data

3.1.3 What should a rule say?

Business rules should be concerned only with the conditions that must apply in a defined state. If you're writing a rule statement, you should resist the temptation to add extra information that goes outside this boundary. The extra information should be covered elsewhere; by duplicating it in a rule, you are only increasing the potential for error.

In particular, a business rule should define *what* should be the case and should not prescribe

- *Who* invokes the rule. (This is usually described in a use case or a process description.)
- *When* the rule is executed. (This is usually described in a business event, a use case, or a process description.)
- *Where* the rule executes. (This will be defined in design.)
- *How* the rule is to be implemented. (This will be defined in design.)

This point sometimes causes confusion, so it's worth being extra clear about it. We're not saying that rules should be prohibited from mentioning people, places, times, and so on. It's more a question of describing a state of affairs that should exist.

For instance, consider a rule that starts

During the final quarter, all managers based in Europe must . . .

This does not specify *who* invokes the rule. It's not necessarily any of the managers referred to. It could be their secretaries, their bosses, an automation system, any combination of these, or different ones at different times.

It does not specify *when* the rule is executed. The rule is applicable only in a given period, but, depending on the choice of implementation, it could be checked at the end of each working day, once at the end of the quarter, with every database transaction, or any other time the business decides.

Nor does it specify *where* the rule is executed. The rule defines what happens in a specific geographical area, but it could be executed at the head office, at each manager's location, in a remote automation system, or wherever is most convenient for the business.

A less obvious case is the question of *why* the rule is applied. Let's pull apart two separate issues:

- *Why* are we bothering with this rule in the first place?
- If processing fails because of a particular rule, can we tell *why* this is happening?

The answer to the first question is a fairly simple consequence of the system scope. The rule is relevant if it's something we need to say to pin down an aspect of the system. If we need it, we say it; if not, we don't. We'll have more to say about defining and recording the source of a rule in later chapters.

The second question is a bit more interesting and reflects a common problem with today's systems. If something goes wrong, how can we tell what's happening? A description of the problem at a technical level might only add to the confusion. For example, an error message, such as "interface method addParty failed" is not very helpful to a businessperson. Such a failure, which, of course, will require rectification before processing can continue, is best explained by the business rule that identified the problem.

For instance, let's say we have this business rule:

R301 A Party must be related to at least one PartyRole.

If we tried to create an instance of a Party without defining the role that the Party plays, what should the system do? Clearly, it should not accept the existence of the Party, given that particular business rule. What would be the best explanation of the failure? It is the business rule itself; read R301 again. This is a point to take on board when creating business rules: Thinking through the immediate business pressures, how could we answer the *why* question?

3.1.4 Levels of expression

So far, we've glibly talked about rule statements as one simple kind of thing. In fact, it's possible to imagine at least three levels of rule expression. All have a structure but occupy different points along the trade-off between accessibility of business meaning and desirable automation properties. The following examples illustrate what a rule might look like at each of the levels. (These aren't meant to correspond to any particular language or notation standard.)

1. *Informal.* This provides colloquial natural-language statements within a limited range of patterns. For example:

   A credit account customer must be at least 18 years old

2. *Technical.* This combines structured data references, operators, and constrained natural language. For example:

   ```
   CreditAccount
   self.customer.age >= 18
   ```

3. *Formal.* This provides statements conforming to a more closely defined syntax with particular mathematical properties. For example:

   ```
   {X , Y, (customer X) (creditAccount Y) (holder X Y) }
   ==> (ge (age X) 18)
   ```

The quest for greater structure points to the most formal option as being the most desirable, but most people at the business level would be far happier with the more colloquial informal option. One way of resolving this is through decent tool support. Figure 3-1 shows a low-technology way of creating and using rule statements.

The analyst creates rules at an informal level, treating the rules as pieces of text. The text does have the advantage of keeping the rules easy to read, but all the control over rule structure, consistency, and so on, has to come from the discipline of the analyst. The translation into formal structures, leading ultimately to one or more implementations of the rule, is similarly a human activity, with consequent opportunities for the introduction of errors. This is roughly the level of support for business rules provided by the current generation of tools.

What's needed is a way of creating the more formal rule structure while retaining the ease of use of the colloquial statements. Figure 3-2 sketches how this might be achieved. The job of the analyst is now to manipulate a set of prede-fined structural units. The various structural forms can be used as a basis for generating the equivalent textual representations; they are not edited directly. Although the appearance to the analyst and to the business is still in the form of text, all the control over the structure is now within the system. Given a reliable structure to work from, it's now also possible to think about generating code from the structure.

We can take this even further. Figure 3-2 shows the analyst as an intermediary between the business owner and the rule definition, but human interpretation allows the introduction of errors. The ultimate goal has to be an arrangement closer to Figure 3-3, with the business owner having direct control over the rule definitions. Because present tools are not sufficiently mature, however, this is not a practical option today, but it's definitely the direction we should be taking.

In the rest of this chapter, we'll talk mainly about text-based rule statements, of the kind described as informal, but with an eye to the improved tool support we can expect from future generations of analysis and design tools.

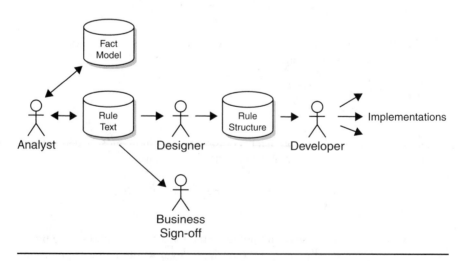

Figure 3-1   Low-technology rule definition

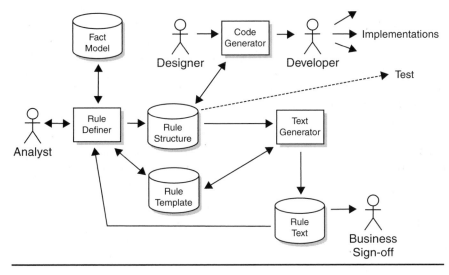

Figure 3-2   Controlled rule definition

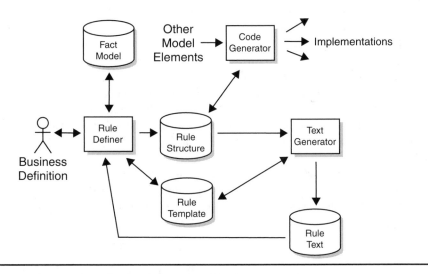

Figure 3-3   Rule definition: long-term objective

3.1.5   OCL

Although we've discussed a number of the notations used in UML, we haven't yet mentioned one of its less well-known features: the Object Constraint Language (OCL), which was added in UML version 1.1. See Warmer and Kleppe 1999 for more details. OCL is a language for expressing constraints on object-oriented models. It supplements the diagramming aspects of UML by allowing the modeler to say things that the diagrams don't support well or clearing up ambiguities that often seem to arise when UML class diagrams try to show complex relationships. In terms of the three levels described earlier, OCL fits somewhere around the technical level but perhaps somewhat on the formal side.

For example, suppose that we have a Person class with an attribute social-SecurityNumber. We want to have a rule that a person's social security number must be unique. That wording is more or less how we would express it in a rule at the informal level. Here's how it looks at a technical/formal level in OCL:

```
Person
Person.allInstances -> forAll (p1, p2 |
      p1 <> p2 implies   p1.socialSecurityNumber <>
                         p2.socialSecurityNumber)
```

If you read this carefully, you can pretty much tell what it's saying, even if you aren't familiar with the OCL syntax. For the average analyst, creating it from scratch might be a different matter, though. And as far as getting the business owner to sign off on something like this, forget it!

To date, OCL's main claim to fame has been its role in cleaning up the UML specification, but there's very little evidence of its achieving widespread adoption in practical information systems, which is a pity. The apparent lack of enthusiasm undoubtedly results from the daunting appearance the syntax presents to the business owner and also to most analysts. OCL is really usable only by a technical specialist, which rules it out as a candidate for the "visible" rule format that we want to present to the business owner in Figure 3-3 and, probably, also to the analyst in Figure 3-2.

Let's not write OCL off, though. It could have a very useful part to play behind the scenes, as a more precise representation that an informal rule might be translated into. For now, we'll put it to one side because we need to focus on the front-end business statements.

3.2 Forming rule statements

The most convenient way of creating rule statements is to select an appropriate pattern selected from a short list of available patterns. Besides saving valuable analysis time, this helps to enforce some consistency of approach. In this section, we discuss a vanilla set of patterns that should be applicable across a range of types of applications and industries.

The patterns we cover are in the form of *statements*, and they're all more or less elaborate versions of one basic form:

```
<subject> must <constraint>
```

This is in tune with the idea that a rule is always true: The rule makes a statement about what must or must not be the case in the operational system. Both the `<subject>` and the `<constraint>` of the rule can get to be fairly complex, as shown in some of the examples that follow later. A range of patterns allows us to have reasonably natural-sounding business sentences without introducing all the difficulties associated with full natural-language processing.

In addition to conforming to an appropriate pattern, the rule also has to make reference to other model elements, principally business objects and their attributes. This is done through a fact model, which we'll look at in more detail shortly. Figure 3-4 shows the position of rule statements in this scheme of things.

There's no standard for how to make rule statements, although it's possible to make some recommendations, based on experience. You should regard the following set of patterns as a suggestion to start from rather than a mandatory requirement. One reason you might want to use a different set of patterns is to fine-tune the wording for the domain you're working in. These patterns might reflect the way things are done in your industry or the kinds of problems that your automation system is intended to deal with. What's important is not the patterns themselves but the adoption of this style of rule definition. We'll see an example in a case study later in this chapter.

The following patterns have a reasonably neutral flavor: They don't assume any particular kind of application. The only presupposition is the existence of a fact model to provide a context for the subject and the constraint.

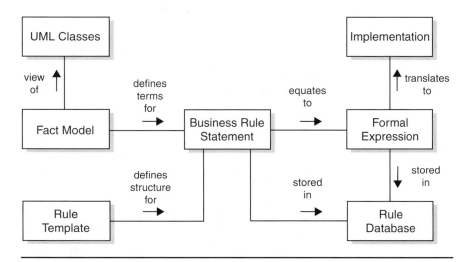

Figure 3-4   Rule statements and their relationships

3.2.1   Pattern conventions

The conventions used in the patterns are as follows.

- Parentheses ( ) enclose a group of terms
- Brackets [ ] enclose optional terms
- Vertical bars | separate alternative terms
- Angle brackets < > enclose special terms, as defined in Table 3-2.

Note that the symbols do not appear in the rule statement but only in the pattern definition.

Table 3-2   Variable pattern elements

Element	Meaning
<det>	The determiner for the subject; from the following, the one that makes the best business sense in the statement: A An The Each Every (or nothing).
<subject>	A recognizable business entity, such as a business object visible in the fact model, a role name, or a property of an object. The entity may be qualified by other descriptive elements, such as its existence in a particular state, in order to specify the applicability of the rule with enough precision.
<characteristic>	The business behavior that must take place or a relationship that must be enforced.
<fact>	A relationship between terms identifiable in the fact model, together with defined constants. The relationship may be qualified by other descriptive elements in order to specify the applicability of the rule precisely.
<fact-list>	A list of <fact> items.
<m>, <n>	Numeric parameters.
<result>	Any value, not necessarily numeric, that has some business meaning. The result is often, but does not have to be, the value of an attribute of a business object.
<algorithm>	A definition of the technique to be used to derive the value of a result; normally expressed using combinations of variable terms identifiable in the fact model together with available constants.
<classification>	A definition of a term in the fact model. This typically defines either the value of an attribute, perhaps called "state" or something similar, or a subset of the objects in an existing class.
<enum-list>	A list of enumerated values. An *open* enumeration indicates that the list may be modified in the light of future requirements; for example, a list of status values for an object as currently known. A *closed* enumeration indicates that changes to the list are not anticipated; for example, days of the week. The distinction is helpful in later implementation.

3.2.2   Rule patterns

Pattern 1: Basic constraint   This pattern, the most common business rule pattern, establishes a constraint on the subject of the rule. Two equally valid variants are provided; choose the option that gives the most natural business style to the rule statement when you read it back. The optional word "should" in this pattern and the next one makes an easier-sounding expression in some circumstances. It does not make the rule optional in any way. If you think that this may cause confusion in your organization, don't allow its use.

> <det> <subject> (must | should) [not] <characteristic>
> [(if | unless) <fact>].

> <det> <subject> may (<characteristic> only if <fact>) | (not
> <characteristic>).

Examples:

> R302   An urgent order must not be accepted if the order value
> is less than $30.

> R303   An account may be closed only if the current balance
> is zero.

Pattern 2: List constraint   This pattern also constrains the subject, but the constraining characteristic(s) is (are) one or more items taken from a list. Again, two variants are provided, so you can choose the one that's the best fit to the particular situation.

> <det> <subject> (must | should) [not] <characteristic> (if |
> unless) at least <m> [and not more than <n>] of the following
> is true: <fact-list>.

> <det> <subject> (may <characteristic> only if) | (may not
> <characteristic> if) at least <m> [and not more than <n>]
> of the following is true: <fact-list>.

Examples:

> R304   A next-day order must not be accepted if at least one of
> the following is true:
> —Order is received after 15:00, Monday through Friday,
> —Order is received anytime on Saturday or Sunday,
> —Order is received between 15 December and 5 January,
> —Postal inhibition is in place.

R305   A customer may be raised from Bronze to Silver status
only if at least one of the following is true:
—The customer's account balance has been positive for
the past 12 months,
—The customer's average account balance over the past
12 months exceeds $500.

Pattern 3: Classification   This pattern establishes a definition for a term in the
fact model. Such terms are likely to have only a short-term, temporary usage. If
the distinction is permanent, it may be better to reflect it in the fact model. The
variants are just choices for readability.

<det> <subject> is [not] defined as <classification>
[(if | unless) <fact>].

<det> <subject> must [not] be considered as <classification>
[(if | unless) <fact>].

Examples:

R306   An order is defined as urgent if delivery is required in
less than three hours.

R307   A customer without credit clearance must be considered
as cash-only.

Pattern 4: Computation   This pattern establishes a relationship between terms
in the fact model sufficient to allow the computation or the establishment of a
value. Note that this is similar to the Classification pattern. Using "is defined as"
instead of the imperative "must be computed as" leaves the computation implicit
in the relationship. This is to avoid an overprocedural style and because it may be
possible to compute various values based on the relationship. For instance, in the
following example R308 it would be equally valid to calculate "total item value"
from "total sale value" and "sales tax". Two variants are provided; the second is
more likely to be favored for mathematical expressions.

<det> <result> is defined as <algorithm>.
<det> <result> = <algorithm>.

Examples:

R308   Total sale value is defined as total item value plus sales
tax.

R309   Pi = 4 * arctan(1).

Pattern 5: Enumeration   This pattern establishes the range of values that can legitimately be taken by a term in the fact model.

```
<det> <result> must be chosen from the following
[ open | closed ] enumeration: <enum-list>.
```

Example:

    R310   Customer standing must be chosen from the following
               closed enumeration:
               —Gold,
               —Silver,
               —Bronze.

3.2.3   Rule sets

For complex cases, it may be useful to group rules into rule sets, or one "master" rule with a number of subsidiary rules. Splitting up a complex problem into smaller parts greatly helps the initial rule definition and is vital for long-term maintainability. An extended example of a rule set is given in the next chapter.

3.2.4   Static models versus rule statements

Some situations require you to exercise judgment about the best way to capture the business logic. The main area for trade-off is between business rules and the fact model. A good example of this is cardinality (also known as multiplicity). Simple cardinality constraints on associations can sometimes be expressed either as a rule or directly in the static model without using a rule statement. A fragment of a fact model with a typical simple relationship is shown in Figure 3-5.

Let's say that we wanted to exercise some control over this and insist that if we hold any information about the existence of a Party, we must also identify the

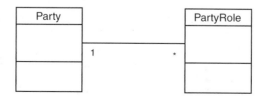

Figure 3-5   Relationship with weak constraint

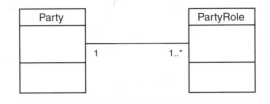

Figure 3-6   Relationship constrained by cardinality on class model

role that Party plays, such as customer or supplier. One way of doing this would be with a business rule, such as:

> R311   A Party must be related to at least one PartyRole.

Alternatively, instead of using the business rule, the constraint could be shown using cardinality markings on the class model, as shown in Figure 3-6. In this case, no rule statement would be needed.

However, in general, you should be very wary about introducing additional classes or associations into the fact model purely to express constraints. The logic will be clearer, and more maintainable in the long term, if it's captured in the form of rule statements. We'll return to this later in the book when we get to rule realizations.

A useful guideline—if you can convince your local UML zealots—is to limit the class diagram to showing just one (1) or many (*) on the association ends and stating any elaborations on this as explicit business rules. That way, it's always clear where you should look for any constraints.

3.3   References to facts

3.3.1   Terms and rules

The rule statements refer to various terms—used as the definition of <subject> and <constraint>—that are visible in a supporting fact model. What ties a rule down to a particular situation is the explicit reference to something that's visible in the fact model.

Business rules build on a known set of facts described in a model. Conceptually, this *fact model* shows business objects, their relationships, and their attributes. In practice, a UML class diagram usually fulfills the role of a fact model. One thing to check, though, is that your fact model is able to distinguish between

- Items of business record: things that are going to be stored in persistent form, probably in a database

• Objects, properties, and relationships that have definitional value but do not exist as recognizable artifacts in the operational information system or, if they do, have at most a transient existence

A convention you can use on your class diagram is to precede any names that aren't to be treated as persistent with a forward slash character (/). So, for example, a class called Entry is persistent, but a class called /EntryInput is not. Some tools may provide other ways of achieving the same end by the use of icons, colors, and so on.

Preferably, references to terms in rules should use the same form as in the fact model. For example, a complex class name might appear as MyComplexClassName. The purpose of this is to reduce the potential for ambiguity. You might want to make exceptions if the use of a precise reference of this sort obscures the business meaning of the rule, but this may equally well point to a need to find a better class name.

You'll have to decide how to refer to attributes of objects; for instance, an "order" business object may have a "total value" attribute. One style is to rely on the normal constructs available in English or whatever language you're using; for instance, "the order's total value" or "the total value of the order" or something similar. The other main option is to use dot notation, producing something like Order.totalValue. This option is much more precise and can use the names from the class diagram, but it may not be acceptable as a form of business expression. This is something that you will have to negotiate within your own organization.

You also have a choice about how to handle complex relationships. One approach is to introduce extra classes and associations into the business model to capture the necessary features. But doing this makes it more difficult to automate subsequent design steps. For instance, the class model is a good starting point for the automatic generation of a database schema, but that's going to be difficult to do if it mixes in some elements that are there only for explanatory purposes. If you do introduce additional classes and/or associations to model your constraints, you must bear in mind that these additions will almost certainly be reflected in the structure of the associated database. Changing the structure of an operational database is generally very difficult, so don't put constraints of this type into the static (class) model unless you are very sure that they are not going to change in the future.

As an example, think about the details of how many cards of various kinds could be held by a bank's customers. A fragment of a possible model is shown in Figure 3-7. Various kinds of customer-card relationships could be expressed by

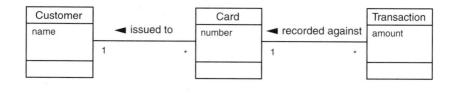

Figure 3-7   Customers, cards, and transactions

defining various specializations of customer and card. Other classes could also be introduced to reify, or make concrete, various abstract features of customers and/or cards. If treated as persistent objects, like records in tables in a database, the resulting structure could be difficult to design and implement, difficult to change, and challenging for the business owner to understand. If the relationship in the business model is kept simple, as shown in Figure 3-7, any necessary customer or card restrictions, special cases, and so on, can be expressed in a much more maintainable way as business rules.

In summary, keep the classes and relationships as simple as possible in your class diagram, and put any constraints on class membership or associations as business rules. Doing so has two advantages:

- The initial database is straightforward to design and to implement.
- Future variations in the constraints can be accommodated by changing the rules rather than the class structure, leading to much greater flexibility.

3.3.2   Individual items

The following examples navigate the relationships from the simple model in a direction that always leads to an individual item. Collections, or multiple items, are discussed later.

Classes—and implicitly the business objects they represent—are indicated by name:

Customer

If the <subject> of a rule is just an unqualified class name, the rule will apply to any object, an instance of that class:

A Customer must . . .

This could be the start of a rule that would apply to any object of type Customer. Attributes can optionally be shown by using dot notation:

Classname.attribute

For example, we could refer to

The customer's name

or

Customer.name

whichever gives the more understandable rule.

Dot notation can be extended for more complicated relationships by using a navigation path. Starting from one class, we can navigate to another by using the role names on the association ends. Remember that the role name defaults to the class name if not explicitly stated, although to be consistent with the UML, class names used as role names should start with a lowercase letter. In Figure 3-7, we could describe the customer associated with a particular transaction as

Transaction.card.customer

This is equivalent to the more verbose English form: "the customer to whom the card was issued that the transaction was recorded against."

Attributes can also be identified in the same way, as in:

Transaction.card.number

A feature of the dot notation is that a navigational reference to a role name has the same syntactic form as a reference to an attribute, as in:

Transaction.card   (a class)
Transaction.amount   (an attribute)

In other words, a reference of this type must be read in conjunction with a class model in order to understand what is being referred to. This feature is taken into account in the UML definitions, which forbid a role name for a class from being the same as one of its attribute names, precisely to avoid potential clashes of this sort.

Where necessary, you can qualify a reference to a class to define a rule that applies only to a subset of the class. In the following example, the <subject> of the rule is any <ContactRequest with a status of Closed>, not any Contact Request:

A ContactRequest with a status of Closed must . . .

Try to keep anything that refines the subject together in the <subject> part of the rule. Use the <fact> part of the rule for other constraints. In the following example, <System.time is greater than 16:00> does not refine the definition of a Contact Request and so is a <fact>, not part of the definition of the <subject>:

R312X   A ContactRequest must (something) only if System.time
         is greater than 16:00.

3.3.3   References to multiple items

In some cases, you will want to make statements about a collection of objects. For example, in the context of a particular customer, the following is a collection of transactions, not a single transaction (see Figure 3-7):

Customer.card.transaction

To be precise, it's all the transactions for all the cards held by the customer. Multiple levels of collections are assumed to be flattened, which is why this example is a collection of transactions, not a collection of cards, each of which has a collection of transactions.

It can feel a little awkward having a singular name when you're referring to many objects. This comes from UML's default use of the class name to designate the end of an association. This problem can be resolved by adding a specific plural role name, such as "transactions," to the association instead of using the default, singular class name. The model would then look like Figure 3-8.

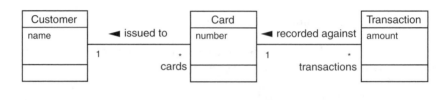

Figure 3-8   Using role names to improve readability

Several operations are relevant to a collection. Some of the most useful ones are summarized in Table 3-3. Obviously, the placeholders <collection>, <element>, and so on, can be replaced by specific references when these operations are used in a business rule. The exact form of words is less important than getting the logical statement correct. Multiple items don't introduce any concepts that we haven't already seen. In complex cases, you might want to use a technique such as Venn diagrams to get a clearer idea of the relationships between various collections and their members. The appendix gives more detail on this.

Table 3-3   Operations on collections

Operation	Usage
Size of <collection>	Defines how many elements the collection contains
Count of <element> in <collection>	Defines how many times the specified element appears in the collection
<collection> includes <element>	True if the specified element is included in the collection
<collection1> includes all <collection2>	True if all the elements in collection2 are present in collection1
<collection> is empty	True if the collection contains no elements
<element> exists in <collection>	True if at least one of the specified elements exists in the collection
<expression> for all <collection>	True if the expression is true for all the elements in the collection

3.4 Business parameters

Business rules act to constrain the operation of a system in various ways, controlling its behavior in diverse situations, ensuring that variable data always conforms to the desired structures, and so on. Business parameters are critical values that have a similar constraining influence. Rules use parameters to define boundaries, identify names used in enumerations, provide specific string values, and many other purposes. Parameters are also used by other model elements. Because they're closely related to business rules, parameters can be defined and managed in much the same way.

A parallel situation arises when common values pop up at various points in software code. If handled in the wrong way, these values seem to materialize out of thin air without visible support, so they're sometimes referred to as *magic numbers*. If the actual values are used directly in the program—called *hard-coding*—maintenance becomes more difficult. A change to a value means searching for all the places where it's been used: no mean feat if it's a large automation system. Instead, the recommended approach is to use *a program constant*. This gives a meaningful name to the value; because it is defined in just one place, it's easy to locate if a change is needed. The result in a program is something that looks like:

```
' declarations
Public Const MAX_CREDIT = 5000
     ' more code ...
If orderValue < MAX_CREDIT Then CreateOrder(items)
     ' more code ...
' and so on
```

The situation is pretty much the same at the business level. Because of the analogy with programming, these values are sometimes called *business constants*. However, this is something of a misnomer; the whole point of specially identifying these values is that they might *not* remain constant. For this reason, it's better to refer to them as *business parameters*.

Business parameters can range in complexity from a single value to a whole database table. For simple values, we can use forms of statements similar to those used for business rules, such as:

Maximum credit limit is $5,000.

For the more complicated cases, this approach soon gets very cumbersome and difficult to maintain. An example that's likely to be needed in a global e-commerce system is a set of standard parameters for individual countries. Table 3-4 shows what this might look like.

Table 3-4   Example of complex business parameters

Country	Code	Currency	Symbol	. . . and so on
Afghanistan	AF	Afghani	AFA	. . .
Albania	AL	Lek	ALL	. . .
Algeria	DZ	Algerian dinar	DZD	. . .
American Samoa	AS	US dollar	USD	. . .
. . . and so on	. . .	. . .	. . .	. . .

This information may not be as static as it seems. Countries merge, split, change their names, adopt different currencies, and so on. Any value that we might need to look up should be treated in the sense of a business parameter. The only exceptions are values that are so fixed that they don't vary from place to place or time to time; for instance, mathematical constants, such as *pi,* always have the same value anywhere in the world and for all time.

The potential for change also introduces the need for change control. If we change a parameter, such as increasing the maximum credit limit from $5,000 to $8,000, we must be able to introduce this at the right time and to align historical transactions with a particular version of the parameter. We'll look at the issues involved in configuration management in more detail in a later chapter.

Enumerations can be represented as business parameters or as attributes of special classes in the fact model as alternatives to the enumeration pattern. For example, a definition of the possible values that could be taken by a status attribute could be defined by the following rule form. (See the earlier pattern definitions for why this should be an open enumeration.)

> R313   A Contact Request Status must be chosen from the
> following open enumeration:
> —Open,
> —Pending,
> —Failed,
> —Delivered.

Alternatively, it could be represented as a special class—the UML recommendation—as shown in Figure 3-9. You will have to decide on the most appropriate method to suit your own local circumstances.

Figure 3-9   Defining an enumeration as a class

3.5   Tips on rule construction

This section discusses some common problems that arise in the construction of rule statements. The examples are intended to illustrate variations in rule syntax and so don't necessarily contain real business knowledge or relate to any particular business model. Also, each example should be taken in isolation; these rules are not intended to form a single, coherent model.

We'll look at potential problems in the following areas:

- Using facts
- Simple constraints
- Quantifications and qualifications
- States and events
- Actors
- Dangerous verbs
- Computation
- Structure and consistency

All these categories should be kept in mind when the rules are created, as well as in reviews aimed at controlling the quality of the rules, covered in more detail in Chapter 5. The example rules have been numbered for ease of reference. Rule numbers ending in X indicate rules that are incomplete, inconsistent, or badly formed.

3.5.1   Using facts

Use a fact model   You should have a fact model available so that the rules can be related to other parts of the business model. The rules should always relate to elements visible in the fact model.

For example, look at the model fragment shown in Figure 3-10.

The following rule produces an ambiguity when applied to the given fact model:

R314X   An Event categorized as 'Agreement' must . . .

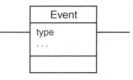

Figure 3-10   Model fragment

It's not clear whether the category stated in the rule is meant to refer to the *type* attribute of an Event business object or whether an Event is intended to have a *category* attribute as well as a *type* attribute.

The act of defining a rule may highlight some modification required to other facets of the business model, so treat the whole model as evolutionary. If it does need to be changed, don't forget to check for possible impact on other rules that have been defined earlier.

Question basic assumptions   Reconsider the rule by reducing it to a simpler form by removing any associated qualifications. For example, we might have as a rule:

> R315   A loan greater than X must be approved by a branch manager of grade Y or higher with at least one year in post.

We can reduce this rule to its most fundamental form as:

> R316   A loan must be approved.

Then ask questions.

- What is the underlying business goal behind the fundamental rule?
- Does the rule fully address associated risks?
- Are there other ways of achieving the business goal?

Of course, if the rule forms part of the fundamental definition of the business, such as a "given" in the business statements of policy, there is no point in questioning the basic assumptions.

Question the terms used   Look for terms that may be too wide or too narrow. For instance, in the example rule R316, we might question whether the term "loan" is too wide and whether we should be concerned only with certain types of loan, such as "unsecured loan." Alternatively, we may want to widen the term to include other financial products. As with the fundamental assumptions, if the terms are "given," there is no point in questioning them.

Explicit relationships   Make relationships explicit, so that it's clear what the rule is constraining. Sentences containing the verb *to have* are a particular danger signal. You don't have to avoid *to have;* it's often the best way to state the conditions under which an attribute should be set to a particular value or business objects should be associated. Just make sure that you are being explicit.

Consider the following:

R317X   Each project must have a manager.

This example does not make it sufficiently clear exactly what the project should "have" a sponsor in management? a manager representing user interests? a line manager? The rule should make this clear:

R318   Each project must be managed by a project manager.

Obscure facts or terms   Look out for facts or terms that are not adequately qualified. The rule may seem clear at the time but could be open to various interpretations. This could lead to a realization that differs from your intention.

Look at this rule:

R319X   All inbound contacts must identify the associated Party.

In this example, the meaning of Party might be defined adequately in the class model, but what does the word "associated" imply: the Party making the contact? the Party responsible for creating the content of the contact? the Party to whom the contact is addressed?

An improved rule might be:

R320   An inbound contact must be associated with the
         originating Party.

Vague terms   Avoid using vague terms, such as "there," as the subject of a rule.

R321X   There may be no more than two overdue payments on a
          type A account.

Make the meaning explicit by moving the focus of the rule to the real subject. The preceding example would be improved as:

R322   A type A account must have no more than two overdue
         payments.

3.5.2   Simple constraints

No permissions   Avoid unqualified use of words such as "can" or "may," in a rule. Unqualified terms such as these might turn out to be permission statements and not constraints. By definition, anything in the underlying business model "can" be true. The purpose of the rules is to define the conditions under which something in the fact model is mandated or prohibited: in other words, a constraint.

Sentences with "can" or equivalent simply say that something might or might not be the case, which is too vague to be useful. For example, the following rule is presumably trying to imply a limitation on the values of loans that can be approved by a branch manager:

> R323X   A branch manager can approve loans up to the value of $10,000.

But the way the rule is stated, it could be optional. It might also imply, but doesn't actually state, that the manager may not approve loans of value $10,000 and above.

The rule should state precisely what is intended, as in:

> R324   A branch manager may approve a loan only if the value of the loan is less than $10,000.

Avoid padding   Don't overelaborate the rules. Keep them short and to the point, and avoid padding them out with filler terms that add nothing to the definition. For example, the following rules are unnecessarily wordy ways of saying the same thing.

> R325X   The payment period allowed must never be greater than 60 days for any customer.
>
> R326X   The time period that's allowed for payment can be for a period of up to but not exceeding 60 days.
>
> R327X   For any order, however it has been raised, the period allowed for payment may not exceed 60 days.

A more straightforward version, containing the same information, would be:

> R328   The allowed payment period must not exceed 60 days.

Using "or"   Avoid joining multiple terms with "or." Such rules can be difficult to understand and to maintain. A particular trap for the unwary is the difference between *inclusive-or* and *exclusive-or;* see the appendix if you're unsure about which is which. It is usually better to split "or" rules into separate rules or to make the nature of the constraint more explicit. For example:

> R329X   A Party is defined as high worth if it is a VIP, has a current balance of at least X, or has held an account for more than Y years.

It's not clear whether this means exactly one or at least one of the conditions. Also, what would happen if the rule changed to two out of the three? A more explicit, and more maintainable, rule would be:

> R330   A Party is defined as high worth if at least one of the
> following is true:
> —The Party is a VIP,
> —The Party has a current balance of at least *X*,
> —The Party has held an account for more than *Y* years.

Of course, establishing whether a Party is to be considered a VIP may well require further rules.

Using "and"   Be careful about using "and" in expressing rules. It should be reserved for cases in which you really do mean "and" in its logical sense. Maintainability is usually improved by splitting "and-ed" clauses into separate atomic rules, especially if the clauses might change independently in the future. For example:

> R331X   A withdrawal from an account may be made only if the
> account is active and the account balance is greater than
> zero.

This example could be expressed in more atomic form as:

> R332   A withdrawal from an account may be made only if the
> account is active.

> R333   A withdrawal from an account may be made only if the
> account balance is greater than zero.

If the "and-ed" terms are unlikely to change independently, another alternative would be to express the rule as a list constraint.

Complex rules   Complex rules are difficult to maintain and may hide terms of business significance that should be defined more explicitly. Such rules are better split into several simple rules or perhaps even a modification of the fact model. A split may introduce a need for some new intermediate terms, each representing part of the result or a step toward its production. These new intermediate terms should be given names that have some genuine business meaning rather than placeholder names that simply link rule statements. Wherever possible, you should prefer names that are already used by the business to describe the term in question. For example:

> R334X   A Party with *X* successive defaults must not be offered a
> new loan exceeding *Y*.

This rule could be easier to maintain if the additional terms "high-risk" and "high-value" are defined in the fact model. (You would, of course, have checked that these terms are the most relevant for the business in this context.) The original single rule can then be restated more clearly in three rules:

R335   A Party with X successive defaults is defined as high risk.

R336   A loan exceeding Y is defined as high value.

R337   A high-risk Party must not be offered a high-value loan.

As well as improving clarity, this type of simplification eases maintenance of the rule population over an extended period.

Starting with "if"   Avoid starting a rule with "if," which can lead to sentences that confuse the underlying logic. For example:

R338X   If an account is overdrawn, the customer may make only cash transactions.

Initially, this rule sounds as though an account, not a customer, is the subject of the rule. A better version would be:

R339   A customer with an overdrawn account may make only cash transactions.

3.5.3   Quantifications and qualifications

Question qualifications   Any qualifications can be assessed by stripping the rule down to its most basic form. Then, progressively add back the qualifications, while asking such questions as

- Are the qualifications necessary?
- Are they appropriate for the purpose?
- Are the specified values or ranges correct?
- Have specified values been defined as business parameters, where appropriate?

Even if the rule forms part of the fundamental definition of a business, the qualifications should still be questioned because they may have been added as embellishments during the evolution of the business descriptions.

Plural terms   Wherever possible, avoid using plurals as terms of rules. For example:

R340X   Contacts with high-value customers must be recorded.

Instead, express the rules as applying to individual instances of the appropriate business object. For example, the preceding rule is better as:

R341   A contact with a high-value customer must be recorded.

Each and every   Don't be afraid to say *each* or *every* if it improves the clarity of the rule. Consider the following rule:

R342X   An account must be allocated to a Customer
         Representative, with effect from 1 January 2002.

This rule might be better as:

R343   Each account must be allocated to a Customer
         Representative, with effect from 1 January 2002.

3.5.4   States and events

Events as subjects   Avoid using a business event, such as a business action, a time, or an external trigger, as the subject of a rule. For example:

R344X   By close of business, all withdrawals must be notified to
         the head office.

Events may well cause rules to be evaluated, but the real subject of the rule is the specific element that's affected, not the event. The preceding rule is better as:

R345   Each withdrawal must be notified to the head office
         before the close of business.

Ambiguous states   Avoid ambiguous states. For example:

R346X   The outstanding balance on a secondary account that is
         being closed must be transferred to the primary account
         before it is terminated.

Do "closed" and "terminated" mean the same thing? Does "terminated" refer to a state of the primary or to the secondary account? Each state should be distinct from other states for the same entity, and it should be clear exactly which entity the state is related to. A better statement would be:

R347   The outstanding balance on a secondary account that is
         being closed must be transferred to the primary account
         before the secondary account is closed.

Ambiguous time frames   Avoid ambiguous time frames. For example:

> R348X   A new account must be approved by at least two
>   managers in the final quarter.

This rule could be taken to mean that any new account must be approved by at least two managers but not until the last quarter. The definition of the period and the nature of the constraint should both be clear-cut. The correct interpretation is more likely to be:

> R349   A new account opened in the final quarter must be
>   approved by at least two managers.

Saying when   Be wary of introducing rules that use "when," which implies that an action is fixed to a particular point. For example:

> R350X   When a policy is issued, it must have a defined expiry
>   date.

Resequencing activities and redefining their interdependencies are typical areas for business process reengineering. This makes the "when" better defined in a business event or a business process, not in a business rule. A rule statement should refer to a constraint that applies in a particular state, not to transitions between states.

It might be possible for the expiry date to be changed after a policy has been issued. We want to eliminate the possibility that a subsequent change may result in a null expiry date, so a better version would be:

> R351   An issued policy must have an expiry date.

3.5.5   Actors

Question actors   If actors appear in the rule, we should ask questions about why that particular actor needs to be specified. For instance, in rule R324, we might question why the approver should specifically be a branch manager. Again, it may be appropriate to consider a narrower or a wider definition.

Consideration of this point may reveal a need for a better classification of actors. This is important because business process engineering activities often involve reassignment of tasks from one actor or group to another.

Even if the rule forms part of the fundamental definition of a business, it's still worth questioning the actors. For example, they may just reflect the current status quo rather than being genuine requirements of the business.

Actors as subjects   If you can, avoid making actors the subjects of rules. As we've said, redefining which actor does which action is a common feature in business process reengineering.

R352X   A customer representative may issue a replacement
         charge card only if the old card expired within the last
         30 days.

Putting this definition of who does what into the process descriptions makes it easier to change workflow patterns. Leave the rules to express the actor-independent logic. Thus, this rule would be better as:

R353   A replacement charge card may be issued only if the old
         card expired within the last 30 days.

3.5.6 Dangerous verbs

Command verbs   Avoid command verb forms. These often appeal to an invisible actor that may or may not exist. Such forms may also indicate related activity that's probably better captured in a process description. For example:

R354X   Don't credit an account with a deposit amount if the
         owning Party is in default.

This rule would be better as:

R355   An account for a Party in default may not be credited
         with a deposit amount.

Action verbs   Avoid action verbs, which are likely to create unclear definitions. For example:

R356X   A facility must not be terminated if transactions are
         pending.

Remember that rules should constrain what must or must not be true in a particular state; they are not intended to be descriptions of processes. Thus, this rule is better as:

R357   A terminated facility must not contain pending
         transactions.

CRUD words   Look carefully at rules that use CRUD words (create, read, update, delete) or other terms relating to possible implementations. Again, these words can refer to an action rather than to a constraint and may represent a procedure that should be scheduled. For example:

R358X   Update the account current balance by adding the new
         deposit amount when received.

Rules should be eventless and express only the underlying business logic. Thus, this rule would be better as:

R359 The account current balance is defined as the previous balance plus the amount of the new deposit.

CRUD-type words may provide useful clues in rule discovery, but the rule statements should decouple the constraint from its point of application.

3.5.7 Computation

Ambiguous computation You can clarify the essence of a computation by making the result of the computation the subject of the rule. For example:

R360X A customer may hold no more than three Type A and Type B accounts combined.

In this example, the computation implied is not immediately clear but is more obvious if the total is made the subject of the rule, as in:

R361 The combined total of Type A accounts and type B accounts held by a customer must not exceed three.

Embedded computations Look out for computations embedded within rules; separate these computations out. An algorithm or a formula might need to change independently from the entity that's being constrained by the rule. For example:

R362X The sum of the repayments to date must be greater than or equal to the cumulative debt.

Separating these concerns makes the rules easier to maintain. This rule could be easier to maintain if expressed as two rules:

R363 The cumulative repayment value for an account is defined as the sum of all repayment amounts to date.

R364 The cumulative repayment value must be greater than or equal to the cumulative debt.

3.5.8 Structure and consistency

Missing rules You can identify missing rules by thinking carefully about the kinds of constraints that would make business sense. A good way to do this is to work systematically through your business objects, especially the relationships among them. At each point, you can ask such questions as, "Does this always apply?" "Are there any special cases or exceptions?" "Is there perhaps a particular situation in which unrelated objects X and Y *could* be related?"

Overlap   Look among rules that relate to the same part of the model to check for overlapping coverage, where one rule is wholly or partly contained within another. In such cases, it may be necessary to rationalize the rules to remove the overlap. Take, for example, the following two rules:

> R365   A loan exceeding $1,000 must be approved by a branch manager or above.

> R366X   A loan exceeding $1,500 must be approved by a branch manager or above.

We can see that the second rule is subsumed by the first, so we could eliminate the second rule without losing any of the business control that the rule implies. Of course, we would also need to look at the source of both rules to make sure that $1,000 is indeed the right value to use in the single rule.

Note that this doesn't contravene the guideline about rules not specifying who applies them. Rule R365 expresses a relationship between a range of loan values and the seniority of the approver. The rule could be applied by a customer service agent checking a set of forms, an automated information system, an external auditor, or perhaps all these.

Duplication   Look for rules that are the same or very similar, perhaps with slight differences in the terms used or a different ordering of the statement wording. For example, the following two rules are duplicates and should be replaced by one rule.

> R367X   The total value of all current loan facilities must not exceed X.

> R368X   The sum of the values of existing loan facilities must not be greater than X.

This situation can arise if the current repository is not properly checked before defining a new rule or where an existing rule has been poorly categorized, making it difficult to find. Use of the standard rule patterns and rooting the rules in a fact model should minimize the occurrence of duplication.

Inversion   Look for situations in which two rules produce the same result, but one rule is stated as the inverse or complement of the other. For example:

> R369X   A new loan may not be offered to an overdrawn customer.

> R370X   An overdrawn customer may not be offered a new loan.

These two rules represent the same logic but with the order of terms reversed. Inversions are particularly likely to appear in the following situations:

- If A exists, then B must exist; If B exists, then A must exist.
- A must be equal to B; B must be equal to A.
- A must be greater than (or less than) B; B must be less than (or greater than) A.

The same is true for the negative (must not) forms.

Take special care with "greater than" and "less than" statements to consider whether the "equal to" case is meant to be included or excluded. Also, check carefully what is really intended by the rule statements. The appendix discusses how logical statements can legitimately be turned into alternative forms and some fallacies arising from incorrect transformations.

Conflict   Conflict arises when two or more rules produce contradictory results. For example:

R371X   An account holder may be issued with only one card.

R372X   An account holder may be issued with no more than two cards.

These two rules would produce conflicting results if an attempt were made to issue a second card to an account holder. Conflicts of this sort must always be resolved; rules with the potential for conflict cannot coexist within the same population.

Rule references   All the references between the rule statements and the rest of the model should be complete and consistent. "Complete" is difficult to be sure about. It would be nice to have the time to gently ruminate on the relationship of everything to everything else, but the realities of life are otherwise. In practice, you're limited to staying alert during the specification stages, especially at review meetings. Some tool support to show what's related to what can help, but it won't do the job for you. "Consistent" is a property that can be helped by some proactive measures, such as the enforcement of naming standards and thorough reviews— again, with decent tool support.

All this applies both to references made from the rules to other model elements, such as to business objects, and to references made to the rules from other elements, such as from use case descriptions. If you have any particular conventions about naming or numbering, they too must be observed.

Repository information   All the relevant fields in the rules repository should be checked to make sure that they have been completed appropriately with the correct information. In addition to the rule definitions themselves, this also covers such fields as supporting notes to provide documentation of complex or unusual cases.

Here, too, good tool support is invaluable. Even something as simple as identifying all the places that a particular term has been used can make a crucial difference to your ability to impose control over a swelling rule population. We'll return to this topic again in later chapters.

3.6   Case Study: Microsoft Outlook

Microsoft Outlook is a desktop program that's designed to help you to manage messages, appointments, contacts, and other facets of modern business life. The program integrates with other Microsoft applications, such as Exchange, to provide a comprehensive range of facilities. Here, we're going to look at the way that Outlook uses rules to automate the handling of mail messages.

Rules in Outlook are composed by using a "wizard" that provides an interactive dialog from which you can define the various parts of your rule. The interface design shows how a potentially complex and technical task can be made much easier for ordinary users, but we're going to concentrate on the way that the rules are structured and the logic that lies beneath them.

Taking Outlook as an example isn't meant to imply that it's a pure expression of an idealistic rule concept. In fact, it violates some of the guidelines that we've already been over, because Outlook, like the rest of us, has to accommodate the realities of today's information systems. Sometimes, the ideal has to be sacrificed for the workmanlike. Among other things, this case study shows the sort of trade-offs you may need to make between the pure and the pragmatic. From that point of view, Outlook is a pretty good example of the kind of compromise that you may need to find in your own applications.

3.6.1   Outlook rule structure

Each rule statement is made up of a number of clauses. The initial type clause defines whether the rule applies to outgoing or to incoming mail messages. There can be zero or more condition clauses, selected from a range of possibilities. When specified, all these must be true for the rule to be activated. At least one action clause must define the action to be taken if the rule is activated. Finally, zero or more exception clauses can be selected from a range of possibilities. When specified, all the exception clauses must be false, or the rule will not be activated. In summary, a rule statement has the following general structure.

```
typeClause    [conditionClause ["and" conditionClause]]
              actionClause ["and" actionClause]
              ["except" exceptionClause ["or" exceptionClause]]
```

A typical rule statement constructed in this way might be:

> Apply this rule after the message arrives
> where my name is in the To or Cc box
>   and which has an attachment
> delete it
> except if sent only to me
>   or except if it is an Out of Office message

All the possible conditions, exceptions, and actions are drawn from pre-defined lists. The condition and exception lists are logically the same, but the text strings are slightly different to create a more natural reading of the rule.

The reason for having both conditions and exceptions is that it's sometimes more convenient to use one or the other. A rule with a large number of conditions might be expressed equivalently by a rule with a small number of exceptions and vice versa. For instance, you could say something like:

> "apply this rule if <condition> and <condition> and ... and <condition>...."

But you would probably find it more natural to say something like:

> "apply this rule except where <exception>...."

Outlook allows you to define rules by using any combination of conditions and exceptions, but it won't necessarily identify problems if you chose an inconsistent combination. For example, what would happen if you use the same clause as both a condition and an exception? It's unlikely that you would make such a mistake, because your Outlook rules will probably be simple enough to make such an error stand out. However, it may be less obvious in more complex environments. Remember that the underlying logic may still produce a result in a case like this: It just might not be the one that you expected.

3.6.2   Conditions, exceptions, and actions

Table 3-5 lists the conditions and exceptions available in the version of Outlook shipping with Microsoft Office 2000. The actions that can be taken, and therefore the action clauses, are also dependent on the type of mail message—incoming or outgoing—and these are summarized in Table 3-6.

Table 3-5   Outlook conditions and exceptions

Condition or Exception Clause (exception wording is slightly different)	Type Clause	
	Apply this rule after the message arrives	Apply this rule after I send the message
sent directly to me	Y	
sent only to me	Y	
where my name is in the Cc box	Y	
where my name is in the To or the Cc box	Y	
where my name is not in the To box	Y	
from people or distribution list	Y	
sent to people or distribution list	Y	Y
with specific words in the recipient's address	Y	Y
with specific words in the sender's address	Y	
with specific words in the subject	Y	Y
with specific words in the body	Y	Y
with specific words in the subject or body	Y	Y
with specific words in the message header	Y	
flagged for action	Y	
marked as importance	Y	Y
marked as sensitivity	Y	Y
assigned to category	Y	Y
which is an Out of Office message	Y	
which has an attachment	Y	Y
with selected properties of documents or forms	Y	Y
with a size in a specific range	Y	Y
received in a specific date span	Y	
uses the form name form	Y	Y
suspected to be junk e-mail or from Junk Senders	Y*	
containing adult content or from Adult Content Senders	Y*	

*Can be used in conditions only, not exceptions

Table 3-6   Outlook actions

Action Clause	Type Clause	
	Apply this rule after the message arrives	Apply this rule after I send the message
move it to the <u>specified folder</u>	Y	
move a copy to the <u>specified folder</u>	Y	Y
delete it	Y	
forward it to <u>people or distribution list</u>	Y	
reply, using a <u>specific template</u>	Y	
notify me, using <u>a specific message</u>	Y	
flag message for <u>action in a number of days</u>	Y	Y
clear the Message Flag	Y	
assign it to the <u>category</u> category	Y	Y
play <u>a sound</u>	Y	
mark it as <u>importance</u>	Y	Y
mark it as <u>sensitivity</u>		Y
notify me when it is read		Y
notify me when it is delivered		Y
cc the message to <u>people or distribution list</u>		Y
defer delivery by <u>a number of</u> minutes		Y
perform <u>a custom action</u>	Y	Y
stop processing more rules	Y	Y

In some cases, the clauses include references to parameters that refine the meaning of the clause. Initially, a placeholder marks the position of the parameter, shown underlined in the tables. The placeholder is a temporary string that makes sense within the rule statement but has not yet been made specific. Later, this placeholder string is replaced by a string that defines the actual value or reference. As with the placeholder, the new embedded string is worded to make for a natural reading of the rule statement. Figures 3-11 and 3-12 show an example of a rule before and after the placeholder values have been refined. The placeholders Outlook uses in condition or exception clauses—indicated in the *c/e* column—or in action clauses—indicated in the *a* column—are summarized in Table 3-7.

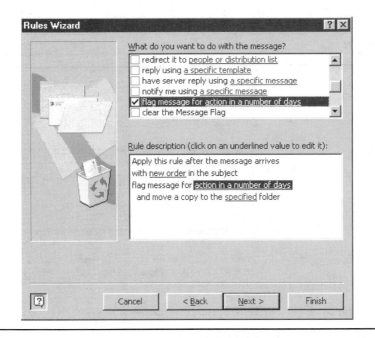

Figure 3-11   Outlook rule with placeholder

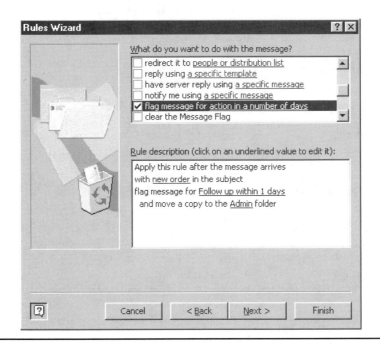

Figure 3-12   Placeholder replaced by value

Table 3-7 Outlook placeholders

Placeholder	Usage	c/e	a
people or distribution list	Entry from normal Outlook mail addresses	Y	Y
specific words	Text string	Y	
action	Entry from list of Outlook message flag types	Y	
importance	Selected from Outlook importance types: Low, Normal, High	Y	Y
sensitivity	Selected from Outlook sensitivity types: Normal, Personal, Private, Confidential	Y	Y
category	Names of categories, separated by semicolons	Y	Y
selected properties	List of properties of documents of forms, with the test to be applied to each property (equal-to, less-than, and so on)	Y	
specific range	Maximum and minimum file size, in kilobytes	Y	
specific date span	After date and/or before date	Y	
form name	Form selected from available form names	Y	
Junk Senders	Entry from list of known junk e-mail senders	Y	
Adult Content Senders	Entry from list of known junk e-mail senders (same list as Junk Senders)	Y	
specified folder	Entry from Outlook's Folder List		Y
specific template	Entry from list of available Outlook templates		Y
a specific message	Text of message		Y
action in a number of days	Message flag type and number of days		Y
a sound	Name of sound file		Y
a number of	Number of minutes		Y
a custom action	Predefined custom actions		Y

3.6.3   Internals

Internally, Outlook contains code to evaluate the rule statements and to carry out the actions. Because this code has to do only one job, it can be optimized for its given role. Without knowing the details of the implementation, you can guess at the likely internal organization by thinking about how you might go about designing the rule subsystem.

The internal representation of rule clauses need not be exactly the same as displayed on the screen, providing that the logical sense is preserved. You can make structures of this sort more efficient by using tokens to represent the various types of clauses (condition, exception, action) instead of the literal text string that was selected by the user. Each token would be linked internally to the following:

- A text string, for display to the user
- Zero or more links to additional parameters, to refine the meaning of the clause

There's also an implied link to some program code that's able to establish true/false values for conditions and exceptions or to carry out the associated action. You could realize this by having your program branch to a particular point in the code when it encounters a particular token type, but we won't bother with the details here.

For a complete rule, you would need to store

- Its name (a text string)
- A token to indicate the type (incoming or outgoing mail message)
- Zero or more condition tokens
- Zero or more exception tokens
- One or more action tokens

You might also choose to store some additional information with each rule. Management information, such as the date and time last edited and the name of the user, can be useful for maintaining the rules. Auxiliary information, such as cached intermediate results, can make the implementation more efficient. However, these don't affect the logical structure, so, again, we'll skip over the details.

3.6.4   Logic

In a similar way, the logic structure need not be evaluated exactly as laid out on the screen. In a closed environment like this, we know that rules are always going to have a consistent structure, so we can always process them in a consistent way. We can write down a simple formula that defines how the clauses have to be processed, using basic logic constructs: `And`, `Or`, and `Not`. Turning the formula into program code is then a straightforward job.

The basic logic structure of a rule in Outlook can be summarized in codelike form as:

```
If      ( And (c₁, c₂, c₃, ... , Not ( Or (e₁, e₂, e₃, ... ) ) ) )
Then    ( a₁, a₂, a₃, ... )
```

where:

> c_1, c_2, c_3, ... are conditions; all must be true for the rule to apply.
>
> e_1, e_2, e_3, ... are exceptions; all must be false for the rule to apply.
>
> a_1, a_2, a_3, ... are actions that must be carried out if the rule applies.

You'll see that this is slightly different from the user's version. On screen, the actions are shown between the conditions and the exceptions of the rule, so that the statement reads more naturally to a human user. However, when you're considering mechanization of the logic, it makes sense to put the statement into a more mathematical form.

Now that we have the stark outline of the logical structure of a rule, it's easy to answer the question we posed earlier. What would happen if we used the same clause as both a condition and an exception? The test applied to decide whether to carry out the action(s) would look something like:

```
And (A, B, C, ... Not ( Or (A, P, Q, ...) ) )
```

where A, B, C, and so on, stand for the clauses, with A being the clause that's common. If we assume that A is true, the Or part must also be true. Because Not (true) is false, we're looking at the truth value of the whole expression as being something like:

```
And (True, ... False)
```

which will always be false. Similarly, if A is false, we're looking at a truth value like:

```
And (False, ... ?)
```

The query indicates that the value of the Or part depends on the other exception clauses, but this has no effect on the overall result; it will always be false. In other words, whatever combination of values we have for the conditions and exceptions in this rule, the associated actions will *never* be carried out.

This illustrates the value of having a clear structure to the underlying logic. We did not need to consider all the possible condition and exception clauses, and maybe their parameters too, in order to come to this conclusion. Just knowing the logic formula—and that a clause must be either true or false—we could establish how Outlook will behave in every instance of this situation.

3.6.5   Outlook rule features

Now that we've seen something of how Outlook uses messaging rules, let's consider how it compares with the general principles we outlined earlier. Here are some of the features of the Outlook rules that you should have been able to spot from the description.

- Rules are built from a range of predefined patterns. The patterns are chosen to be relevant to the nature of the domain; in other words, they allow Outlook users to say what they need to say.

- Rule statements are expressed in constrained natural language. Because the rules can be read as simple sentences, they are easy for nonexperts to create and to understand.

- The rule clauses use canned text to avoid the problems of natural-language processing. Users have no option to create free-format text, and so the clauses available can be designed in advance to be clear and meaningful in the places they appear.

- Rules may make references to terms that have a standard meaning in the context of the domain. The context is electronic mail, so the terms cover such objects as *sender* and *message* with such properties as *address* and *subject,* which make sense in that domain.

- All defined rules are maintained in a repository. Rules are identified by descriptive names and can be checked out for editing, if required. Some meta-information, such as whether a rule is active, can also be viewed and edited.

- The internal representational structure does not necessarily line up one to one with the rule statement structure. Once a rule or a set of rules has been defined, the system can exploit knowledge of the rule structure to turn the statements into an appropriate form for processing.

- Internally, rule clauses are combined strictly in accordance with standard logic. There's no need for special-to-purpose algorithms. Evaluating the logic expressed by the rule statements is all that's needed.

All this is pretty much in accord with the ideas discussed earlier in this chapter. There are some differences, though, arising from the size and the scope of the application.

- There's no explicit fact model. Because the scope of the application is limited, it's not too difficult to remember what all the terms mean, and it's very unlikely that users would disagree about them. This would not scale up to a full business system, for which a fact model would be necessary to provide an agreed point of reference.

- There's no opportunity to use rules for any other purpose or in any manner but the way they're hard-wired into Outlook. Here the rules are contained inside the application and invoked at a fixed point in its operation. This is a trade-off worth making; the resulting gain in simplicity far outweighs the uncertain benefits that might be gained from using Outlook features elsewhere.

- The conclusion of the rule is tied immediately to a procedural action. This departs from the declarative style recommended as a general practice, but, again, the additional complexity would be difficult to justify in the context of the Outlook application.

Although it is not a complete business system, Outlook provides a useful example of a small-scale usage of business rules. As we'll see in later chapters, using rules on a wider scale requires some industrial-strength features that are not necessary in Outlook, particularly when dealing with the practicalities of using rules in distributed information systems.

3.7   Rule description summary

Rules are used to describe the conditions that *must* apply when the system is in a stable state. In other words, a rule violation may exist temporarily, but the system should take some automatic corrective action whenever such a situation is detected.

For business rules to be used effectively, a wide range of people must be able to read and to write them without needing special technical expertise. The best way of achieving this is for the original source rule statement to be expressed in a fairly colloquial natural-language form. Many of the difficulties of unconstrained natural-language processing can be avoided by defining a suitable set of rule patterns to be used as templates.

Behind the scenes, the source rules can have other, equivalent, forms that might be better suited to subsequent automation activities. Regardless of how this is achieved, it must still be possible to create and to maintain the rules in their more natural form.

The terms referred to in the rules must have a consistent and well-defined interpretation. This can be achieved by insisting on a supporting fact model in which the business rules can be rooted.

Rule statements are a key element in defining the intentions and the needs of the business. Many downstream decisions will depend on what the rules say, so it's worth spending some up-front effort on making sure that they are accurately stated and properly aligned to the aims of the business.

4

Discovering
Business
Rules

4.1 That which we call a rule

We now have a good idea of what business rules might look like and their underlying logic. The problem we tackle in this chapter is how to spot a rule, or, to be
more accurate, how to position our focus at the right distance.

At one extreme, it's possible to see rules everywhere. In principle, a complete
business description can be produced by using nothing but rule statements—plus,
of course, their related facts. Although the result might be completely accurate,
it's not a very practical approach to analysis. Some tortuous definitions might be
required to force-fit every aspect of a business description into a rule format. Particular features, such as associations between business objects, are much easier to
express using other kinds of definitions, such as UML class diagrams. Also on a
practical level is the need to accommodate tools, packages, and other things that
don't deal directly with rules. The inevitable conclusion is that rules must take
their place as one aspect of a business model—albeit a very important one—
alongside the other model elements we looked at in Chapter 2.

At the other extreme, it's possible to go into denial and push all rules down
into a general mush of description from which it's difficult to pick out the logic.
Again, the description is still correct, in the sense that other people—with the
right background—could read it and understand it. The problem is that computers
are not people. In order to make use of automation, we have to give the machine
something to get a grip on. A human interpretation of a description brings into
play a large amount of knowledge: making connections and filling gaps without
our necessarily being aware of what we're doing. The job of the business analyst
is to make important nuggets of knowledge explicit, available both to people *and*
to machines. This is where business rules come into play.

A related issue is scope. At some point, we have to draw a line in the sand and say, This is our limit. Just because something *could* be formulated as a rule doesn't mean that we have to do it. For instance, something might be very important to the business but classified as out of scope by the project sponsor. We need to strike the right balance. A coverage that's too wide will not be wrong in the logical sense, but we'll have expended valuable effort on things that will never give us a payback. Ideally, an important rule that's out of scope for us will be in scope for someone else. This is where knowledge reuse starts to pay off. If you have a good strategy in place for managing business model(s), you don't have to dump everything onto one project. (Project managers have been known to object to that sort of thing!) Instead, you can build up a comprehensive model or set of models incrementally, without imposing the whole cost on one individual project.

4.2   Where rules come from

Before we look at practical techniques for identifying rules, it's useful to understand something about their origins. In the business world, it's doubtful that anyone ever sits down and says, "I think I'll create a business rule." The rules are reflections of the way that the organization works or the way it intends to work in the future. If the rules reflect established practice, they may have been around for a surprisingly long time, although perhaps not specifically identified as business rules.

Let's say that you have to analyze a new e-commerce application, which will, of course, involve business rules. You understand the importance of isolating rule statements to encapsulate important aspects of this application, you know what they should look like, and you know how to find good ways of expressing them. But where do they come from? Who says that a particular piece of text in a document is a business rule? How do you recognize a rule in a description of a business activity?

What's needed is an approach to pulling together the right kind of information. On rare occasions, this is made straightforward because the business owner has anticipated what's relevant to the project. More likely, you will have to roll up your sleeves and dig out what's needed. You need to think in terms of hard evidence: clear statements that are about the business and that can be attributed to a source. These statements should stand apart from any flavor-of-the-month preoccupations.

You're likely to come across three main kinds of rules:

1. *Structural* rules describe constraints or relationships among various elements of a model or system. Here's an example:

   R401   An order that is fillable must have a recorded
            assignment to a specific packer.

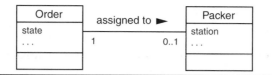

Figure 4-1 Association between Order and Packer

In terms of a UML class diagram, this could be shown as an association between an Order class and a Packer class, as in Figure 4-1. We can imagine that the Order class has an attribute called *state,* one possible value of which is *fillable.* The rule is saying that the association between Order and Packer is mandatory if `Order.state = fillable`. Otherwise, we can assume that there is no association—unless, of course, another rule comes into play.

2. *Behavioral* rules define a course of action to be followed in a particular situation. Rules such as the following add detail to the process model and are common features in workflow environments; Figure 4-2 shows a fragment of a workflow corresponding to this rule. Behavioral rules also define the recognition of, and the response to, business events. The initial trigger may be the arrival of a piece of data of a particular type. But this on its own may not be enough to categorize the exact nature of the event. Rules can be used to pull together the clues needed to form the right assessment. Once this has been done, further rules can use the event identity, along with other data, to decide on the appropriate course of action.

R402 An urgent order must be routed to Packing Supervision for expediting.

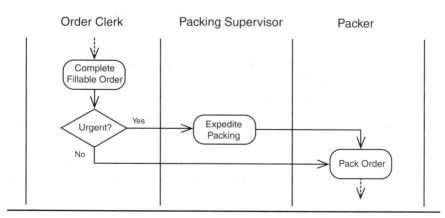

Figure 4-2 Fragment of "packaging" workflow

3. *Definitional* rules provide a definition of a term or a quantitative or a qualitative relationship between terms.

R403   Billable amount is total item value plus sales tax.

This rule can be seen both as a definition of *billable amount* and as a formula for calculating it. In fact, it's a bit more than that: The relationship it expresses among three terms is such that any one of them could be calculated, knowing the other two. More complex quantitative relationships can be expressed by rule sets, but it's often clearer to leave them in the form of a mathematical equation.

True though all this may be, knowing the classifications won't necessarily help you to find rules. It's easier to classify rules once they're safely in captivity, although even then, there may be scope for disagreement. For instance, behavior can be controlled through constraints on information structures, and information structures can be created by behavior.

Some rules may well sit in a gray area, where they could plausibly be assigned to more than one category. You may be able to spot this in the first two example rules. Rule R401 mandates a record of the packer in persistent storage but may also have workflow implications, as shown in Figure 4-2. Similarly, the business may decide in the future to record details of the "expediting" step shown in Figure 4-2, although rule R402 as expressed does not ask for this.

It's important not to waste time in sterile debates about whether a rule should be classified as one thing or another. Instead, the focus should remain squarely on making clear and precise statements about the business.

4.2.1   Information sources

You can consider four main types of information source. We cover them briefly here and then come back to them when we get into more detail about analysis techniques.

1. *Documentation.* Source documents can become relevant in a number of ways. They may be the *trigger* that lies behind the initiation of a project, *supporting material* that underpins a business objective, or *historical statements* that lay down the creed that the business observes. The reason for their relevance is less important than the fact that the business owner has *said* that they are relevant. The documents may be primary—"This project will implement the recommendations of the New Business Task Group Final Report"—or secondary—"Obviously, moving into home loans implies that we must conform to the official regulatory requirements"—see Figure 4-3.

2. *Tacit know-how.* Many, perhaps all, organizations have an internal culture that defines "the way we do things around here." There's also general industry experience about what will or won't work. This is often the richest source of information but, frustratingly, also the one that is least well documented. As we'll see, a large part of the analysis effort is teasing out what is already "known" but restating it in a more specific and concrete form.

Primary
(given)

Secondary
(referenced)

Implicit
(may be hidden)

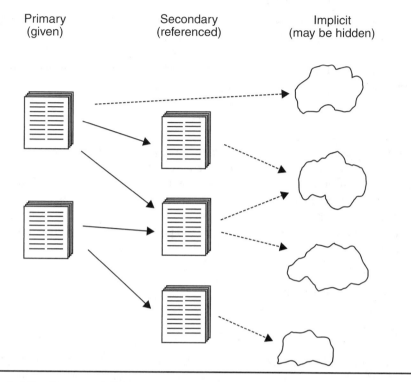

Figure 4-3   Documentation sources

3. *Automation systems.* If the project overlaps with an existing business activity, which is quite likely in a clicks-and-mortar situation, it's almost certain that an automation system is already operational and may have been so for an appreciable time. The collateral associated with this may provide useful input to a new initiative: for example, in e-commerce.

4. *Business records.* Even though your application might be tied to a new business venture, there may be records of earlier business activity that can be trawled for relevant facts. Typical examples of this can be found in production "recipes"—the way that particular customer requirements have been satisfied in the past—and marketing categorization—segmenting customers into groups that are handled in different ways.

4.2.2   Common indicators

The following indications are often associated with business rule definitions, even if rule-like expressions aren't immediately obvious in the way that they are described. Their appearance is a signal that one or more business rules might—or might not—be lurking just beneath the surface. These are indications, not guarantees! However, they do tend to be associated with classifications, constraints, and other features that fit very comfortably in business rule descriptions.

To recap: These are not business rule categories but rather signs that a rule—or perhaps a whole load of rules—may be close at hand. Don't expect all these to apply in any one project. Don't expect them to be mutually exclusive; clues to the possible existence of the same rule or rule set might be provided by more than one indicator.

Features defined by external agencies   These entities, values, or relationships are relevant to the business but are not controlled by it. Setting these out as business rules is useful for two reasons. First, it makes it easier to demonstrate compliance with the external source. Second, it's easier to assess the impact of changes in the external information and to make any necessary modifications to the system. These agencies tend to be those that impose regulatory influence or perhaps even a legal duty:

- Government departments
- Professional associations
- Standards bodies
- Industry codes of practice

Systematic variations among organizational units   Most large organizations are subdivided. Even if the division is not formalized, business practices are likely to vary from one part to another. Sometimes, this variation is so pronounced that it's easier to treat different parts of the same organization as different organizations. There may be varied ways of describing the subdivisions, and business rules may be required for several ways of slicing the cake. The following are typical types of variations:

- Geography: regions, areas
- Business function: divisions, departments
- Hierarchy: head office, branch office

Entities with multiple states   It's often convenient to describe a business object as being in one of a number of possible states; for instance, a real estate office might denote properties as for sale, under offer, or sold. There's no absolute about what the states might be or how many of them can exist. It just depends on how many degrees of discrimination are useful to the business. Often, the various states indicate conditions under which a different set of business rules apply. Here are a few more examples.

- A loan application might be submitted, pending, or approved.
- A contact with a customer might be open, delivered, failed, or closed.
- A customer order might be received, collected, or packed.

Specializations or subclasses   Some kinds of business objects may be defined in terms of a generic type plus specialized variants. On a UML class diagram these business objects appear as classes and subclasses, using the open-arrowhead symbol. These classes have a family resemblance to states; in practice, subclasses might be realized by adding subtype property to the generic class. As with states, it's common to find that rules are required to deal with the differences among the categories. Typical examples are

- Customer contact, specializations: inbound, outbound, interactive
- Business event, specializations: marriage, death, name change
- Party, specializations: individual, commercial organization, nonprofit organization

Automated business decision making   Some categories of complex decisions are ultimately based on a set of relatively simple values, although the process of getting from the values to the conclusion may be quite convoluted. Such decisions are ripe for automation, once the nature of the decision making has been explored and made explicit. The realization can be in the form of a rule set, which has one header rule that triggers a cascade of other rules, depending on the specific details of the problem. Putting it another way, the problem is completely deterministic in the sense that a particular combination of base data will always lead to the same conclusion. Writing a procedural algorithm to calculate the conclusion may prove to be utterly impossible, given the vast number of combinations possible. It's usually much easier to write a set of business rules embodying the business principles involved and let these constrain the result. The example later in this chapter illustrates how this can work.

Definitions of boundaries   Another way that organizations define their business is by setting thresholds that split the space of possibilities into bands of values. Having a small, discrete set of possibilities is often easier to handle than is a continuum. This makes it possible to assign different rules to each band. Sometimes, the thresholds seem fairly arbitrary; sometimes, they're backed by a law: statutory or natural. The most common threshold value is 0, which divides numerical quantities into positive or negative. Typical ways of defining bands of values are

- On one side/on the other side
- Above/below
- Within/without

Conditions linked to time   Some business conditions are relevant only at a particular point in time or during a particular time span. Specific business rules may come into play only at these times or outside these times. This is another example of taking a continuum and highlighting regions that are of particular interest to the business. Typical examples are

- Calendar-related data, including public holidays
- Definition of business hours
- Data or activities valid from `<date>`, up to `<date>`, or between `<date1>` and `<date2>`

Quality manual   Many large organizations, particularly in Europe and Japan, have adopted a formal approach to quality management. If you're working in an organization accredited to ISO 9000 or equivalent, it's bound to have a company manual. This is a gold mine for business rules, because its whole objective is to make "the way we do things here" absolutely explicit, in terms that leave no room for doubt. If a company manual or equivalent does not exist, you will effectively be creating bits of it as you define your business rules. If it does exist, a lot of the work has already been done, and you just need to express the salient points in your particular rule format. Some examples of the kinds of thing you're likely to find are

- Defined processes: who does what, where, when
- Levels of authorization
- Mandatory business records that must be generated or retained

Significant discriminators   Descriptions of business activity sometimes refer to factors that can be used to classify a process, a business object, or another aspect as being of a particular kind. This discrimination is necessary because the business treats the various kinds of things in different ways. The basis of discrimination can be unique to a particular business—such as the definition of which customers are considered "local" for delivery purposes—or something that's acknowledged more widely, such as an overdrawn account. Other typical indicators are

- Major branch points in business processes
- Characteristic patterns of behavior that recur frequently
- Important categories of business objects

Activities related to particular circumstances or events   Business events are often associated with business processes: initiating them, stopping them, or changing their course. Some rules may be required to characterize the event accurately or to filter out those that are superficially similar to meaningful ones. Typical examples are

- Time events: at end of month, at end of year, and so on
- When `<event>` happens or when `<event>` does not happen as expected
- When defined conditions—particular combinations of circumstances—exist

Information constraints   It's sometimes valuable for the business to set limitations on the way that its information is structured. This may arise organically from the nature of the business or may be an artificial constraint that's imposed to control an automation system so that it is capable of handling only acceptable values. Rules provide a clear and natural way of expressing such constraints. Common examples are

- Values that are permitted only in a particular range or from a limited set
- Data items that must go together
- Combinations that are not allowed

Definitions, derivations, or calculations   Rules are a good way of capturing the many definitions a business uses to identify or to generate data. Most businesses use a variety of simple formulas that are convenient to express in this way. One common business example is pinning down a precise definition for terms in casual use, such as "profits" or "overheads." Typical definitional areas are

- Identifying subclassifications of business objects, usually transient
- Algorithms for computing values
- Definitions of quantitative or qualitative relationships

4.3   Finding rules

To start your list of rules, try sitting with a notepad in a quiet room and thinking about the business. Trying to think things through from first principles is a good discipline. But for an information system of any realistic scale, it's unlikely to be adequate.

- It's unlikely that an individual analyst will have the breadth of knowledge and experience to understand the business at the right level, especially if the system is breaking new ground.
- It's important to cover the ground in a systematic way so that no gaps are left. A well-known law says that any holes left in the system will gape open at an embarrassing point, typically just as the system becomes operational.
- The rules have to be expressed at the correct level. Too much detail, and the analysis will become bogged down and the system difficult to implement. Too little detail, and openings for misinterpretations when the system is realized will ensue.
- The short timeframes imposed by such demands as e-commerce make it necessary to spread the work over several people, who must be organized as a team to be effective.

We need to find some organizing principles that can be used to make locating business rules less of a hit-and-miss affair. Three main approaches can be used for rule discovery. These approaches can be used alone or in combination, depending on the size and the nature of the system in question.

1. *Static analysis* is the best approach when relevant documentation is available. This involves careful checking of source documents for potential rules.

2. *Interactive sessions* bring together analysts and business specialists to explore areas where business knowledge is not readily available in a documented form.

3. *Automated rule discovery* can be used in particular cases to find rules through machine analysis, providing that suitable source data can be made available.

A systematic approach to rule discovery may meet resistance in some projects because it can increase the amount of effort needed in the analysis phase. Of course, the aim is that the short-term costs will be more than offset by gains in the longer term. The right way to tackle a particular topic will depend on a complex interplay among available resources, acceptable risk levels, budgets, accepted industry standards, and many other features. The most sensible way forward is to understand the pros and cons of each approach so that the most appropriate combination can be selected to fit the circumstances.

There's a certain amount of correlation between these discovery methods and the various sources of information we looked at earlier (see Table 4-1). This might be overridden in particular special cases; for instance, if a large amount of highly structured material exists in a machine-readable form.

Table 4-1 Applicability of discovery methods

Source	Static Analysis	Interactive	Automated
Documentation	High	Moderate	Unreliable
Tacit know-how	Not applicable	High	Not applicable
Automation systems	Low	Moderate	High
Business records	Depends on source	Low	Depends on source

4.3.1   Static analysis

Static analysis is the best starting point, even if you're sure that a fair degree of interaction will be needed eventually. It's a good idea to do at least a first pass through any available material before involving business experts. Working through the documentation is a great help in bringing analysts up to speed on the relevant issues and it will also avoid wasting time rediscovering what's already known or losing credibility with business experts, who will assume that you are professional enough to do your homework properly before wasting their time.

Although some documentation will probably be on the table from day one, other materials will emerge during the analysis, and so this process will be interleaved with interactive sessions. It's also likely that any document will reveal questions that will need to be resolved with the relevant business experts. These questions can be postponed to future interactive sessions at which the appropriate business expertise is represented.

Types of source documents   A wide range of source documents might be available. As a first cut, these can be categorized into *internal* or *external*. Internal documents are exclusive to the organization and tend to be kept private, particularly from competitors. External documents are, in principle, available to other parties, although obtaining them might involve some cost or effort.

It may not be practical to hold a physical copy of the document, but the project files should at the very least contain a reference to any document that's agreed to be in scope. If you're working in an organization with an effective document management system, you may be able to create a references document that has hyperlinks to online copies of the source documents over an intranet.

Internal sources can include

- Specifications covering the system you are analyzing
- Slides, handouts, and other materials from internal training courses
- Business plans
- Marketing brochures
- Internally generated reports
- Deliverables produced in earlier projects
- Commissioned reports—for example, from a firm of management consultants
- Internal directives, manuals, and other forms of guidance provided for staff
- The organization's quality manual
- Minutes of meetings at which relevant issues have been discussed
- Correspondence relating to the system or business area

External sources can include:
- Legislation affecting the business area concerned
- Standards defined by official organizations, such as ISO, or industry groups
- Voluntary codes of practice observed within the industry
- Standard references for common facts, such as scientific or geographic data
- Information produced by postal, telecommunications, and electrical and other utilities
- Subscription reports from analyst companies

- Magazines, journals, and other publications containing relevant materials
- Information provided by suppliers, customers, or business partners

You'll need to make sure that each document being used is the right one. In particular, check that it's the most recent version of the document and that it's not about to be overtaken by a new version. This may sound obvious, but under the pressure of deadlines, it's all too easy to pick up an old photocopy, without realizing that events have moved on. Having a solid repository helps here, so it just becomes a matter of checking out the current version of the document. Otherwise, positive confirmation from the relevant stakeholder may be needed. Similarly, you may need to check the authority behind the document. It must be something that all stakeholders can agree as being relevant and correct, not just one person's favorite set of ideas. Once this has been done, you can record the agreed source references in the project files so that you or your fellow team members don't have to have the same discussions several times over.

One thing to be wary of in source documents is that the granularity of the points you detect may be very uneven. Statements that initially appear perfectly innocent may turn out to have a sting in the tail. Here's a scenario.

A quick scan down a page of a requirements document shows ten points or so that you need to cover. "Fine," you think, "should be done by lunchtime." You read the first point:

Para 6.8.4.1:   The business loan system shall be available for operation before the start of fiscal year 2003 to 2004.

No business rules there, and nothing to worry the project manager either, so you move on:

Para 6.8.4.2:   The system shall provide a unique identifier for each loan.

A quick check with the business model shows that the loan business object has a uniqueId property, so this looks OK so far.

Para 6.8.4.3:   The system shall maintain a record of the interest rate applicable at the point that the loan was approved.

You see that the class model has an association between the Loan and the Rate business objects, but that won't do. You need two associations: one for the opening rate and one for the current rate. You also need a business rule to specify that the association between the loan and the opening rate is mandatory and applied at the date of loan approval. Some work to do, but no major problem.

Para 6.8.4.4:   The system shall comply with current tax
                     regulations relating to loans advanced for
                     capital purchases.

What? You must be joking! "Tax regulations" means 200 pages of legalese to wade through! And we may need to bring in specialist expertise. And it's likely to be a moving target—note the little word *current* in the specification—how do we intend to cope with that?

At this point, alarm bells may start to ring in your head. It's also goodbye to lunch.

Another syndrome that afflicts some organizations is excessive secrecy. There's no reason why an analyst should be handed sensitive materials that have nothing to do with the project, but equally, there's no logical reason to hold back on relevant information. Sad to say, people are not always logical, and getting the right documents can come to resemble the dance of the seven veils, otherwise known as progressive disclosure. The existence of some source documents may emerge only as a result of questioning during the analysis stage. A little tactful forbearance on the part of the analyst may be required, along with a determination not to be fobbed off. The obstructions are almost always at the lower levels of the organization; in the extreme, an appeal to the sponsor usually releases the information quite quickly.

Analyzing documents   The general approach for any kind of document follows pretty much the same pattern. We've already seen the sorts of clues to look for as you comb through the document. Here are some additional issues that are worth bearing in mind during static analysis.

- Try to get an electronic copy of the document. You can then use a word processor to mark up tentative rules directly against the associated document text. (In Microsoft Word, you use the Insert I Comment menu item.) You can also note any queries as you go along and, on a big document, checkpoint how far you've gone. This is a great help in keeping the analysis work organized. It's easy to copy the comments and paste them elsewhere, so you don't have to reenter them later. Save your marked-up version separately from the original document.

- Work through the material in a systematic way. The most obvious strategy is to start at the start and end at the end; for large documents, there may be times when it's better to change this a little. For example, if a crucial subsystem or module is going to be used many times, it might be worth coming to grips with this first. A clue to this is where the feature in question is referred to in many places. If the source document is large, it pays to spend a little extra time up front to understand the structure of its contents, before trying to pull out particular rules.

- Work in a consistent way. Try to apply the same level of analysis to all documents, even though they may vary in style, quality, size, or other attributes. If you suddenly realize that you've been missing something important, be honest with yourself and decide whether it's necessary to go back to earlier results. For large documents, it may be necessary to spread the load over several analysts, and all should be working to the same standards. For a big effort of this kind, it may be necessary to hold an initial workshop so that all the analysts involved can agree on the rules of engagement.

- The document is likely to contain lots of clues about potential rules, even if they are not stated explicitly. When reading it, be sensitive to wording that might imply a logical statement. If you're lucky, you'll get absolute statements that you could put into some quasi-logical form, such as

all instances of X are handled as follows . . .

If you're unlucky, you may find lots of limp statements, such as

X is mostly . . .
X sometimes . . .
apart from special conditions, X is . . .

Such cases point to "nearly rules" for which you'll need to pin down a more exact formulation. If the necessary clarification is not in the document, you will have to request a ruling from the relevant stakeholder or, in particularly tricky cases, schedule the whole issue for discussion in a workshop.

- Aim to get rules expressed in the right form as early as possible. All analysts should be looking to make definitive statements about the business in a standard way. If this seems difficult, wonder why this is so. Have you really hit on something that can't be expressed as a set of simple statements in the agreed form? More likely, you've stumbled into some weasel wording that was designed to cover over a compromise when the document was written or a complex situation that hasn't been thought through properly. The right answer is not to perpetuate any vagueness but to create a crisp and unambiguous statement of what you think is being said. Your results will be subject to review, as discussed in the next chapter, so there will be later opportunities for the relevant stakeholders to comment on your understanding.

- Don't get distracted by with numbering and cross-reference systems. Don't try to consolidate rules into the agreed rule base too early. You're sure to change your mind many times as you work through. What seemed obvious in section 20.1.2 of the document might be called into question by the time you get to section 20.3.4 and is clearly wrong by section 20.8.9. Use a temporary rule identification scheme at this stage. As long as your results are locally consistent, standardization is less important. After the rules have been reviewed and accepted, it should be straightforward to put then into the standard form, whatever that might be.

- Check for agreement with the current business model as you go along. In particular, check that the terms used in your tentative rules are the same as those used in the latest version of the model. A common situation is when you find a need to talk about a subset of a model term; for instance, instead of just "customer," you need to refer to "customer with some special characteristic." You have a few choices here.
  - If this is likely to be a one-off situation, leave the special characteristic as part of the rule statement.
  - If it's going to be referred to many times, either make a new rule(s) that provides an explicit definition for this subset, or change the model to make the distinction clear, perhaps by creating a new subclass of business object.

- Focus on stakeholder understanding. Even though you're not aiming at polished presentations, you should always be wondering whether your tentative rules would be understandable to the relevant stakeholder. Ideally, your rule mining should produce a restatement of something that one or more stakeholders has said already and so should be happy to acknowledge as a business truth. In more complex or contentious cases, you might want to take special care with the way that the rules are expressed or, at least, make a note to emphasize them when they are reviewed.

- Be sensitive to political issues. Although rarely discussed in a technology context, these issues can make or break a system. In some ways, the analyst is in a good position here because he or she can take a detached view. However, it's necessary to know that particular stakeholders may have a position that they have to—or have been told to—uphold. The temptation on politically sensitive issues is sometimes to fudge. The reaction from the analyst should be to coax, however gently, a definitive position and to express this in an objective way.

- Insist on clarity. As we've said many times, it does no good to perpetuate vagueness. Remember that automation is cold-blooded. There may be uncertainty about whether a particular business situation should be treated as X or as Y. The job of the analyst is not necessarily to reengineer the business but just to insist that whatever X and Y might be, they at least have a clear definition. The computer that automates the process won't know, or care, about the background. It will relentlessly do X or do Y under the conditions specified.

4.3.2 Interactive sessions

Interactive sessions are designed to bring analysts together with one or more sources of business expertise to explore a particular area or topic. The two main kinds of interactions are structured interviews and analysis workshops. These differ mainly in the scale of what's being attempted. A typical project will include a mix of interviews and workshops, depending on the circumstances.

Table 4-2 summarizes the main characteristics of each type of session. These are only general guidelines, and there may be good reasons to depart from them. For example, if the expertise in question is particularly deep, and thus difficult to acquire, it might be appropriate to carry out an in-depth interview over a longer period and to build in appropriate breaks.

Table 4-2   Some characteristics of interactive sessions

Feature	Session Type	
	Interview	Workshop
Typical number of participants	Two or three	Six to ten
Typical duration	Half-hour to a few hours	Several days
Areas of business expertise explored	Single	Multiple
Logistics	Simple	Complex
Typical venue	Personal office	Conference room

Structured interviews   As with any successful analysis technique, the key is structure. Just turning up to chat with a key businessperson does not count as an interview. Some level of structure is important to make sure that you make the most of what might turn out to be a scarce opportunity.

Follow these guidelines to put your efforts on the right path.

- *Find out about the interviewee.* What makes him or her relevant? Does the person have a special skill or is privy to particular knowledge that's difficult to access? Or is he or she just filling in because the person you really need to speak to is unavailable? (If so, ask the project manager whether this project has a high enough profile.)
- *Observe the courtesies.* Be punctual, courteous, logical, precise, cheerful, diplomatic, and so on, even if your interviewee is none of these things. It will count in the long term.
- *Keep notes.* At the very least, you should take scribbled notes during the interview. Some analysts like to use a dictation machine to record interviews, but you should always check whether your subject has any objections. If you take handwritten notes, make sure they are correct. Recap the salient points with the interviewee if you need to be certain.
- *Make records.* Leave a permanent record of the interview in the project file. The best approach is to use your notes to create a document that summarizes the interview. This is best done immediately after the interview, while things

are still fresh in your mind. The interview summary should not just be a verbatim transcript of what was said, although in some cases, it may be useful to have that as well. Instead, try to understand what was said and arrange it in logical groupings rather than simply the order in which it was covered.

- *Feedback.* Check on the channels by which the interviewee will get feedback on the project. He or she will want to see that personal views have been taken into account. If the project is going in a direction that the interviewee recommended, there's no real problem; the person will assume that his or her ideas are driving the project. If the project ends up going in a different direction, it's a good idea to schedule a follow-up session to explain, with some care and sensitivity, why a different approach is being adopted.

Analysis workshops   All kinds of workshops follow a very similar pattern. In a way, it's a small life cycle that's repeated as many times as necessary. The general stages are as follows.

1. *Define goal and approach.* It's rarely practical to analyze a complete system in one sitting, although attempting to do so might be a way to kick off the analysis work at the start of a project to bring home the scale of what needs to be covered. More likely, it will be necessary to focus on something that's achievable within a short timeframe and to select the right way to tackle the issue in question. If you're uncertain about the goal of a workshop you're organizing, postpone it until you have a clear mind on the matter.

2. *Prepare for workshop.* A certain amount of preparatory work will help to make the most of the workshop opportunity, especially if it's difficult to get access to some of the attendees. Preparation includes housekeeping arrangements—suitable room booked? appropriate attendees confirmed? resources, such as whiteboard, flipchart, pens, and so on, available?—making sure that any required reference materials are available, and setting out a suitable agenda, including, of course, adequate comfort breaks.

3. *Conduct the workshop session.* This will depend on the approach being used. Several lines of attack can be used, and particular techniques might be useful in given circumstances. You don't have to stick with one approach. Sometimes, changing the angle can be a good way to get around an analysis blockage. We'll look at an example of a workshop style shortly.

4. *Pursue immediate follow-up activities.* These actions arise directly from the workshop and can be completed quite quickly after the session ends. Examples are checking assumptions made during the workshop with the relevant authority, filling in minor details from reference materials that weren't available at the time, and sending copies of materials to individuals who did not attend.

5. *Follow up with consolidation and research.* These follow-up actions are more significant in scale, usually delegated from the workshop to avoid loss of impetus during the session. It's sometimes more appropriate to allocate

activities to an individual to complete later rather than taking the time of the whole group. Examples are cross-checking with other analysis results; extracting noncontentious facts from reference materials, such as look-up tables; and establishing new sources of information to meet needs identified in the workshop.

6. *Review.* We'll look at reviews in detail in a later chapter. For now, it's enough to note that the review exposes the results of the analysis to a group suitably qualified to assess their quality, bearing in mind that only interim results may be available at the time. Although analysis workshops and reviews may seem like similar group activities, it's generally not a good idea to try to combine them. They have different aims—discovery versus confirmation—may involve different people, and may need organizing in a different way.

The typical cycle follows the sequence shown in Figure 4-4. Completion of a particular stage of analysis is always through a review, but several workshops might be needed before a review becomes appropriate. On a large project, several of these analysis cycles may be going on at the same time. Once the team involved with a particular topic has completed its work, the members become free to join other teams or to start new topics.

The team is likely to include at least one business expert having specialist knowledge about a particular area: marketing, accounts, legal, shipping, and so on. The expert is responsible for providing information about how that part of the

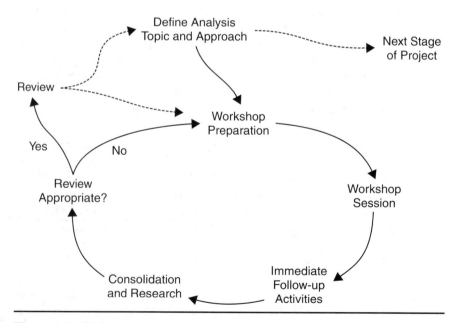

Figure 4-4 Typical workshop activity cycle

business works or, more likely, how it's intended to work in the future. This will come both in the form of direct input and as feedback on tentative results that emerge during the workshop. If it's proving difficult to get the business expert to volunteer information, it's sometimes useful to float a model that's known to be deficient and invite the expert to explain what's wrong with it, so the difference between input and feedback does not matter in practice. Of course, at the end of the day, the expert must be willing to agree that the model that's been developed is an accurate reflection of his or her particular part of the business.

4.3.3   Automated rule discovery

Automating the process of rule discovery sounds like a grand idea, but it's not one that's generally practical. The reason is that even when business knowledge is available, it's expressed in natural language, without too much in the way of consistent structure. Machine interpretation of this is beyond the state of the art at present, which is why the analytical skills discussed earlier are so important. However, machine processing can be brought to bear in a few special situations, and we'll consider a couple of examples here.

Data mining   Data mining uses inductive logic and neural networks to identify previously unsuspected patterns in data. The most common application is the examination of sales records to try to identify interesting customer behavior.

A common example is the known association between diapers and beer. Husbands sent out to get disposable diapers for the new addition to the family also pick up a six-pack while at the drugstore, possibly anticipating a long, sleepless night ahead. Once this association was identified from sales records, store presentation could be arranged to boost sales further. (This is also an example of a geographical rule: It works only if the local culture includes stores that sell both kinds of article, which may not be true on a wider scale.)

Of course, this can't be a totally automated process, because many patterns are appallingly obvious, such as "Sales of product X increased when the price was reduced." A human observer can direct the process, diverting effort away from useless information—such as "Nobody under 16 years old made purchases with a credit card," which is pretty obvious, as credit card companies don't open accounts for youngsters—toward areas that may have more significance, such as "Can we quantify the increase in sales against the reduction in price?"

For business rules, this may be a productive approach to determining the types and positioning of categories. Let's say that you have a mortgage loan facility that you now want to offer online. You have records about loan conditions, corresponding property valuations, applicant details, amounts advanced in the past, repayment histories, and all kinds of other information. You can use this as the basis for generating a set of rules that distinguish good loan opportunities from bad ones. Once the rules are set out, you can see the kinds of decisions that are important and the boundary values that can be adjusted to meet current business conditions.

Most data mining is carried out using commercial tools. This isn't the place to go into a detailed tool evaluation, which would quickly date anyway. From the larger perspective of business rules, data mining is a niche activity. That's not to say it's irrelevant. Setting the right criteria for advancing loans can make or break a finance company. The important point to bear in mind is that the rules that emerge from data mining must be put into the same framework as the rules derived via other routes.

Code analysis   Many organizations are the reluctant beneficiaries of earlier automation systems that deliver their bread and butter—if only the organizations knew how! For instance, a major international bank is totally dependent on a mainframe accounting system that has no reliable documentation. How good would it be to understand what that system really does? What's it worth to have control over a resource that could make or break your business? It's a very one-sided equation, because "break" is the most crucial. If the system's working, there's no incremental benefit; you just keep on doing whatever you do. If it fails, though, the business might cease to exist.

One way out of this blind canyon is to reengineer the system, working backward from the code to generate the kind of description that could be used to implement the system again, using newer technology but, more important, having control over exactly what the system does or does not do. Again, this is a toolcentric business. The conversion is likely to be a one-time process involving retrospective skills. It's really a question of extracting the critical business features from the mist and then trying to move on.

Several companies and tools provide the kinds of code-analysis facilities that we're talking about here. Again, evaluation of commercial offerings is not the aim; products come and go. More important, you should understand how the analysis of legacy systems could provide rules that could form part of your broader business information infrastructure.

Several systems have claimed great success in the kind of code analysis we're talking about here. If this is a problem you face, it's worth investigating further. But be aware that not all legacy code was developed from a strict business perspective. Some constructs are there just to deal with storage limitations, to optimize calculations, or generally just to get around the limitations of the computational machinery relevant when the program was written.

The most important clues are in the branching structures, the IF-THEN-ELSE constructs, or the equivalent in whatever language was used to create the system you're looking at. A branch in a program does not necessarily indicate anything of business importance. But it just might.

Perhaps the most useful thing that automated code analysis can perform is to highlight important decisions. Why do we check A before we do B? Why do we create X and Y at the same time? The rationale may be lost in the mists of time. Who cares? We certainly do, because it's part of our business. What we have to do is to distinguish between pragmatic decisions that were forced by computational limitations of the time and decisions that reflect an underlying truth about the business. Sadly, the code gives only veiled clues. There's rarely any supporting documentation, so the only real option is to try to follow through the same thought processes.

That's not to say that code analysis is a waste of time. It can greatly help in many reengineering processes. Just don't expect it to deliver ready-to-go business rules without at least a little manual intervention.

4.4   Case study: loan approval

The Very Big Bank (VBB) wants to automate the initial processing of loan applications. The bank has some effective indicators of bad risks and wants to use these criteria to eliminate unsuitable applicants. Information given by each applicant will be screened, using a rule set based on the bank's criteria, the result being a straightforward accept/reject decision on the loan or a referral for further investigation if the information given by the applicant is not sufficient to reach a decision.

In a real-life situation, the definition of a suitable rule set would probably require the efforts of a team of analysts over several weeks of elapsed time. For reasons of practicality, the rule set we cover is only a simple version of what might really be required. We'll discuss the ways in which a more comprehensive version might differ a little later. For now, though, it's worth remembering that the overall process won't be very different for a full-sized industrial example. For similar reasons, we won't cover all the steps along the way to defining the rule set but just pick out some points to highlight.

4.4.1   The early stages

The initial stages involve the creation of a business model, along the lines discussed in Chapter 2. This model will define VBB's goals for its loan program, the anticipated business process, and the relevant business objects. The organizational units involved will all be within VBB, but the actors and the roles will include at least one external entity: the loan applicant.

At least one use case will describe what a loan application looks like from the applicant's perspective. This might become more complex if VBB allows applications through multiple channels: through independent financial agents, direct via the Internet, in person at a VBB branch office, and so on. Here, we'll just assume that the applicant has provided the answers to a set of questions, and these answers will form the input to the loan process. Unfortunately, we don't yet know what questions to ask.

In this case, the analysts have taken the initial step of representing the loan decision by a single business rule in the model, along with a note that this is expected to be replaced by a rule set later. During the discovery stage, the analysts have interviewed the VBB staff concerned with the existing manual loan-approval process and checked any documentation that might be applicable. What they've found is not enough to give a definitive picture, and they need to find an alternative way to move forward.

In this kind of situation, a good bet is to schedule a workshop or, if the problem is particularly messy, maybe more than one. The objective of the workshop is to allow the relevant stakeholders to make their individual inputs and to work toward a consensus view of the rules needed. We'll take a look at a particular workshop technique that's well suited to cases like this.

4.4.2   Fishbones

The concept   The workshop is built around a concept called a *fishbone diagram,* or an *Ishikawa diagram,* after its inventor. The basic idea has been used in many industries and applications, and at least one tool provides direct support for creating and animating of fishbone models.

Here, we're going to apply it to identifying a rule set. When completed, the diagram will show the overall result of the rule set at the head and the factors contributing to the result as a series of ribs leading off from a backbone. Each rib may have successive levels of smaller bones, depending on the levels of decomposition needed. Each branch of the bone structure represents a potential rule, showing how the input values, which appear at the tip of the subsidiary bones, are combined to reach the final conclusion. The concept is illustrated in Figure 4-5, which makes it pretty obvious how this style of diagram gets its name.

Working up the fishbone structure is likely to be highly interactive. Lots of space will be needed to lay out the work in progress so as to give the participants sufficient access. A big whiteboard is a useful asset here, as is a good supply of sticky notes. Concepts, or just simple reminders, can be written on individual notes and then moved around quite easily as the picture develops.

Finding the VBB rules   Here's how the VBB analysts might work through their problem in the workshop. The obvious first step is to start at the head, with a statement of the result required. This might get modified during the workshop as a better understanding of the problem is gained, but an initial peg in the ground is necessary. In this case, the head might start with a statement: "Loan decision: accept, reject, or refer." Any argument about the wording of this is good because it provides useful clues for directions to follow up on later.

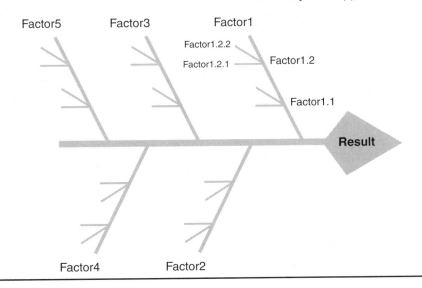

Figure 4-5   Fishbone diagram: concept

The next step is usually a pause while everyone stares down at the table and thinks, "But I knew that anyway." Now it's time for the lead analyst to find a theme that the participants can rally around. In this case, covering all the ways that the applicant could be accepted doesn't look very promising. Most applicants won't go through the hassle of applying unless they expect to succeed. A better line of attack might be to think about reasons why applicants would be refused, with the option of referral in the background for borderline cases.

Some answers are fairly obvious: "The applicant couldn't afford the repayments." The fact that they're obvious doesn't negate their value, so they can be added as new bones. Once a diagram has started to evolve, it becomes much easier for the participants to react to the emerging picture: debating existing points, adding new strands, or whatever. The growing consensus arises almost by stealth, bit by bit, as the diagram is refined.

During the workshop session, the group may encounter difficulties over how to express a feature. It's important that the facilitator not allow the workshop to become sidetracked into debates over modes of expression, methodology, or other fine points. In such cases, the way forward is to agree on some working assumptions or conventions, and to move quickly back to the main analysis task before impetus is lost.

Figure 4-6 shows how the diagram might look at an intermediate stage. At any point in time, the diagram should reflect the mindset of the participants, and so it's unlikely to be neat and tidy while the workshop is in full swing. We won't follow every twist and turn in the definition but instead will fast-forward to a point when the structure appears to be reasonably well developed.

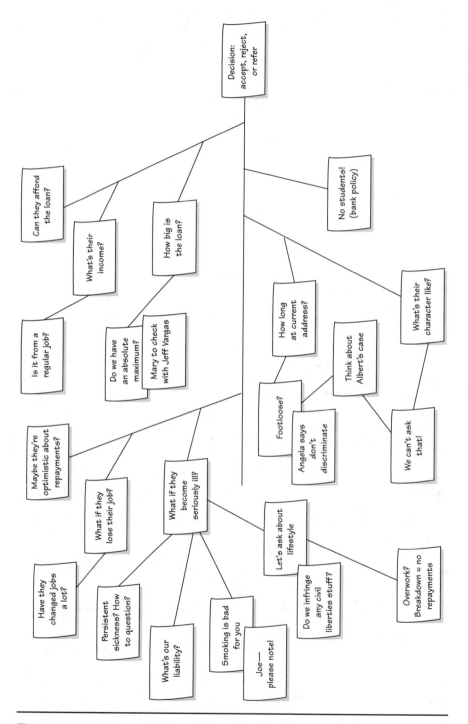

Figure 4-6 Fishbone workshop: intermediate position

The emergence of a stable position is a good time to assess the consistency of the current picture with other materials. Does the rule set fit with prior assumptions that have been made about the business process? The use case(s)? The organization? The goals of the business? These thoughts may spark new rounds of refinement, which will proceed until the participants reach a suitable accord.

Several tasks must be carried out once the bare bones of the business logic have been defined and agreed. They don't necessarily need to be done in the workshop session, but they do need to be done soon after, so that any errors get picked up and rectified while they're still fresh and actions get carried out before they're forgotten.

- The workshop results must be captured and expressed in a form that can be distributed to the participants easily. The simplest thing to do is to play back a cleaned-up version of the fishbone diagram, along with any supporting notes and actions. These don't need to be elegant, but they do need to be accurate.

- In this case, a key issue was the lack of a suitable set of questions that should be asked of an applicant in order to assess the loan opportunity. Tracing down the bone structure will reveal the input data needed. At this stage, it would be too early to start designing application forms, but it should be possible to list the items of information and the ranges of values expected.

- Along with this, it should be possible to produce an initial set of rules that take the defined input values and deliver a specific result. At this stage, the rules will be somewhat tentative. Even in the simplified case we're considering, it will be difficult to check the rules by eye, so a wise business analyst will schedule some testing to check the correctness of the logic defined by the rule set. In the next chapter, we'll see how this happens.

One final point to note is that the workshop results should be lodged in the project filing system. The notes may not be a configuration item in their own right, but they are valuable supporting material that might be referred to again in later stages, particularly when the rationale behind the logic is being examined in a review.

4.4.3   Input data

This is the information that applicants will be asked to supply. At this stage, we aren't concerned about how this will be acquired—for example, in paper form or via Web browser—or how and where it is made available to the rule set. We can just assume that the information is accessible to the rules whenever needed. However, we are making the additional assumption that the information has already been validated to some extent, so we won't be defining rules to check that values are within a sensible range. For example, "Years at current address" can't have a negative value.

Table 4-3 summarizes the list of applicant questions to emerge from the workshop. The answers to questions 1–5 will result in a string drawn from a limited list, that is, an enumerated value. The answers to questions 6–11 and 15–17 will result in an integer value. Questions 12–14 will be defined in terms of whatever currency is applicable, but the choice of this won't affect the logic.

Table 4-3 Loan application questions

Question	Information	Possible Values
1	Residence type	Owner occupier, living with parents, tenant, other
2	Employment type	Public sector, private sector, military, homemaker, student, unemployed, other
3	Health	Good, poor, unknown
4	Smoking habit	Heavy, light, non
5	Marital status	Single, married, divorced, widowed, cohabiting, unknown
6	Years at current address	Integer
7	Years at previous address	Integer
8	Years in current employment	Integer
9	Years in previous employment	Integer
10	Average hours worked per week	Integer
11	Number of children	Integer
12	Amount of loan requested	Integer
13	Average weekly income	Integer
14	Average weekly outgoings	Integer
15	Loan period in years	Integer
16	Present age, in years	Integer
17	Expected retirement age, in years	Integer

4.4.4   Loan-assessment rules

Here's the kind of rule set that might emerge following the workshop session. Don't take the rules too seriously: They're not meant to be a recommendation about the right way to run a bank! You might also consider some to be overdiscriminatory—for example, VBB clearly doesn't like students—but this is just for the purpose of illustrating some specific cases.

You'll see that the rule constraints apply to situations in which a loan should not be approved. In other words, a loan is assumed to be approved unless one or more of the rules indicates otherwise. It would have been possible to construct the rules differently—for instance, with a default assumption of rejection. However, the positive underlying assumption is probably a reasonable reflection of the commercial outlook of the bank. As mentioned earlier, it's also likely to be more efficient, as applicants won't bother to apply unless they feel there's a good chance of being accepted.

The rules here include some embedded constant values, such as "5 hours per week." In practice, these values would be maintained as rule parameters, and the rule statements would refer to the parameter name rather than to the literal value. This greatly improves maintainability, for the same reason that symbolic constants are used in programming. For the purpose of this case study, they've been left as literal values, to avoid tedious cross-referencing as you work through the rules.

R404X	An applicant who works more than 5 hours per week must be referred if one or more of the following is true: —The applicant is unemployed, —The applicant is a homemaker.
R405	An applicant must be rejected if at least one of the following is true: —The applicant is a stability risk, —The applicant is a health risk.
R406	A lone applicant must be considered a lifestyle risk if all the following are true: —The applicant has one or more children, —The applicant's average hours of work per week exceeds 35 hours.
R407	An applicant must be considered a lifestyle risk if average hours of work per week exceeds 65 hours.
R408X	An applicant must be referred if he or she is a lifestyle risk.

R409   An applicant must be rejected if his or her average hours of work per week exceeds 80 hours.

R410   An applicant's weekly disposable income is defined as (average weekly income – average weekly outgoings).

R411   An applicant's working years is defined as (retirement age – present age).

R412   Address mobility is defined as (years at present address + years at previous address).

R413   Employment mobility is defined as (years in present employment + years in previous employment).

R414   An applicant not employed in the military with address mobility less than 2 must be considered a stability risk.

R415   A working applicant with employment mobility less than 3 must be considered a stability risk.

R416   An applicant must be considered a health risk if one or more of the following is true:
—health is poor,
—smoking habit is light,
—smoking habit is heavy.

R417   An applicant who is a student must be rejected.

R418   An applicant must be considered as working if his or her employment type is any one of the following:
—public sector,
—private sector,
—military.

R419   A working applicant must be rejected if the loan period is greater than the applicant's working years.

R420   An applicant's available funding is defined as (weekly disposable income) * 52 * loan period in years.

R421   An applicant's funding ratio is defined as (applicant's available funding / loan amount).

R422   An applicant must be rejected unless his or her funding
       is adequate.

R423   An applicant must be considered as lone if his or her
       marital status is one of the following:
       —Single,
       —Divorced,
       —Widowed.

R424X An applicant must be considered to have adequate
       funding if all the following are true:
       —Applicant is an owner/occupier,
       —Applicant is not unemployed,
       —Applicant's funding ratio is greater than 2.

R425   An applicant must be considered to have adequate
       funding if all the following are true:
       —Applicant is working,
       —Applicant's funding ratio is greater than 3.

R426   An applicant must be considered to have adequate
       funding if all the following are true:
       —Applicant is an owner/occupier,
       —Applicant is a homemaker,
       —Applicant's funding ratio is greater than 4.

R427   An application may be accepted only if it does not fall
       into one of the following categories:
       —Referred,
       —Rejected.

The phrasing of these rule statements is broadly in line with the suggestions made in the previous chapter. In practice, the terms used in the rules would have been drawn from a supporting model, which we've omitted here for brevity.

As you might expect, the first attempt at defining a fairly complex rule set may not be perfect. In the next chapter, we'll return to this example to see how we can identify any problems that might be lurking within it.

4.5   Rule-discovery summary

Rules can be categorized into a number of types: structural, behavioral, and definitional is one such classification. But knowing that won't necessarily help to locate the rules in the first place. Rules are found mainly in:

- Documentation
- Tacit know-how
- Other automation systems
- Business records

The job of the analyst is to identify the underlying logic and to turn it into a series of crisp statements. The main techniques for doing this are

- Static analysis of information resources
- Interactive sessions, including structured interviews and workshops
- Automated rule discovery

5

Controlling Rule Quality

5.1 Developing quality rules

So far, we've looked at how we can find business rules, turn them into statements with business meaning, and relate them to a wider context as part of a business model. Before we can think about technology realization, however, we need to check the quality of the rules.

A quality review should always precede a handover: for example, before the rules are passed to the business owner for approval or given to a designer to plan their realization. However, you shouldn't wait until the last moment before you think about quality. Experience shows that it's a bad idea to treat quality like a condiment to be sprinkled, like salt or pepper, over an endeavor as it's being dished up. Rather, you need to plan quality measures as an ongoing activity during your project.

Well-timed quality controls save money. The longer that rules exist, the more work is done on them. This work ultimately represents additional cost. If the rules are good, the cost of the work is offset by the additional value generated. On the other hand, bad rules consume cost but don't add value. By resolving issues early, you avoid spending time and money on activities that are going to bring you no return.

Having ongoing quality control also makes the evolution of a rule population a more predictable process. You can feel happy about the reduced opportunities for nasty surprises, and the metrics that you gather from reviews will help you understand the true state of your project. In some ways, this improved discipline is more valuable than cost cutting alone. You can always plan for a given level of cost, but unexpected overruns will seriously damage the credibility of your project.

It's certainly true that applying quality controls will improve your deliverable product, but that's only part of the story. A well-designed quality system will also help to improve your *process*. A better process means that you can deliver the appropriate level of product while using less time and less money. An important contribution to achieving this is made by collecting appropriate measurements, or metrics, during the quality control activities.

This book is mainly about business rules, so we're not going to discuss wider quality issues. The measures described here should form part of a quality plan that will also span other elements in your project. You should follow your local guidelines for overall quality management, but make sure that the rule-specific aspects are included at the appropriate points.

In this chapter, we look at three quality control mechanisms that you can apply during the evolution of a rule population.

1. *Walkthroughs* are workshop-style review sessions in which a group examines a group of rules by considering them, step by step, in the context of business scenarios. The main benefit of a walkthrough is the early elimination of poorly framed rules. Walkthroughs are easy to set up and to carry out, so they can be used reasonably often.

2. *Inspections,* a more formal type of review, involve closely examining a rule population in the context of its designated business domain. Because they often involve representatives from many areas of the business, inspections involve more effort, and so they are used mostly at major milestones. Inspections also require a reasonably complete rule population before they can produce truly meaningful results.

3. *Testing* is used mainly to ensure a clear understanding of complex rule sets. Individual rule statements don't require testing; they should be short and simple enough to have obvious results. Rule sets contain an interconnected group of rules, and although it's easy to understand each rule individually, it may be difficult to see the logic of the whole set. Testing applies a series of specific cases to a trial implementation of the rule set, so that the full implications of the combined rules can be appreciated.

These three mechanisms are not substitutes for other types of reviews and tests applied during and after development. The three should be used well before realization, weeding out recognizable problems at an early stage before expensive development effort is invested in bad rules. At the analysis stage, we're questioning rule populations from two main perspectives.

- Are the rules correct in a business sense?
- Are the rule definitions well structured and consistent?

Although the quality controls should be applied as soon as possible, you should not review a rule population or test a rule set until you've assembled enough material. The general pattern is as follows.

- Begin walkthroughs as soon as enough rules have been defined to support a business scenario.
- Plan for at least one inspection before the end of a phase.
- Carry out testing as soon as you've defined a rule set that's worth testing.

Figure 5-1 illustrates the sort of sequence of activities that you can expect.

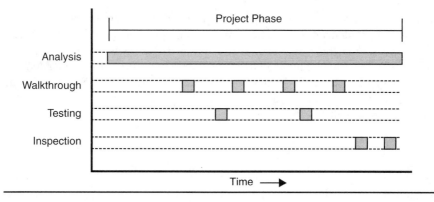

Figure 5-1   Typical assessment activity pattern

Remember that the quality controls here aren't concerned with such issues as where the rules should be located or how to run them efficiently. What we *are* concerned about is ensuring that the rule statements form an accurate description of the business logic that we want to use. The rest of this chapter looks in detail at how to apply each of these mechanisms.

5.2   Reviewing rules

5.2.1   What to look for in reviewing rules

There's little to add here to the advice given in Chapter 3. Basically, you're going to be looking for such problems as

- Rules that are malformed, that don't conform to your local standards or preferred rule patterns
- Rules that are incomplete, typically found when a reviewer points out a situation that's not been properly covered
- Rules that are inconsistent, leading to ambiguous results with different rules
- Rules that are redundant, that serve no business purpose or are covered by another rule
- Rules that use terms not properly rooted in the supporting fact model

Reviews are the main mechanism used to assess and to control rule quality. They're primarily a group activity that's intended to bring a wide range of experience to bear on a rule population during its evolution.

Although we discuss problems with rules in the context of group reviews, awareness of the need for accuracy should be built into your normal working practices. As you write rule statements, you should form them in ways that avoid the sorts of problems described here. With a little practice, you'll learn to define well-formed rules that won't need correction later. The reviews are there to provide a safety net; they're not intended to be the primary forum for rule creation.

Two types of reviews—walkthroughs and inspections—differ mainly in the level of completeness they aim for. We can start by thinking about the aspects that are common to both.

5.2.2   Roles

A number of roles need to be allocated among the participants before the review proper begins. These positions are not permanent; they apply only for the duration of a particular review session. An individual may take on different roles in successive reviews.

A *moderator* acts as the chairperson for the review. The moderator's responsibilities include securing appropriate attendance, managing the session, making sure that appropriate records are kept, and following up on any resulting actions to see that they have been carried out properly.

The rule *author*—or one of the authors, if several—is required to lead the group through the rule population in an orderly way, so that each rule can be understood in its proper context. The rules under consideration will need to be grouped and sequenced so that they tell a coherent story. One way of doing this is to step through realistic business scenarios, introducing each rule at the appropriate point in the flow of activity. Another way is to categorize the rules under a number of headings relating to a business aspect, such as credit control, invoicing, delivery, and so on.

A *scribe* must be identified to note comments and actions that arise during the session. It's worth separating out this role, if you can, to make sure that a decent record is kept. Reviews are not very effective if the participants are confused about what the resulting actions should be. The notes can be produced by marking up review materials, maintaining a separate list of points raised, or combining the two. In any event, the record must be placed in the project files for future reference.

The remaining participants are *reviewers* as are, to a lesser extent, the three special roles just identified. The reviewers examine the rules against an agreed set of criteria. They'll be trying to identify rules that fail to give clear, accurate, and consistent statements of business logic. We'll look at some common pitfalls shortly.

In a large group, you should always separate out the three special roles. The moderator is often someone who already has a coordination function, such as project manager or a team leader. The role of scribe can be given to a different person in each review session, so that no one feels unduly loaded. In a small group, it may be necessary to combine the moderator and scribe roles or author and scribe. Privately, it's good practice to mentally combine all these roles into one, as you review your own work. Figure 5-2 shows the general structure of a review.

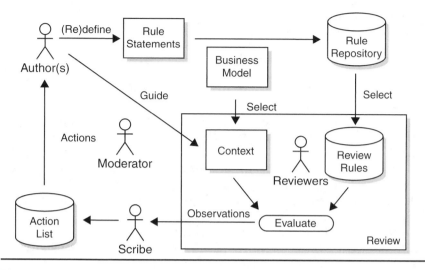

Figure 5-2   General structure of a review

5.2.3   Rule context

It's very likely that a review will be considering something less than a complete rule population. You will therefore need a way to refer to the group of rules that you're reviewing. Rules can be grouped in many ways, each grouping corresponding to a different context, or frame of reference within which the rules are being considered. The groupings will not form a neat hierarchy: An individual rule might be relevant in several contexts. For example, you might find that one rule could be considered in the context of use case 123, financial controls, the Sunrise project, IRS compliance, and the HR department.

Although the groupings we're considering here are for review purposes, you should still identify them in a way that preserves some business significance. For instance, it's easier to understand the business relevance of "rules associated with use cases 123, 456, and 789" than "rules reviewed on August 15."

The rule repository is a crucial resource here because it allows you to record and to track the rules in relation to their various contexts. We'll see more of this in a later chapter.

For a review, you'll need to be clear about which context(s) you're considering. The context defines not only which rules are in scope but also the viewpoint from which you should be reviewing them. The context(s) must be agreed before the review is planned and must form part of the review record. When you mark a rule as reviewed in the repository, you'll also be recording the context(s) within which the review took place.

It's also very convenient to apply a version number to each group of rules. Neither the identity nor the version number of the group has any meaning in an operational system after the rules have been implemented. However, version numbers are useful in managing the evolution of a rule population. We'll look at management issues in more detail in a later chapter.

5.2.4 Tone

It's important to set the right tone for review sessions. To meet their objectives, review sessions need to be informal and open. If they regard reviews as hostile inquisitions, rule authors will lose their enthusiasm, and they'll feel forced into defensive positions, even against helpful criticism. It's possible to mismanage a review as a courtroom drama, with the moderator as judge, the author as defendant, and the reviewers as jury. This is usually counterproductive and should be resisted. The moderator has a key role here in managing the personalities involved to provide a supportive and collaborative environment.

Reviews demand and deserve a fair amount of concentration from the participants, so it's important for the moderator to include appropriate comfort breaks. Don't let any session run for more than 2 hours without a break, and try to keep the whole review within this sort of timeframe. If you have to cover a large rule population and/or many complex scenarios, don't try to cram everything into one review. The participants will lose concentration, errors will pass undetected, and the whole point of the review will be lost.

5.2.5 Review outcomes

As with the other quality controls, the review outcome will be recorded in the project files. It is likely that a number of actions will result from a review. They must be clearly documented and allocated to individuals so that their completion can be tracked. It may also be necessary to raise additional change requests—not necessarily relating to the rules themselves—because of observations made in the review. These items should be raised through your local change control mechanisms in the appropriate way.

You're likely to find that most of the issues raised during a review fall into one of the following categories:

- Corrections to the rule statements. The review will have picked up incorrect use of terms, poor structure, ambiguous wording, or another problem relating to the phrasing of the rules. These corrections are usually straightforward to put right and rarely require a new review.
- Problems with auxiliary information. This is typically the support information that's linked to the rules in the rule repository. Possible issues might be naming and numbering, cross-referencing, rule categorization, and so on.
- Missing rules. The review will have identified areas where the rule coverage is unexpectedly incomplete or even totally absent. The amount of work

needed to fill the gap will depend on the scale of the problem, and a new review may be necessary.

- Problems elsewhere in the business model. The rules may be satisfactory, as far as they go, but they might have highlighted something amiss with other model elements. The most common example is where a close look at the business logic has revealed a discrepancy in a business scenario or a use case. The explicit and logical nature of business rules can often be the catalyst that flushes a previous misunderstanding out into the open.

In your own environment, you may want to add extra categories for local circumstances, and you'll probably also want to include an extra category called "other" or "miscellaneous."

If a rule is rejected in the review, you should note the reason for rejection by recording the appropriate category. This will prove useful as part of your collection of metrics.

The main outcome of a review will be the list of actions. Depending on their scale, it may or may not be necessary to schedule another review to cover the same ground. If the actions are relatively minor, their completion may be sufficient for the rule population to be deemed accepted. In more complex cases, completing the actions may change the situation sufficiently to warrant another review of the same materials. In either case, it's up to the moderator of the review to make sure that all the actions have been properly completed within the agreed timeframe.

Typical actions are

- Tidying up cross-references between rules and other parts of the business model
- Correcting rule statements that aren't sufficiently clear
- Adding missing rules to make sure that the logic joins up properly

5.2.6 Review records and approvals

You can keep the review records as handwritten notes, but it's better to complete them in machine-readable form. It may mean a little more work in the short term, but it usually pays off later. You can copy-and-paste into reports, automating the collection of metrics and ensuring that you won't have problems with the handwriting! The ideal is to store the review records in a database and to generate any hard copy required from database reports.

Figure 5-3 shows a typical example of a review record that could be filled by hand or entered as a table in a word processor. Your own organization may already have its own standards for this sort of thing; if not, you can use this layout as a basis. You may need to add local embellishments, such as cost center codes, departmental identifiers, and so on.

Review Type			Review Date		Review Sheet No.		
Rule Context Reference					Version		
Participants	Name		Signature		#Rules Examined		
Moderator					Review Duration		
Lead Author							
Reviewer					Review Standard		
Reviewer							
Reviewer					Version		
Reviewer							
Rule(s) Ref	Issues/Action Required				#Rules	Issue Type	Rework Checked
Rules Accepted After Rework			Approval Signature			Approval Date	
New Review Required							

Figure 5-3 Typical review record

Once all the actions relating to the rules have been completed and checked—with a new review, if necessary—the rule population can be released. Again, the precise mechanisms for this will vary according to your local circumstances, but they should include all the following, in one form or another:

- Sign-off by the responsible authority, to indicate acceptance of the rules
- Updating the rule repository to identify the rules as reviewed and approved
- Publishing the rules, in read-only form, so that they become available for wider use
- Raising any related change requests for previously released items that may be impacted by the results of the review

5.3 Walkthroughs

These review sessions are one of the primary means of providing quality control on rules.

5.3.1 Planning and preparation

In addition to their primary function of ensuring rule quality, walkthroughs have some useful side benefits. They provide an opportunity for team members to gain a wider appreciation of the work they're engaged in, contribute a qualitative feel for the state of progress, and help to kick-start a rule population that's become stuck in analysis paralysis.

You should plan to hold several walkthroughs during the evolution of a rule population. The exact number will depend on your project circumstances. A rule-intensive project involving many analysts might arrange a weekly walkthrough meeting to review the rules defined or changed during the previous week. A project spread over a long period with only a couple of analysts might choose a lower frequency. It may also be useful to schedule walkthroughs so that they link up with other project activities, such as the completion of a set of use cases.

Before starting a walkthrough, it's important to give the participants a good definition of its intended scope. It's quite likely that you'll be considering an incomplete rule population, and the group must avoid becoming bogged down in issues relating to rules that don't yet exist. The main things to establish are

- The business objectives and requirements relating to this rule population
- Any standards or guidelines that are applicable
- The status of other elements of the business model
- The boundary of the rule population that's to be considered
- The end point of the session, aiming at a duration of less than 2 hours, if you can

5.3.2 Conducting a walkthrough

The walkthrough session itself is reasonably straightforward. Depending on the members of the group, some background material may need to be introduced at the start of the session. However, most of the time should be taken up with the author's explaining how each rule meets a facet of the business requirement. The best way to do this is to walk through one or more realistic business scenarios.

The source of these scenarios will vary according to the circumstances of your review. In a standard business modeling exercise, you should base your walkthrough sessions on use cases, but other situations may also arise, such as a fault report that needs to be investigated.

While you're working up a business model, you need to bear in mind that most parts of it—rules, class diagram, use cases, and so on—are likely to be in an unfinished state during a walkthrough. Although we're concentrating here on the rules, you shouldn't ignore the possibility that other elements, such as use cases, may themselves require changing as you iterate toward your final position.

Use cases normally contain the possibility of alternative courses of action, and you will need to be guided by your local practices for accommodating them. The easiest way to get good coverage in a walkthrough is usually a depth-first approach. Here, the author takes the group through the whole use case, following the most likely path. The walkthrough is then restarted from the first branching point, then the next, and so on, until all required branches have been examined. It's not necessary, and usually not practical, to follow every possible branch; you should stop when you feel that you've achieved sufficient coverage. Another common approach is to consider just two scenarios for each use case: a "happy day" scenario, covering the normal flow of events and a "rainy day" scenario covering a common business problem.

While the author takes the group through the business scenario, the other reviewers will be looking out for rules that are poorly framed. We'll look later at ways in which this can happen. Any suspect rule should be questioned until

1. It's accepted

2. A suitable modification is agreed

3. A need for more work is identified, to be completed outside the review session

Apart from the obvious items of record—project name, review date, and so on—the main results from the session are contained in the list of action points, each of which is allocated to a specific team member, usually the author of the rule. It's the job of the individual to carry out the action appropriately. The moderator will follow up in due course to make sure that all actions have been properly addressed and will sign off the walkthrough record.

5.4   Inspections

This type of quality control examines rules in the context of their business domain.

5.4.1 Planning and preparation

An inspection is a more formal activity than a walkthrough, taking in a wider perspective because it looks at a whole rule population in its business context. Therefore, an inspection needs a complete or almost complete rule population; a walkthrough, in contrast, may be aimed only at an identifiable subset.

An inspection of a rule population is usually the last stage before it's accepted by a business unit or before it's released to another group for further work, such as realization, which is why it tends to be a more formal and detailed activity than a walkthrough. For the same reason, an inspection usually involves people from outside the team that defined the rule statements. In particular, an inspection normally includes reviewers representing

- The business owner
- The designers who will be responsible for the subsequent rule realization

It may also be necessary to recruit additional reviewers with special knowledge or skills, depending on the review material and scope.

The other main difference is that an inspection meeting does not need to be as interactive as a walkthrough. Each reviewer can work through the review material individually and in advance, creating a list of points before attending the inspection meeting. The purpose of the meeting is to assess these points and to merge them into an agreed list of actions. Because the reviewers may be geographically separated, it may be more practical to designate a virtual review meeting, with electronic rather than physical participation from the reviewers.

Before starting the inspection, you should ensure that all the reviewers have adequate access to the following:

- A clear statement of the review objective and scope and the meeting format: electronic or face-to-face
- The rules repository, containing the definitions of all the rules to be reviewed, as well as, perhaps, others that are out of scope for the review but that are needed for a full understanding
- The source business descriptions from which the rules were mined. Descriptions of the flow of events in use cases are likely to dominate, but other possible sources are business process descriptions and miscellaneous external collateral, such as specifications provided by clients
- Other elements of the business model used as a basis for rule definition, including class diagrams, sequence diagrams, state transition diagrams, and so on
- Materials that define the business goals and intentions stated by the business owner and the associated levels of business risk that have been deemed acceptable
- Results from any testing that's already been carried out, typically relating to complex rule sets

It may be worth providing participants with individual copies of some of these items for ease of reference. For a large or important review, it may also be useful to have a prereview meeting to guide the participants through the material. This helps to avoid possible misunderstandings that could hold up the review later.

5.4.2   Managing an inspection

Given good preparation, the inspection itself need not be a complex affair. The moderator will need to lead the meeting through the review material in an orderly fashion. Deciding how best to work through the material is the crucial step, and this choice will be guided by the nature of the inspection.

A useful technique is to make inspections more manageable by defining a series of subsets of the whole rule population. Each subset provides a context within which a moderate number of rules can be considered. It's quite likely that a rule will end up being considered more than once, but you should view this as a positive benefit. Each context illuminates the rule from a different angle, and this may highlight factors that were not previously visible.

Here are some of the ways that you can break a rule population into subsets that are easier to manage.

- Focus on business functions. These are clustered by the various kinds of activities that are carried out in the business. Examples are marketing, operations, and finance and their various subdivisions.

- Focus on organizational units. Examples would typically include particular divisions, departments, and groups within the business. These units may correlate closely to business functions, but that's not always the case.

- Focus on business objects. These will be important entities relevant to the business. The objects will have been exposed in your current business model. Typical examples might be agreements, products, and parties.

- Focus on geographical locations. Examples of the kinds of geographical distinctions that might be important could include head office, northern region, or Europe. This can be especially useful if you need to consider rules that are heavily influenced by locale, such as regulatory requirements or currencies.

- Focus on a business perspective. These are usually identified with a strategic goal of the organization. Typical examples are customer relationship management (CRM), operational excellence, or product leadership.

- Focus on specific market offerings. For example, in a financial service organization, these could be such products as flexible mortgage packages, unsecured loans, or savings accounts.

- Focus on business partners. These are parties with which the organization has done, is doing, or wishes to do business. Examples could be specific types of customers, suppliers, and third-party associates.

As you can see, a rule population can be subdivided in many possible ways. The classifications are not mutually exclusive, and you can combine them in various ways to obtain the right level of granularity. The main guiding principles are to make sure that your grouping makes business sense and that every rule in scope is covered *at least* once. This is one of the times when having a good rule repository really pays off. You can easily tag rules to mark their different groupings and check that you haven't left any gaps in your coverage.

Given a context or a series of contexts, the reviewers can work through the rules systematically. The questions to be asked about each rule are similar to those in a walkthrough, along with additional examination of the completeness and consistency of the rule population as a whole. We'll look at testing for possible rule deficiencies shortly.

All reviewers record their own observations and submit them to the moderator either during a face-to-face review meeting or, if this is not possible, remotely. The moderator resolves any queries and combines the observations of all the reviewers into a consolidated list of action points.

All the action points should be addressed before the rule population is approved for release. Disagreements over fundamental issues can be less easy to untangle in an inspection than they would be in a walkthrough, because of polarization caused by the contractual nature of the result. The moderator must make sure these are escalated to a level at which they can be resolved. It's important not to just take these offline and deem the inspection complete. They may represent major obstacles to the eventual delivery of a successful system. Glossing over major disagreements usually results in a lot of rework later.

5.5 Testing

The third mechanism for controlling rule quality focuses on complex rule sets.

5.5.1 The use of testing

Any significant rule population has areas of special complexity. These usually arise where a constraint is based on a combination of many factors. Even where the possible outcome is as simple as a true/false distinction, it can be difficult to get your mind around the precise combinations that could lead to a true or a false conclusion.

Although the review procedures in walkthroughs and inspections provide a useful control on the quality of the separate rules, it can still be difficult to be sure that a whole rule set works together to provide the right results. This is where testing can help. Figure 5-4 shows the general structure of the testing environment.

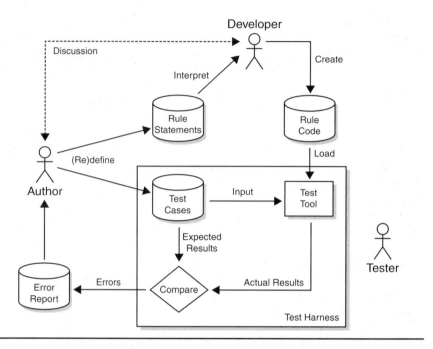

Figure 5-4   Overview of testing environment

The basic idea is to create a simple implementation of the relevant rules and to feed it with representative data. The test implementation does not have to conform to the sorts of constraints that will be necessary for the real implementation later; in particular, efficiency of operation is less important here. However, the test implementation, the test data, and the test results will be preserved in the project files, so normal good housekeeping practices should apply. We'll look at an example of testing a rule set shortly.

Roles   As with reviews, a few special roles are relevant to testing. The rule *author*—or one of the authors, if several—will have defined the rule set that's being tested. Before the tests are carried out, the author must also define a suitable set of test cases that will exercise the rules, accompanied by the expected results. The expected results are crucial here; without them, it will be impossible to say whether the test results show the rules as correct or not.

A *developer*—perhaps more than one for a large rule set—is responsible for coding the rules in the testing environment. The way that the business rule statements are translated into code depends on the tool being used. The main contribution of the developer is technical, rather than business, knowledge. A good understanding of the features of the test tool is obviously a prerequisite.

If it looks as though you're going to have a significant testing load, it may be worth designating the special role of *tester*. Having a dedicated resource provides a clear focal point for test expertise, helps to streamline the testing process, and makes sure that standardized and consistent procedures are followed.

If you have access to a particularly easy-to-use tool and testing environment, it may be possible to combine all these roles into one; in other words, the author also becomes the developer and the tester for the rule set. This can be more efficient, but it does remove an implicit layer of reviewing that would have resulted from the need for the developer to understand the author's rule statements.

5.5.2 Test implementation

Most of the implementation effort is tied up with coding the business rule statements in a form that can be executed by your chosen test tool. The coding may also be helped by other results from previous analysis. For example, you might have access to workshop notes and diagrams that show how the rule statements were derived.

The ideal tool would be one that's designed specifically for rule set testing, but at present, such things aren't generally available. It may be possible to press another test tool, such as one designed to test standard program code, into service, but this may turn out to be more trouble than it's worth. It's a good idea to make the test environment interactive, if you can, so that you can try out new scenarios quickly. You can realistically consider three main approaches, and we'll look briefly at each of them. The case study later in the chapter shows more clearly how they appear in practice.

Spreadsheet   The tool that's most likely to be available is a spreadsheet, which can be organized with the columns representing data values and the rows representing test cases. The rule author enters the input data for each test case and the corresponding outputs expected from the rule set. The developer creates formulas for cells containing intermediate and output values, which are entered in the first row and then copied down to all the succeeding rows. Figure 5-5 shows the general layout.

The columns containing intermediate values can be hidden once the formulas have been entered, so that attention can be focused on the inputs and outputs. It's also easy to highlight any differences between the actual and expected values, using another formula cell in each row.

The main advantages of the spreadsheet approach are its availability and immediacy. It's simple to experiment with different input values once a worksheet has been set up, and management is simple because the test values, coded rules, and test results are all kept together. The downside is that the formulas are sometimes a little opaque and difficult to debug if they're not working properly.

Custom program   The next alternative is a custom program. It's fairly straightforward to write a one-off program in Visual Basic or other languages that have a

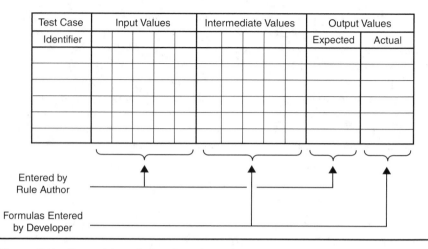

Figure 5-5 Spreadsheet layout for rule testing

similarly accessible user interface. The simplest technique is to replace each rule statement by an appropriate program statement, so a large proportion of the program code usually ends up a series of IF-THEN statements. Most developers find these easier than spreadsheet formulas to get right, and most modern programming environments provide good debugging facilities. Some additional code will also be needed in the program to handle the inputs and outputs. The input values and the expected results will have to be stored in a file that the test program reads in. This is fairly easy to produce as a text file or from a table created in a spreadsheet. The test results can be output in whatever format is most acceptable.

This approach has the advantage of maximum flexibility over the way that the testing is done and the outputs that are produced. It's also possible to set up a standardized framework that cuts down the effort needed for each new rule set. However, this approach does require more technical expertise, as well as access to a suitable programming environment. Managing the materials is also a bit more difficult because you're likely to have three files to look after: inputs, outputs, and the test program.

Rules engine If you imagine a programming framework elaborated to the extent that all variable elements have been taken out, you arrive at the third approach: a rules engine. Instead of the rules being in the program code, they, like the input values, are held in an external file to be read in at runtime. Each rules engine has its own specific syntax in which the rules must be expressed, but this is normally straightforward to understand. It's unlikely that you'll want to create your own rules engine, because they're generally easy to find. Several that are suitable for testing can be found on the Internet as freeware.

The big advantage of using a rules engine is that all the necessary mechanisms are already in place. This means that you can be pretty sure that differences between the actual and expected results aren't just side effects of an implementation error. Development effort can be focused solely on creating appropriate rule statements, and it's usually practical for business rule authors to learn the language of the rules engine, avoiding the need for an additional development resource. The main disadvantages of using a rules engine are a reduction in flexibility and, potentially, the higher cost of ownership if it's used only for rule set testing.

Other approaches   The alternatives discussed so far cover the main options, but there's plenty of scope for variations on the themes. One example is the use of the Prolog language to code the rules. Prolog has a built-in inference mechanism, and so it provides the best of both the programming and the rules engine approaches. However, Prolog has a learning curve that most business rule authors and developers find a little too steep. Another example is the use of a macro language in conjunction with a spreadsheet. These days, that usually means VBA (Visual Basic for Applications), making the implementation more of a hybrid between the spreadsheet and the programming approaches.

Procedural implications   One point to bear in mind is that your rule statements will be declarative, but your realization may have to be procedural. This implies some sequencing of the rules during evaluation, and you need to understand the implications of this.

Figure 5-6 shows a hypothetical set of dependencies, where the nodes A, B, C, and D represent input values and the nodes W, X, Y, and Z represent rules and their results. Instead of defining one complex rule (Z) that depends on all the inputs (A, B, C, D), this rule set follows the guidelines from earlier chapters and

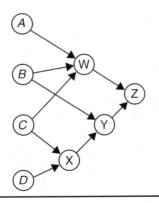

Figure 5-6   Dependency relationships

introduces some intermediate rules (W, X, Y) to improve the clarity of the rule statements.

The dependencies of the result Z on the input values A and D are straightforward, with B and C less so. For example, if input value C changes, it could affect result Z through two paths: C-W-Z and C-X-Y-Z. In theory, this need not matter, as declarative rules effectively assume that all changes propagate instantaneously. However, in a procedural implementation, we must make sure that we are never in a position where rule Z is seeing the old value of C along one path and the new value on another path.

With dependencies that are more complex, the outcome can be sensitive to the order in which the rules are evaluated, or fired. Practical implementations require a strategy that defines this ordering. The most common is sequential; that is, the rules are tested in the order in which they are stored. In more sophisticated schemes, rules can be given priorities that change their ordering.

The upshot is that you should be aware of the strategy that your implementation uses. If you obtain unexpected results while testing a complex rule set, it may be worth looking at sequencing of intermediate results to make sure that the outcome isn't an artifact of the test implementation.

5.5.3   The process of testing

Setting up the tests   The rule author takes the leading role in setting up the test cases. Each case will require both the relevant data values and the expected results. It's important to record the test cases in machine-readable form, because they will ultimately be used to drive the test harness, although perhaps mapped into a different structure. For complex rule sets, it may be valuable to review the proposed test cases before proceeding, to make sure that they reflect the proper business viewpoint.

In parallel with this, the developer codes the rule set, using the language defined by the choice of test tool. For any problems about the meaning or the intent of a rule, it's essential that the developer raise the issue with the rule author. Apart from avoiding subsequent difficulties in testing, this may also provide a strong hint to the author that the rule statement could benefit from improved wording.

The simplest approach to testing is to take a black-box view of the rule set. From this viewpoint, we're interested only in the results produced by the rule set under a given range of circumstances: in other words, just the relationship between the inputs and the outputs of the rule set. However, knowing something about how the rule set works can help you to define a reasonable set of inputs. We could call this a gray-box viewpoint. These two viewpoints are shown in Figure 5-7.

It's rarely possible to carry out exhaustive testing of every possible combination of inputs. The difficulty does not come so much in generating the test data or carrying out the testing itself, because both of these aspects can be automated. Rather, the real obstacle is the need for the rule author to define the expected results for each input combination.

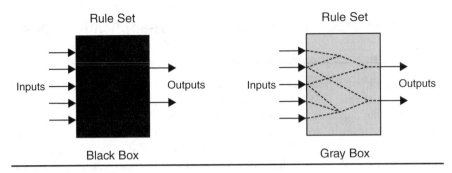

Figure 5-7   Two viewpoints: black box versus gray box

Using the test results   We can expect three kinds of issues to show up in testing:

1. Incorrect business logic. The testing of the rule set has revealed some deficiencies in the rule statements it contains.

2. Errors in the realization of the rules. The source rule statements are correct, but the developer has implemented them incorrectly.

3. Errors made in predicting the test results. The rules and the implementation are both correct, but they have produced results that the author did not expect. This can be only too easy with a complex rule set.

Although we're interested mainly in the first of these issues, the other categories can also provide some useful hints about rules that might benefit from revision. Errors in realization can arise because the intent of the rule statements is understandable only to their author. Errors in predicting results can arise from overcomplex rules or a poor understanding of the underlying business context.

Testing proceeds by alternately running the tests and changing the rules and/or the test cases, until the required test coverage is achieved with no errors. See Figure 5-4 for a high-level summary. A few important points are noteworthy.

- Any changes needed to the rules must be made at the source. In other words, the rule statements must be changed by the author and then the revised rules recoded by the developer. It's bad practice to fix a problem by patching the test implementation, because it's so easy to lose track of what you're testing.

- Think carefully about any cases in which the logic gives an unexpected result. Once you've eliminated coding errors, the remaining explanations may indicate a more fundamental problem with the rule set. Don't assume that just because a computer has worked out the logic correctly, it must be right in a business sense.

- Make the collection of metrics a routine part of your testing. Save all the tests and results, including, *especially* including, failures of all kinds. If you can, it's also useful to keep a note of auxiliary information, such as time spent on various activities. We'll look at metrics in a little more detail later.

5.6   Case study: testing the VBB loan-application rules

5.6.1   Setting up the ABC testing

In this section, we'll return to the VBB loan application rules that we developed in the previous chapter. We left them after a workshop effort had produced a set of definitions that appeared to meet the needs of the business. Although the individual rules appear fairly straightforward, it's not easy to see whether the rule set as a whole does what it should. This kind of situation is one that calls for testing.

Before we start planning the tests, it's useful to get an idea of the potential combinatorial complexity involved. We can do this by looking at the questions that are asked of an applicant. Looking back at Table 4-3, we can see 17 questions. The first five questions have a limited number of possible responses (4, 7, 3, 3, and 6, respectively), so we can easily calculate the number of combinations of all the alternatives (about 1,500). The remaining questions will each produce a numerical response. If we make a simplifying assumption that we would need to test three numerical values for each of these questions, we can come up with a figure for the total number of combinations that we would need for a comprehensive test. The answer is more than 800 million—not a very realistic amount to manage. We obviously need a way of focusing our efforts on a smaller number of tests by being smarter about the number of combinations we take on.

Faced with a set of rule statements like the VBB loan rules, it can be difficult to know where to start organizing the test cases. If you're not sure how to begin, it may be helpful to draw a dependency diagram, showing how the constraining and constrained values are linked by the rules. In the VBB case, we have a head start because the project files contain the workshop notes, including the final fishbone diagram showing the relationships among the various factors. Even if you don't have a starting point like this, it's fairly straightforward to construct a suitable diagram.

Take a large sheet of paper or a whiteboard. List the input values on the left or the top and the result values on the right or the bottom so that the general direction of constraint is from left to right or top to bottom. Work systematically through the rules, adding each one to the diagram as you go. Draw lines connecting the constraining values to the rule and the rule to the value it constrains. Don't expect the results to be tidy; just focus on showing the dependencies clearly. Figure 5-8 shows the VBB loan rules redrawn in this way. A diagram of this sort provides an opportunity for the analyst to assess the rule structure before too much effort is invested in the test implementation.

5.6.2   Assessing the rules

Once you have a picture of the dependencies, any major discontinuities, or places where the rules don't join up properly, should be obvious. Examples are rules that depend on quantities that aren't defined or intermediate results that don't seem to be used for anything.

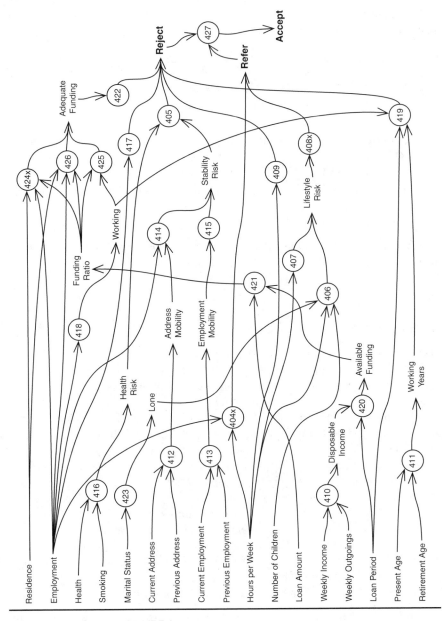

Figure 5-8   Rule set for VBB loan

In the VBB case, comparing the constraining values used by the rules with the input values shows some possible values not used by any rules. For example, the only value of residence type used is "owner/occupier" in rules R424X and R425.

Why should VBB allow for other categories if they're not going to be used? In fact, there might be several good reasons.

- It avoids exposing too much of the business logic to the applicants, who might cheat by guessing the preferred answers, and also to competitors, who would know the grounds on which they can compete.
- It can help to reinforce the customer relationship ("Yes, I see that VBB does cater to people just like me").
- It's useful to decouple the input information from the rules to some extent so that, within limits, the bank can change the loan-assessment rules without necessarily affecting data collection.
- The extra information can be used for future refinement. For example, a data mining exercise on past loans could reveal significant relationships that should be covered by new rules.

When choosing the possible values allowed for a property like this, you should focus initially on subdivisions that arise naturally in the data rather than the way that you intend to use them. Business intentions can change!

5.6.3   Choosing test cases

As we've seen, no simple recipe will provide the right set of test cases. The real limiting factor is the amount of effort available for defining the result(s) expected for each test case. If you think of all the possible combinations as defining points in a multidimensional space, you're going to be able to test only a comparatively small number of sample points in this space. Sampling is a reasonable concept if we assume that other points in the region of the sample will all behave in the same way. There are bound to be regions that are not sampled, and the result(s) from the rule set in these regions will be undetermined—by the tests, at least.

If you're making assumptions to simplify testing, you should keep a note of them, along with the test cases so that other reviewers can at least identify untested areas. For instance, in the VBB example, we decided not to test for "impossible" dates, such as retirement age earlier than current age, because we assumed that these would be checked and eliminated by another part of the process, before the rule set comes into play. This assumption would have been checked out in an earlier review.

Following are some general guidelines for selecting test cases.

- Make sure that you've covered any aspect that's been explicitly identified as a requirement.
- For this rule set, scenarios that are described in business narratives, such as use cases, should be checked by test cases appropriate to the narrative.
- You should note any significant boundaries or thresholds and test on and around the boundaries.

• You should test any rule set paths that are especially important to the business, such as commitment to significant expenditure or exposure to serious risk.

If your definition of test cases highlights regions of input space that seem important but don't appear to be covered by any definite business statement, a deficiency in the requirements or in the use case analysis may exist. In such cases, it may be necessary to challenge earlier assumptions and to revise the business model accordingly.

For example, in the assessment for the VBB loan rule set, we may be considering possible test values to use for loan amount. What range of values would be sensible? How big a loan would VBB be prepared to give? A financial product such as this is normally targeted quite carefully. In noticing that no rule specifies the maximum loan, we might suspect a missing requirement.

Other danger areas can be created by "get-out" values that bypass some of the rule checks. Our loan rules appear to eliminate potential borrowers who may be unable to repay because of poor health (R405 and R416). However, an applicant in poor health only has to leave the health question blank: The value of "unknown" is currently not checked, although presumably it should at least lead to a Refer decision. Querying the business owner about these points may reveal extra rules that will need to be added to the rule set.

A slightly subtler example from this rule set occurs with the calculation of the applicant's remaining working years (R411). We might test for some marginal values here, such as current age 59 retirement age 60. But this should raise some doubts about the quality of the rule, which presumably is intended to assess the length of time over which the applicant could maintain payments. With the rule as stated, applicants anywhere between their fifty-ninth and sixtieth birthdays would all be assessed as having one working year remaining, even though it may be just one day before their retirement. Again, this possible discrepancy would need to be raised with the business owner for clarification. Possible outcomes are changing the computation to months rather than years or adding rules to specify that this loan product is available only for long terms, thereby making the discrepancy unimportant.

5.6.4   Implementing the rule tests

Here, we'll look at some fragments of alternative test implementations to show how the alternative approaches appear in practice.

Spreadsheet   The VBB test spreadsheet uses built-in functions to implement the rules as cell formulas. The main point to be aware of is that some formulas can become very clumsy; in these cases, it's best to introduce extra columns to hold additional intermediate results. You can always remove them from view—in Excel, Format | Column | Hide—once you're happy with the logic.

Here's an example in Excel. Let's say that we've set up columns AN, AT, and AU to represent the Refer, Reject and Accept outcomes, respectively. To make the result easier to see, we've also created an extra Result column that tells us directly which of the three possible outcomes we have, making it easier to check against the expected result. We should have only one of the three, but just to be on the safe side, we'll indicate an error otherwise. Using row 3 as an example, gives us the following formula in the Result column:

```
=IF(AND(AN3,NOT(AT3),NOT(AU3)),"Refer",IF(AND(NOT(AN3),AT3,
NOT(AU3)),"Reject",IF(AND(NOT(AN3),NOT(AT3),AU3),
"Accept","ERROR")))
```

This is ugly! It's not very easy to create or to understand, even though it does work. A better idea is to break up something like this into smaller formulas, using as many extra columns as it takes; you can always hide them later.

To show this, we'll take a different example and show how we can derive the Reject value. Looking at Figure 5-8, you can see that Reject can be affected by five rules: R405, R409, R417, R419, and R422. We can implement these rules individually, and they're going to be defined by formulas in columns AO to AS, respectively. Again using row 3 as an example, we get the relevant formulas shown in Table 5-1. Now, given these intermediate results, the formula in the Reject column (AT) can be quite simple:

```
=OR(AO3:AS3)
```

Table 5-1 Breakdown of Reject formula

Column	Rule	Formula in cell (row 3)	References
AO	R405	=OR(AC3,T3)	Column AC is Stability Risk (Boolean)
			Column T is Health Risk (Boolean)
AP	R409	=K3>80	Column K is Hours Worked per week (integer)
AQ	R417	=C3="student"	Column C is Employment Type (string)
AR	R419	=AND(AB3,P3>Z3)	Column AB is Working (Boolean)
			Column P is Loan Period in years (integer)
			Column Z is Working Years (integer)
AS	R422	=NOT(AJ3)	Column AJ is Adequate Funding (Boolean)

Breaking up the logic in this way gives us a more understandable spreadsheet. Instead of using column numbers, you can also use named ranges, although whether this makes the formulas easier to create or to understand is a matter of opinion.

You might find that the best way to develop the formulas is backward: from the results toward the inputs. If you create the result formulas first and enter temporary values in the cells they refer to, you can check out the logic. Then, move to a referenced cell and enter *its* formula, entering temporary values in the cells it refers to. Repeat this process until you reach the input values.

Custom program   Implementing the rules in a programming language is a bit more verbose because you have to spell out a lot of the machinery that's built into other approaches. A skeleton of a Visual Basic program showing the same Reject rules might look like the following:

```
Option Explicit
Public Enum employmentType
       publicSector
       privateSector
       military
       homemaker
       student
       unemployed
End Enum
Public stabilityRisk As Boolean
Public healthRisk As Boolean
Public working As Boolean
Public adequateFunding As Boolean
Public reject As Boolean
Public loanPeriod As Integer
Public workingYears As Integer
Public workHoursPerWeek As Integer
Public loanPeriod As Integer
Public employment As employmentType
' ... other declarations
'
rFile = FreeFile
Open ruleFileName for Input As #rFile
Do While Not EOF(rFile)
       ' code to read in test case input values
       ' ...
       ' code to calculate intermediate values
       ' ...
       ' Rules R405, R409, R417, R419, R422
```

```
reject = (  (stabilityRisk Or healthRisk) Or _
            (workHoursPerWeek > 80) Or _
            (employment = student) Or _
            (working And (loanPeriod > workingYears)) Or _
            (Not(adequateFunding)))
      ' other rules
      '  ...
      ' code to output results
      '  ...
Loop
Close #rFile
```

It's well worth laying out the code to make the rule implementation as open and explicit as possible, so that the correspondence between the code and the rule statements is easy to understand. The easiest way to manage the program input is to create a *.CSV file with a spreadsheet, reading in each row as a separate test case. For simplicity, you can arrange the program to output only unexpected results.

Rules engine   If you're using a rules engine, you're dependent on the syntax of its rule language. We'll assume here that we're using a simple expert system shell that's able to match named values and to evaluate a limited set of straightforward expressions. The rules can be created as a formatted text file for readability; the rules engine strips out the formatting as white space, leaving just the symbolic values. A typical representation of the Reject rules might look like the following:

```
Rule405A    If
            stability_risk = true
            Then
            reject = true


Rule405B    If
            health_risk = true
            Then
            reject = true


Rule409     If
            work-hours-per-week > 80
            Then
            reject = true


Rule417     If
            Employment = student
            Then
            reject = true
```

```
Rule419      If
             working = true and
             loan_period > working_years
             Then
             reject = true

Rule422      If
             adequate_funding = false
             Then
             reject = true

. . . other rules
```

As you can see, this is quite close to the original rule statements, with only a few concessions to the technology. For example, the rules engine can be simplified by implementing only logical conjunction (AND) and using multiple rules as the way of realizing logical disjunction (OR). This makes it necessary to split conditions, such as R405, into two rules, whereas R419 can be accommodated in a single rule.

One thing to be aware of when thinking about using simple expert system shells for testing is the need for file input and output. A number of systems provide impeccable logic but are arranged for the input values to be input in response to a user dialog. Unless your rule set is very, very trivial, you won't want to type in the values for each test case.

5.6.5 VBB test results

We won't spend time here covering an exhaustive testing of the VBB loan rules. We've already seen a few points that would make us go back and query the initial rule set, based on issues that may arise while setting up the tests. Now we'll look at a couple of problems that may not initially be quite so obvious. The main reason for testing rule sets is to highlight and to locate these deficiencies. We'll use the spreadsheet test environment to illustrate how problems may appear in practice. You can assume that all the rules (R404X to R427) have been implemented in a spreadsheet in the way described earlier.

One problem is obvious straightaway. Figure 5-9 shows a sample of the output values for a few rows. We have a number of error conditions, because some combinations of values produce more than one outcome. (It's a good thing that we put in that ugly result formula!) The actual input combinations don't matter here. The problem lies in a deficiency in the logic: We have lots of situations in which an applicant can be simultaneously rejected and referred.

Presumably the intention is to refer applicants whose status is uncertain and to reject them if they are clearly unacceptable. In this sense, Reject has precedence

		AM	AS	AT	AU	AV
1					RESULT	
2		Refer	Reject	Accept	Actual	Expected
3		TRUE	TRUE	FALSE	ERROR	Refer
4		TRUE	TRUE	FALSE	ERROR	Reject
5		TRUE	TRUE	FALSE	ERROR	Reject
6		FALSE	TRUE	FALSE	Reject	Reject
7		FALSE	TRUE	FALSE	Reject	Reject
8		TRUE	TRUE	FALSE	ERROR	Reject
9		FALSE	FALSE	TRUE	Accept	Accept
10		FALSE	TRUE	FALSE	Reject	Reject

Figure 5-9   Errors in VBB rules

over Refer, but this isn't reflected in the rules. What to do? The first thing is to check with the business owner about the real intention. If the situation is as we expect, we could leave the rules as they are and sort out the multiple Reject/Refer cases manually, outside the rule set. The better solution is to modify the rules to resolve the problem.

One answer is to make the Refer result dependent on the Reject result. This requires modifications to two of the existing rules and the addion of one new rule. The modification to the dependency diagram is shown in Figure 5-10.

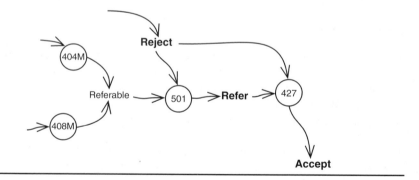

Figure 5-10   Modifications required to dependency diagram

R404M   An applicant who works more than 5 hours per week must be considered as referable if one or more of the following is true:
—The applicant is unemployed,
—The applicant is a homemaker.

R408M   An applicant must be considered as referable if he or she is a lifestyle risk.

R501   An applicant must be referred if both of the following are true:
—The applicant is referable,
—The applicant is not rejected.

The next problem is shown in Figure 5-11. This shows a few selected rows and columns to highlight an unexpected result. (Several columns have been hidden to make it easier to see the key values.) Rule R426 says that this type of applicant requires a funding ratio of at least 4, but we seem to be accepting applicants with a lower ratio.

The root of the problem is a common error: Casual interpretations of everyday terms are not necessarily strictly logical. Rule R424X is likely to be aimed at setting a lower threshold for applicants who are working and own their own homes, because those people are more likely to be reliable payers. Unfortunately, the rule as specified stipulates Not Unemployed rather than Working. Rule R418 defines what we mean by Working, but a slip by the author of R424X allows other categories to creep in. Because Unemployed is one of the seven categories of employment type defined, Not Unemployed means any one of the six other categories. Apart from the three we intended to include, defined in R418, this also includes Homemaker, the dreaded Student, and the catchall Other.

The resolution is a fairly straightforward change to rule R424X.

R424M   An applicant must be considered to have adequate funding if all of the following are true:
—The applicant is an owner/occupier.
—The applicant is working,
—The applicant's funding ratio is greater than 2.

It's worth repeating that the ways in which problems appear from the tests may be influenced by the rule implementation. This is especially true for rules coded in such general-purpose programming languages as Visual Basic. For instance, constructs that pick the first of a number of possibilities can hide other unexpected conditions. For example:

```
If x = a Then
    DoFirstThing
    '...
    Else If x = b Then
        DoSecondThing
    '...
        Else If x = c Then
```

Res	Empl	INPUT							INTERMEDIATE				RESULT	
		LoanAmt	WkInc	WkOut	LoanPrd	PresAge	RetAge	AvFund	WrkYrs	FundRatio	AdqFund	Actual	Expected
owner-occupier	homemaker	1000	50	35	2	30	60	1560	30	1.56	FALSE	Reject	Reject
owner-occupier	homemaker	1000	50	25	2	30	60	2600	30	2.6	TRUE	Accept	Reject
owner-occupier	homemaker	1000	50	15	2	30	60	3640	30	3.64	TRUE	Accept	Reject
owner-occupier	homemaker	1000	50	10	2	30	60	4160	30	4.16	TRUE	Accept	Accept

Figure 5-11   Unexpected results from the VBB rules

```
            DoThirdThing
              ' ...
        End If
     End If
  End If
     ' ...
```

This code might mask an unexpected condition, such as `a = b`. In such a case, the program would just take the first branch to `DoFirstThing`, and the existence of the other possibility may not be noticed.

An aside: loan applications in the real world   Even if you're not a financial expert, you may suspect that the process for loan applications described here is a little simplistic. Of course, you would be right, and it's worth looking briefly at the possible complications that would arise in a more realistic setting. These don't remove the need for testing; in fact, it's even more important to control quality in these more complex situations.

In the case study, we deliberately limited the number of factors considered, in order to make the example easy to follow, but nowadays the trend is to use more, not less, information. Before the second half of the twentieth century, it was still common for applications to be assessed by a local branch manager, whose decision would be based mainly on many years of experience and knowledge of the local community. We can think of this as being a set of rules and speculate that much of the status of bank managers in earlier days came from their exclusive access to this store of intangible knowledge. The world is now a more complex place, and the knowledge has to be captured explicitly, often appearing in such material forms as procedure manuals. Getting the rules right has a big impact on commercial performance, and we're now using not human experience but rather techniques such as data mining in order to identify the core knowledge. A realistic rule-based implementation of loan-application processing might involve hundreds of rules, not just the 20 or so used in the example.

The case study used rules in a very straightforward way, but this is by no means the only route to automation. A common solution in situations like this is to use a numerical scoring algorithm, which allocates points to various features of the loan application. The points are added to determine a score, which can then be compared to a threshold value that defines a go/no go boundary. We could also make use of more sophisticated algorithms to calculate ratios that highlight key features. Yet another approach is to train a neural network on past loan examples, so that it learns the features that were associated with previous good and bad loans. A big advantage of rules over some of these other mechanisms is that the rule statements can be used to explain why a particular application has been rejected. In practice, it's likely that several methods would be used in combination, with the aim of fusing the best elements of each approach.

For simplicity, our example assumed a single accept/reject/refer check on the loan application, so that we could look at the rules in isolation. A real bank would be likely to move the application through several stages of processing, and the related workflow implications might well influence the structuring of our rules. In addition, decisions on applications are not as open-and-shut as they might appear. For example, at a particular point in time, commercial conditions may encourage the bank to accept higher risks in order to increase its loan business. Rules may therefore need to be sensitive to areas outside the loan application itself. The key message is that you need to keep the rules coupled with other elements of the business model, so that you're able to appreciate the wider context within which they are applied.

All these complications may seem daunting, but you can still control rule quality in more realistic cases by using a divide-and-conquer strategy. Break down complex clusters of rules into rule sets that have a simple outcome. Temporarily isolating one part of the problem from the whole business model allows you to focus on it more clearly. Testing it by simulating its interactions with the rest of the model will allow you to assess its quality. Once you're confident about it, you can move on, without continually questioning its validity. Good test records allow you to review previous work quickly, without having to repeat it. They also provide a useful indicator of progress.

5.7   Metrics

Metrics, in the sense used here, are measurements that you make as an integral part of your reviews and tests. Their value is as indicators of the quality of your rule population. To be a good metric, a value must be both measurable and useful. We'll discuss some typical metrics a little later in this section.

The kinds of quality indicators and results you're after will fall into one of the following categories:

- Establishing development status
- Assessing risk exposure
- Estimating productivity and return on investment (ROI).

For each of these, you'll want to know not only the current position but also any identifiable trends.

You can apply metrics at various scales. A project manager may be interested in a specific project; a lead analyst may be more concerned about the behavior of a group over a number of projects. However, both simply take different views of the total information. The key point is that if you don't make the basic measurements, you won't have anything to analyze.

Metrics can also provide a basis for benchmarking one process against another. This needs some care, though; you need to be quite sure that you are comparing like with like. There's no recognized standard for rule metrics, so if you want to make valid comparisons, you'll first have to study the environments involved to understand their similarities and differences. This often identifies the need for conversion factors to correct for different measurement bases.

There's no magic value that's right for any of these measures, because they are so dependent on project size and type, the maturity of your development process, the experience of the individuals involved, and a whole host of other factors. By setting up a metrics-gathering process, you'll start to lay down the baseline that will allow you to calibrate you own environment.

5.7.1   Guidelines

Given the lack of any hard criteria, there's no simple answer to the question, When is enough enough? You're looking for the point at which it's no longer cost-effective to try to improve quality. The following guidelines might help.

Understand the cost of failure   Improved quality reduces the risk of subsequent failure. For many commercial systems, failure equates to the nonavailability of a desired business functionality. The cost of failure is the cost of the business impact plus the cost of rectifying the problem. Usually, a workaround can be used to reduce the business impact, and so the cost of fixing the problem often dominates. As a rule of thumb, the cost of maintenance in many organizations runs at about three to four times the cost of development.

The costs must also be taken in relation to the likely system lifetime. Sometime during this period, which is often much longer than assumed by the original developers, the cumulative costs of weak quality will overtake those of strong quality, as shown in Figure 5-12. In other situations, it may be the impact of the problem that's more serious. Air traffic control, nuclear power, and the manufacture of toxic chemicals are obvious examples. The cost pattern can have a very different profile if the failure has a catastrophic impact. Catastrophic costs threaten not just the integrity of the information systems but also the viability of the organization itself. It's therefore worth setting higher quality standards that are more appropriate to the risk.

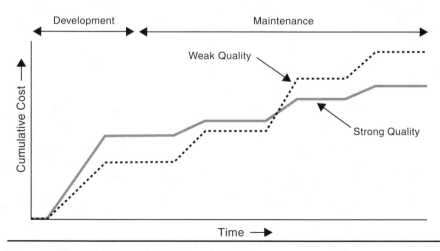

Figure 5-12   Cumulative effect of quality

To give the right perspective on the investment you're making in quality, you'll need to produce a figure for the cost of failure. You could do this in various ways. You should be able to find past information for your organization or perhaps your industry to use as a basis. For example, if the dominant cost in your organization arises from bug fixes in the code, you should be able to estimate the average cost per fault report. This is typically:

(hours to investigate + hours to rectify) * hourly rate

There are only a few special situations in which the costs of quality can't be justified. These usually arise only in systems that are deliberately built to meet a short-term objective, such as a customer demonstration or a trade exhibition.

Establish a baseline   You can produce first-cut estimates for your metrics, based on various elements of your business model. For instance, you might expect that a typical use case would involve about 20 business rules, but half of these would also appear in other use cases. You might also expect an average of three integrity rules per business object. Your first-cut estimate of the expected number of rules would therefore be:

10 * (number of use cases) + 3 * (number of business objects)

At the same time, you should estimate the problem rates that you would expect. For example, this might be 5 percent of rules incorrect prior to first review; 80 percent of problems corrected at first review. Initially, this may be based only on intuition, but as you build up a history of metrics, you'll be able to refine this figure for future projects.

Establish a policy   Even if you're just starting out, you should try to frame a quality policy in terms of metrics that make sense in your environment. If it turns out to be unsatisfactory, you can improve it incrementally in the light of experience. If you don't have a policy, you won't have any rational basis for making decisions. You can base your policy on the rate of problems that you are detecting. Table 5-2 gives an example. Obviously, you'll also have to define the metrics that you will use to determine the appropriate policy level.

Table 5-2   Possible quality policies

Problem Rate	Action
High	An underlying problem should be rectified before proceeding further. Examples are a poor understanding of the problem domain, insufficient clarity of project scope or purpose, and staff inexperience or lack of training.
Moderate	Problems identified appear to have little in common in terms of context, type, and so on. Reviewing and testing should continue or perhaps be extended.
Low	Adequate quality controls have been applied, but the problem-identification rate is acceptably close to zero. It may be possible to scale down reviewing and testing, but only if quality continues to be monitored for any impact.

Know where you are   In order to track your progress toward an acceptable level of quality, you can use the metrics to understand your current position. This is a vital element in both project control and quality control. Assessing current status is difficult because there's no standard measure. If you were building a wall that needed 1,000 bricks and you had 400 left, you could guess that you were about 60 percent complete. Unfortunately, the components of IT projects don't come in standard shapes and sizes, so your estimates will be a little fuzzier.

At any point in the project, you should know how many rules have been defined and how many problems you've identified, along with additional information to categorize them somewhat. It's difficult to express the values accurately as a percentage, because you have only an estimate of the total. Tracking the metrics as they evolve can help to reduce this uncertainty. In many ways, the changes in the values give more information than the absolute numbers.

5.7.2   Minimum metrics

Following is a suggested set of metrics. You can expand the measures covered here to include others that make sense in your environment. From time to time, you'll also need to look at selected areas in more detail, so you may gather more metrics than you use on a regular basis. The minimum set is summarized in the Table 5-3. You can keep your running totals in a simple worksheet like this, based on the inputs from team meetings, reviews, and other sources.

Table 5-3   Metrics worksheet

Metric	Total Anticipated	Total to date
Rules defined		
Individual rules checked (see below)		
Rules covered by reviews (see below)		
Problems identified through reviews		
Staff hours spent in reviews		
Rule sets defined		
Rule sets tested		
Problems identified through testing		
Staff hours spent in testing		

As you can see, you need to track the totals to date against the anticipated total figures. You can expect the anticipated values to change during the project;

for some reason, they always seem to go up, never down! The number of rules defined will exceed the number of rules checked to date, but you need to keep this within limits. If rule definition starts to outstrip rule checking, you're building up a backlog of review work and running the risk of extra difficulties caused by undetected rule deficiencies.

By the end of the project, the number of rules defined should equal the number of individual rules checked. However, some may have been checked more than once; for example, a rule may have been considered in several contexts. For this reason, the value of "rules covered by review" may well be greater than "individual rules checked." The ratio of these two values gives an indication of the number of perspectives from which a rule has been covered. From the point of absolute quality, more is better, but this runs into the problem of diminishing returns.

Tracking the problems identified against the rules covered by review and/or test will give you some idea of the rate of detection. Remember that even if this reduces to zero, it doesn't necessarily mean that your rules are perfect; latent defects may still exist. Assessing the likely number of latent defects is not really practical until you've built up a historical record.

The measure of effort expended will give you an estimate of the cost of your quality measures, calculated as:

(staff hours expended) * (average rate per hour)

This, coupled with your estimate of the cost of failure, will allow you to understand the return on investment (ROI) of your quality controls. In other words, by spending X on quality, you've probably saved Y in failure costs.

From time to time, you'll probably want to assess some aspects in more detail. For example, does a particular type of problem dominate? Are problems more easily detected in certain contexts? Deciding to expend effort in such situations is a matter of judgment, and the only possible advice is to do it if you feel that it's going to produce useful results.

Finally, it's worth noting that none of the metrics described here is particularly difficult or expensive to collect. Gather them as a routine part of the quality process, and analyze them at points that make sense in the framework of your project.

5.8 Quality summary

Table 5-4 summarizes the main features of each type of quality control discussed in this chapter.

Table 5-4   Summary of quality controls

Feature	Reviews		Testing
	Walkthroughs	**Inspections**	
What's examined?	Rule population, possibly incomplete	Complete rule population	Rule set
When used?	As often as practical, starting as soon as a reasonable body of rules is assembled	Toward the end of a project phase, before a rule population is released	When a sufficiently complex rule set is defined or changed
What's checked?	Rule clarity and business relevance	Rule clarity and business relevance, along with consistency of rule population	Logic of rule set
Focus defined by	Selected business scenarios	Business scope of rule population	Facts constrained by rule set
Purpose of meeting	Work though rules and raise actions	Work through pre-prepared comments and consolidate into actions	Work through test results and raise actions
Results on file	Observations and actions from each walkthrough, checked as completed	Observations and actions from each inspection, checked as completed	Test harness; test data; test results; any resulting actions, checked as completed

PART III

IMPLEMENTING BUSINESS RULES

6

The Technology
Environment

6.1 More about architecture

We now turn to the practicalities of making rules work in a realistic computing
environment: the sort found in most organizations of any reasonable size. The first
part of this chapter reviews how the major technology elements are orchestrated in
modern systems. If you're familiar with this kind of infrastructure, you probably
won't find anything new, and you can skip to the later sections, which discuss how
rules fit into the picture.

Up to now, we've simply considered all the apparatus of information technology (IT) as contained in one undifferentiated lump, vaguely called "the system."
Until the mid-1980s, this was often remarkably close to the truth, as corporate
computing was largely contained within very clear boundaries. Apart from a few
remote job entry stations and communication controllers, "the system" could be
considered as a unit by everyone except the few people intimately concerned with
its operation.

The big change came with the growth of distributed computing, which turned
out to be both a blessing and a curse. On the plus side, raw processing power
became much cheaper, allowing decisions about IT to be made at progressively
lower levels of the organization. The negative impact, not well understood initially, was the potential for additional costs hidden in the complexity of creating
and operating distributed environments.

Nowadays, many organizations have varied environments that include, for
very good reasons, a heterogeneous mix of machine types and sizes, some of
which we'll see shortly. There's no practical way of going back to a single mainframe, even if we were convinced that it might be a good thing. Any business
model is going to have to be implemented in an empirical, evolving environment,
and we'll have to make sure that our practices reflect this.

It's not quite as bad as it may seem. Although most computing infrastructures are likely to contain a mixture of offerings from competing vendors, practical constraints tend to force convergence around a few key ways of doing things, so the differences are not always as wide as they might seem on the surface. These days, most vendors recognize customer dislike of the lock-in that was so much a feature of mainframe environments and instead emphasize the positive virtues of open standards, although even the word "open" has come in for some misuse over recent years.

The term we use here to describe the elements that make up a particular computing environment is *technical architecture*. The word *architecture* is deliberately borrowed from its bricks-and-mortar equivalent, because the job of the architect in both cases is strikingly similar. We discussed architecture in Chapter 2, mainly in the context of business architectures. Much the same types of issues emerge here; the role of the architecture is still the same, except we're now concentrating on technology.

A technical architecture prescribes the building blocks for particular situations and defines how they can be put together. There's no one single technical architecture; each is defined to suit a particular set of circumstances. However, the need for blocks from various suppliers to interoperate involves at least some standardization. In the extreme, this can mean strict compliance with a designated standard. Alternatively, it could be a recommendation to adopt a particular style. References might be shorthand descriptions that might look something like HTML (Hypertext Markup Language) or might be more specific indicators, such as //W3C//DTD HTML 3.2//EN. Specifics like these tend to pepper any technical architecture, but its main structure is likely to refer to an overarching vision—a *reference architecture*—that lays down broad principles while leaving flexibility for localized implementation and future evolution.

Before going into more detail, it's worth briefly reviewing some high-level architectural principles that are worth fighting for. (You might reflect on how these are applied in your particular organization.)

- *Decouple technical architecture from business model.* The technology and the business are going to evolve in their own ways and at their own rates without any particular synchronization. For instance, upgrading your technology platform might improve performance, reduce costs, or bring other benefits. You don't want to be prevented from going ahead because the change would upset important business functionality. Similarly, the business is likely to demand the freedom to adapt to meet changing market conditions and will not want to be artificially impeded by technology constraints.
- *Consider system availability very seriously.* This factor needs to span much more than choosing the hardware and developing the software. Operations and support, connections to utilities—power, cooling, and so on—disaster recovery, and many other areas need to be integrated with the architecture picture. The key issue is maintaining a reliable service to customers. With

the onset of e-business, customers are no longer shielded by front-office staff but are looking directly at your system(s). Downtime will result in immediate revenue loss. Even worse could be the future business lost because your customer switched to a more reliable competitor.

- *Build in scalability options.* Trying to predict the future is particularly difficult if you're dealing with an innovative e-business offering lacking an established exemplar that could give guidance. Your architecture should allow systems elements, such as communications bandwidth, processing capacity, and data storage, to scale well beyond their initial design sizes and to do so at very short notice—hours or days, not weeks or months.

- *Organize different elements into clear layers, or tiers.* This makes it easier to manage the inevitable complexity. Each tier need handle only its own concerns, safe in the knowledge that other tiers will be handling theirs. At the same time, layering provides the decoupling that will be needed to allow flexible, on-demand reconfiguration of business services. Finally, organizing elements into tiers also provides opportunities for optimizing each tier to be particularly good at the specific functions it performs.

This is not meant to be an exhaustive list of desirable architectural properties; others, such as reliability, security, and so on, are also important. However, the ones here are particularly interesting in the context of business rules, as we'll see later.

6.2 A typical reference architecture

To make these ideas a little more concrete, we'll take a look at an example. This is based on Microsoft's high–level vision of a Distributed interNet Architecture (DNA). Nothing is particularly unique about the Microsoft perspective; other, comparable architectures are equally valid, and Microsoft will undoubtedly be evolving it's own views as the .NET initiative crystallizes further. Figure 6-1 shows a simplified view of Microsoft's DNA, based on published materials.

Bear in mind that the author of a reference architecture—Microsoft in this case—is not saying "all systems must be built like exactly like this", but simply "here's a basis for rational discussion". It's up to you to take away the essential messages and evaluate them in the light of your own circumstances. To illustrate this, we'll look at just a few interpretations of Figure 6-1.

A simple example is the block labeled External Applications in the Data tier. You would probably want to take this to mean "applications external to the Windows infrastructure", not "applications external to the organization".

A more complex example is the label Presentation for the first tier—and the visual hint that this is implemented on laptops, hand-held organizers, and so on.

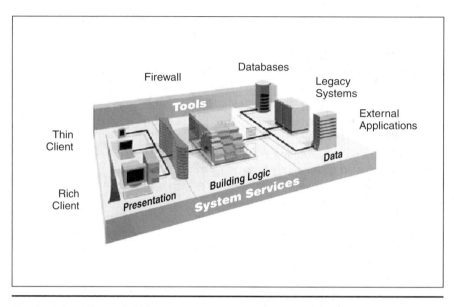

Figure 6-1   Microsoft DNA

The label suggests that this layer is all about issues such as screen layouts and formatting. This may be true in a few limited cases, but more generally it's about handling the various paths through which clients can access the business logic. For instance, an e-commerce system dealing with business-to-consumer operations is likely to require a front end to handle HTML, and this may well include elements of presentation, in the graphic sense. However, a business-to-business system may be concerned only with electronic data interchange using XML forms, with no (visual) presentation element being necessary. A better label for this layer might be "Channel", and so, with apologies to Microsoft, that's what we'll call it from now on.

As a final example, there's the issue of the area labeled Business Logic, which is the tier where the bulk of the business processes happen. These may, of course, contain some logic, but in this chapter and the next we'll show that this is not the only place that logic exists.

The type of scheme shown in Figure 6-1 is often called a three-tier architecture; however, as we'll see shortly, a more accurate term is *N*-tier architecture. It's important to remember that this is a *logical* view of tiers of processing. In spite of the visual appearance of Figure 6-1, the machine room won't necessarily contain three—or even *N*—neat rows of computers. Logical tiers can be colocated at the same physical level; finer subdivisions may exist in any tier to handle variations in services.

Let's see an example of how this might happen in an abstract way, putting aside the specifics of the business functionality. Figure 6-2 shows some possible variations.

- We'll assume the original system (a) provides a basic service X—it doesn't matter what it is—via the first (channel) tier.

- We could add a new service, Y, by modifying the existing channel tier so that it can handle both types of service (b). This might be a good choice if the new service is similar to the existing one, and the differences can be handled by selecting between the alternative operations for X and Y, using fairly simply mechanisms.

- Another possibility is to add a parallel channel tier (c) to handle the new service. This might be a good choice if the nature of the service or its traffic profile is very different from the existing one. All the special things to do with service Y are handled separately, so there's no impact on the existing service. However, the new first tier can make use of the existing functionality of the second tier, which now provides services to both the X and the Y channel tiers.

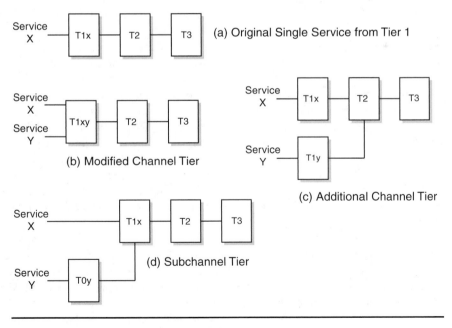

Figure 6-2   Variations in the channel tier

• Finally, we could provide an additional subtier to supplement the existing channel processing (d). This could be useful if the new service is a specialization of the existing one, so the new subtier effectively becomes a front end to the original first tier, translating service Y into service X.

Of course, this sort of flexibility doesn't just apply to the first tier; comparable discussions could be had for each of the other tiers, and there's plenty of scope for variation. However, it's obviously important not to take this sort of thing to extremes. The flexibility of a distributed architecture comes partly because we carefully organize our processing into defined stages. Introducing too many new tiers compromises this organization and defeats the very flexibility that we wanted to achieve. The main point to take away is that we don't have to be rigidly fixed on exactly three tiers; we have a little leeway to optimize the architecture to meet particular conditions.

6.2.1 Business flexibility

We can look at flexibility from another angle: that of preserving investment in IT.

Any organization will have to interact with several kinds of external agents—customers, suppliers, and so on—whether they are individuals, other organizations, or even other computer systems. Each of these agents is reached through one or more channels that may vary in speed, format, and reliability. A range of business processes may be deployed, with new ones added and old ones removed, as the business reacts to its environment. Data is stored in a reliable and accessible way so that it can be produced by, and used by, the business processes.

In former days, new business initiatives were often accompanied by new systems. For example, a bank might decide to move into the home loans market, requiring a new system to hold details of customers, mortgages, and so on. The various elements—screen handling, processing, databases, and the like—were closely coupled so they could be quite efficient (see Figure 6-3). The blocks are sometimes known as stovepipe, or silo, systems, because they look that way if drawn on end.

Unfortunately, it's very difficult to reuse any part of these systems. A subsequent move by the same bank into, say, insurance, would require a different set of business processes, but it would be very nice to be able to use the existing customer database and maybe some of the existing channels. Sadly, in such architectures, it's not really practical.

In the world of e-business, this is not good enough. The ability to react quickly is absolutely essential not only for success but also for basic survival in a world of global competition. Figure 6-4 shows the position that most organizations would much prefer to adopt. The present-day business mantra is the ability to use *any* data to support *any* process through *any* channel to reach *any* agent.

Even if it were possible to predict the right cross-coupling ahead of time, the structure would still need to change as the business adjusts to meet new threats or

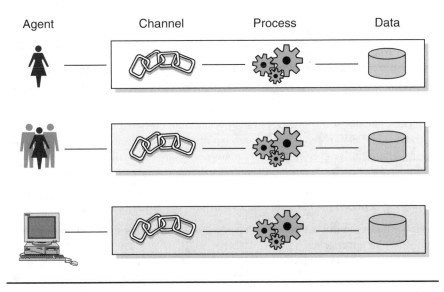

Figure 6-3   Stovepipe systems

opportunities. The sensible solution is to build in a modular capability, adding the cross-couplings as and when they are needed. To do this, we need an *N*-tier architecture.

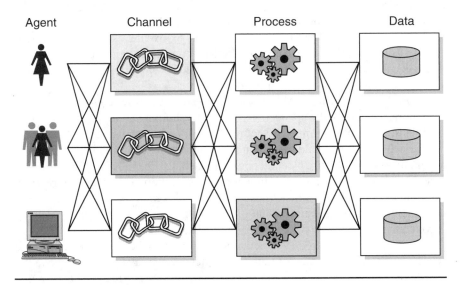

Figure 6-4   Fully connectable systems

6.2.2   Shared resources

Another role of the *N*-tier architecture is making efficient use of shared resources, principally a back-end database. We're certainly going to want to do this if we expect our e-business to handle large numbers of customers. Looking at the world from the database end, we see that a couple of factors are significant.

1. The database machine needs to set up a connection over which its retrievals and updates can pass. Each database connection requires resources, so the machine can't afford to have too many simultaneous connections.

2. The time taken to set up and to close down a database connection is much greater than the time taken to carry out a retrieval or an update over an established connection. The difference is around two orders of magnitude.

To understand the impact of these factors, it's worth taking a step back to look at some simpler approaches.

Perhaps the most obvious solution would be to connect all the users directly to the machine holding the database. (It doesn't matter here whether the users are customer service agents or the customers themselves.) However, this creates two problems. First, the number of simultaneous users is limited by the available database connections. Second, to make efficient use of the database facilities, we might need to eliminate time spent in enriching the user interface; so no interactivity, no nice graphics. You can try the difference at home. A system such as Linux will run happily in character mode on an old i486 machine. Add a graphical shell, and you'll want to be running on a reasonably fast Pentium machine.

We can solve the second problem by providing more processing power closer to the user. Now there are two layers of machine: *client* machines on the user side, optimized for presentation; and a *server* machine handling the database. Relieving the server of responsibility for the GUI allows us to give the users a better experience but does nothing to get around the limit on open database connections. Because each connection is idle unless the attached user carries out a data-related action, the server is used very inefficiently.

Now that we have a machine at the client end, perhaps we could use it to be a little more clever with the connections. Instead of holding on to a connection that sits idle for most of the time, why not make the client machine wait until it really needs one? The client could then create the connection, use it, and close it down, making it available for use by another client machine. The killer here is the set-up time. The client has to wait a long time for the connection to be set up before it can carry out a comparatively quick update or retrieval. Again, the server is used very inefficiently because it's now spending most of its time setting up and tearing down connections instead of operating on the data.

The answer is to introduce a new tier of processing between the clients and the server, allowing a somewhat modified strategy. Let's say that a machine in the middle tier acquires a database connection to the server. The machine is then in a position to offer this to any client machine. Because switching attention from one

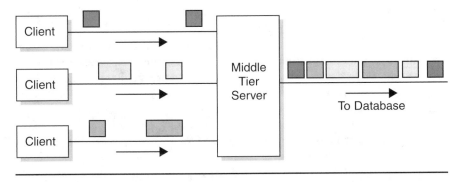

Figure 6-5   Middle tier as a multiplexer

client machine to another is relatively quick, database requests from many client machines can be packed, one behind another, in boxcar fashion. Effectively, the middle-tier machine is now able to multiplex a database connection between many clients, as shown in Figure 6-5.

Holding on to a database connection no longer locks out other clients, so the set-up time is much less of an issue. Database requests are concentrated into streams, cutting out the user's "thinking" time, so the server is used much more efficiently—again, orders of magnitude difference.

The hardware cost of the additional middle-tier servers is negligible compared to the total system costs. The main price to be paid is the significant increase in the complexity of the overall system. On the whole, though, it's worth it, and distributed computing is clearly here to stay.

6.3   Component architecture

The other essential architecture we introduced in Chapter 2 dealt with deployable units of functionality. We'll use the term *component architecture* for this, although exactly what's meant by "component" is somewhat fluid these days. Components are the latest buzzword in development, and anyone entering the scene for the first time could be forgiven for thinking that using them is the only way to produce software. That's not quite true, but if you're developing outside a legacy environment, the component story is pretty convincing, and you would be crazy not to at least consider component-based development (CBD).

In one sense, components are nothing new but rather represent the latest position in the ongoing quest for modularity: another way of breaking potentially complex software structures into more manageable chunks. There are (of course!) differing views on the One True Way to develop components. We won't dwell on the finer details of the various approaches because, in truth, they all pretty much agree on the most important concepts.

First, software components provide their functionality through interfaces. You can think of an interface as a commitment to do something: "If you ask me to do X and provide the necessary supporting information, I promise I will either do X or tell you why I could not do it." A proper component environment has no back door. The only way to talk to a component is through its published interfaces.

A corollary of this is that you don't need to know what goes on inside the component. In fact, you're positively discouraged from peeking! If you want to use the services of a component, you renounce all rights to know *how* a component does what it does. You are entitled to know only *what* it does. The benefit is that the innards of the component can be changed, if necessary, without impacting other pieces of software that rely on its services, providing that it continues to honor its interface promises. A component can sprout new interfaces and make new promises, but it can't break a promise that it has already given. For example, the growth of traffic in an e-commerce system may overstress a particular component service. The solution may be to implement a more efficient algorithm in the component. If the component is well behaved, the changes needed in the remainder of the software will be, well, nothing. The whole system will just work faster.

Another benefit of software components is the discipline that has to be imposed on the packaging, or the way that the component interacts with its environment. Because we want components to talk to one another in a consistent way, they have to conform to certain standards. If they all use the same basic mechanisms, albeit with an infinite variety of business functionality, they can all be handled in the same way. In principle, we need to have only one way of distributing a new piece of software, one way of loading it into the system, one way of releasing new versions, and so on.

A further point that emerges from such a high-level view is the scope for standard services. Some common problems appear frequently in designing any significant piece of software and certainly in the sort of complex functionality we need for e-commerce. For instance, it's good to handle transactions in a consistent way. We'll get to more details on transactions shortly. A standard approach to building components allows us to move some of the common problems out of the components and into a shared substrate: the component environment. There may be several component environments or frameworks—true, unfortunately—but within one framework, all components can work in a consistent way.

Finally, and perhaps the most telling of all, is the synergy between software components and the ideas surrounding business objects that we saw in Chapter 2. That's not to say that one business object is exactly equal to one software component, although that may sometimes happen. It's more about a shared desire to tame complexity through a divide-and-conquer approach. In both business modeling and software components, a common aim is to define an *architectural* methodology, which could be summarized as "here are the building blocks you can use, and here are the rules governing how the blocks can be put together."

The biggies in component frameworks are Enterprise JavaBeans and COM (component object model, actually, COM+ now in Windows 2000). Both of them meet the sort of criteria we've talked about here. Both can be used to build large, complex systems. Sadly, they're not directly compatible, although there are ways of bridging them. This means that you have to opt for a particular choice, which pretty much comes down to Microsoft (a company) versus Java (a programming language), which seems like a strange sort of choice to have to make. Nonetheless, that's the way it is. Whichever path you take, there's plenty of proof that you can develop whatever kind of e-commerce system takes your fancy.

To provide a coherent frame of reference, we'll assume from here on that our new e-commerce functionality will be developed within a component framework. That doesn't preclude interoperation with existing systems. It's perfectly possible to wrap existing systems to provide component-style interfaces so that they can participate fully in business activities. As we saw earlier, an *N*-tier architecture could potentially accommodate existing systems wrapped to provide data resources, business process resources, or channels of communication.

Before drilling down to more detail, let's summarize some important points about components. The main features are shown in Figure 6-6.

- Components encapsulate some functionality that's realized in software.
- The functionality is accessible only through the interfaces of the component.
- Components may not make ad hoc changes to published interfaces.
- Components use an underlying set of common services, provided by the component framework.

Some diagrammatic notations for components are defined in UML. One particular convention, used in Figure 6-6, is the use of a "lollipop stick" to denote an interface. Other notations, which we won't go into here, deal with such things as grouping components into packages.

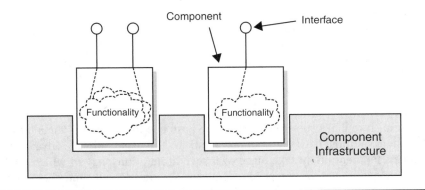

Figure 6-6 Software components

6.3.1 Interfaces

The concept of interfaces is arguably the most profound aspect of software components. All component frameworks expect their components to interact via their interfaces. Unfortunately, the exact details of the workings are specific to each framework. For example, a COM component cannot talk directly to an Enterprise JavaBean, although various companies have developed connectors, or adapters, that can bridge the various environments.

Interface definitions are couched in terms that resemble function calls in a programming language, which shows the heritage of their designers. In COM, for example, interfaces are described using the interface description language (IDL). Here's a fragment of a typical interface description in IDL for IPassword—interface names start with I, by convention—which supports two methods—services as far as we're concerned—called Check and NewPasswordList.

```
. . .
[ object, uuid{4657A891-CC3B-41AC-A166-97EB7E5D0172} ]
interface IPassword : Iunknown
{
HRESULT Check( [in, string] char *word, [out, retval]
    BOOL *isValid );
HRESULT NewPasswordList ( [in, string] char *filename );
}
. . .
```

Intuitive, no?

One reason frameworks came to differ in how they define interfaces is that there was no real candidate language that everyone could rally around. However, the rise of XML offers some hope that future evolutions will lead to standardization and improved readability. For example, the NewPasswordList service in the IPassword interface might come out something more like:

```
<interface>
<component> Password </component>
<service> NewPasswordList </service>
<passwordFile> filename </passwordFile>
</interface>
```

Better, yes?

A mistake that's sometimes made is to postpone finalization of the interface definitions until the later stages of development. The usual rationale advanced is that development might take place over several iterations, any of which could change the design of the component, requiring early work on the interface definitions to be redone. This is incorrect. The time to debate the interfaces offered by a component is *before* any serious coding work begins. Just as an interface is a kind of specification of the behavior of a component, it's also a specification of its functionality: *what* it should do, remember, not *how* it should do it. If this is not clear before coding starts, a great many disappointments are sure to follow.

A walkthrough of an appropriate set of scenarios will show whether the functionality provided by the interfaces correctly meets the requirements, before any of the functional code is written. A good practice is to start development with a set of empty components that have the right interfaces but only stubs or dummy code behind them. As development progresses, through a number of iterations, functionality can be built up behind the interfaces and tested incrementally.

6.3.2   Component interaction

How does one component talk to another? The underlying component framework provides functionality to facilitate this. The aim is to insulate the component developer from the runtime environment. At the time of its creation, many factors relating to component deployment may still be unresolved. Even if all factors were completely defined, it's quite likely that a component could be redeployed in the future. Add to all this the need to deploy different *instances* of a component in different situations, and you can see why this decoupling is more than just a convenience.

A particularly crucial issue is the distinction between the place where a service is requested and the place from which it is provided. Most architectures support modular decomposition, so that one piece of code can request the services of another, perhaps written by somebody else at a different time. Subroutines are an example of this, and they've been around since the earliest days of computing. However, in the world of distributed components, it's not quite so simple. The service requester—roughly equivalent to a subroutine call—does not know whether the service provider—roughly equivalent to the subroutine—lives in the same process, in a different process on the same machine, or on a different machine altogether.

One possibility could be to create multiple versions of each component, but this would be expensive and error prone. Instead, most component frameworks, including all the recent ones, provide an integral capability for managing component interaction. The following discussion is based on Microsoft's COM standard, but other approaches work in a generally similar way, although they aren't necessarily consistent in their use of terms.

To get an idea of how it all works, we need take only a pair of components: one requesting a service and one providing a service. It doesn't matter which architectural layer they sit on; for convenience, we'll refer to them as client (requester) and server (provider). Figure 6-7 shows the main elements.

The first important notion is a *stub,* which is created for the server component. This is a placeholder for a full-fledged instance of the component. To

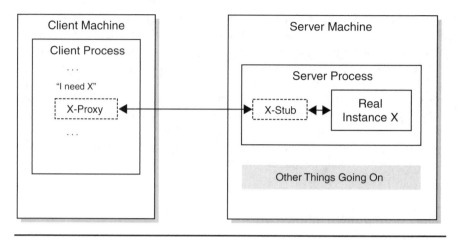

Figure 6-7   Stubs and proxies

economize on scarce resources at the server end, we want to minimize the number of instances present at any one time. A stub is something that fools the outside world into believing that an instance exists, whether it does or not. Behind the stub, the real instances can be managed in a couple of ways. One is to hold a pool of waiting instances and then associate them with a stub as required. Another, the one apparently preferred by Microsoft, is to create an instance only when it's needed, referred to as *just-in-time (JIT) instantiation,* or just *JIT*. Remember that the client might be hanging around doing a whole bunch of things, talking to the server only occasionally. The server needs to keep busy, so it can get on with servicing other clients while the first continues its meditations.

Because the instances are the "real" component, it's reasonable to ask what happens between instantiations. At the server end, a component instance can disappear part way through carrying out a business activity. Although the stub hides this from the outside world, won't we lose information? In fact, the component instances flit in and out of a database that holds the current *state* of the component. The state is what distinguishes one instance of a component from another. The word is used in a somewhat different sense here than in the states of objects and processes in the business model.

For example, a customer component is a generic container: Given a particular name and address, this container has a state. The program code for services associated with this component will be the same all the time, but the data will be different. This is why developers are exhorted to design components to be *stateless;* that is, don't keep data in an instance of a component. Doing so will mess up all the good work that the component environment is attempting to help with.

To talk to the stub, the client has a corresponding *proxy*. To the client, the proxy looks like the actual component: The component environment protects it from having to know anything about where the component really exists. Again, the component environment arranges the communications between proxy and stub, inserting the right kind of proxy/stub setup, depending on its assessment of the different *contexts* involved.

Another particularly cunning feature of all the modern approaches is *interception*. The service request does not go directly to the component instance via the stub but instead gets intercepted by the component environment. This provides an opportunity to trap the communications between client and server, examine them, and, if appropriate, provide some additional service. All this happens without the client (or the proxy) having to take any action. However, the client does have to disclose information that can be used to make decisions about added-value services.

Some of the neat things that can be done at this point are

- Checking security. Is this client allowed to use this component instance?
- Load balancing. Should the traffic be (re)distributed to handle the current load?
- Defining transactions. Is there a chunk of activity that should be treated as an indivisible unit?

The last of these has some particular implications for the realization of business rules, so it's worth a closer look.

6.4 Transactions

Here's one of the complications of distributed processing. It's all very well to split up the functionality in a modular way, but several fragments sometimes need to be treated as one integral unit. For instance, say that we have a business process that transfers an amount from account 1 to account 2 on behalf of a client. This may sound innocuous enough, but let's take a closer look. As pseudocode, the operations might look more like:

```
1. CustomerId = getCustomerIdFromClient()
2. Amount = getAmountFromClient()
3. V1 = getFromDatabase (DB1, CustomerId, Balance)
4. Temp1 = V1 - Amount
5. V2 = getFromDatabase (DB2, CustomerId, Balance)
6. Temp2 = V2 + Amount
7. writeToDatabase (DB1, CustomerId, Balance, Temp1)
8. writeToDatabase (DB2, CustomerId, Balance, Temp2)
```

Recall that the middle-tier machines are busy interleaving client requests in order to work the database as hard as possible. What happens if another client changes the values of the customer balances in databases DB1 or DB2 between steps 3 and 8? The values changed by the first process will be overwritten by the second process, resulting in confusion about the true values. Other things can go wrong too: machine crashes, communication errors, and so on. It's obvious that no serious business could accept such uncertainties, even without the higher visibility that e-commerce brings.

The solution is to define selected blocks of processing to be handled as a single unit, which will either succeed completely or fail completely. If a failure is caused by a transient condition, a retry will usually succeed without the outside world's being aware that it has happened. The term for a block of this sort is a *transaction.* This technical use is related to, but not quite the same as, the use in a non-IT business context.

Writing software to handle transactions is very tricky, even more so in a distributed system. Fortunately, you don't have to do it all by yourself, because most component frameworks provide support for transaction handling. Microsoft's approach provides a good example. An early version appeared during the life of Windows NT 4.0, but it's now much better integrated into Windows 2000 and beyond, as part of the COM+ component framework.

COM+ supports an algorithm, called two-phase commit, that synchronizes the distributed resources involved in a transaction. The key player is the distributed transaction coordinator (DTC) that comes as part of COM+. In the first phase of the transaction, the DTC collects information from each piece of software taking part in a transaction, which could be distributed in several places. Each piece of software in the transaction does its thing and then tells the DTC whether it's happy with what's been done. At this point, no irrevocable changes have been made.

Once everyone in the transaction has reported in, the second phase begins. Based on the responses from the various transaction elements, the DTC will decide either to *commit,* making the changes permanent, or *abort,* undoing the changes. If all the distributed pieces of the transaction are happy, the transaction will be committed. If any of them reports a problem, the whole transaction will be aborted.

An important implication of this is that for a short while, a component has exclusive ownership of the resources it needs for the transaction. The only safe way for another component to see what's going on inside a transaction is to become part of it.

From a development point of view, it's not too difficult to make this work with COM+. A component need only tell the DTC when it wants to start a transaction or join one that's in progress. The component can then go ahead with the reassurance that no other component is going to sneak in and change the data under its nose. When it's completed its work, such as updating a database, the component declares whether everything looks OK from its own local point of view. The component does not have to know anything about how the other components are doing; the DTC looks after all that.

Transactions are one of the scalability issues that can't be avoided in realistic business systems. Fortunately, the facilities provided by COM+, and the equivalents in other component frameworks, hide most of the complexity and reduce the development task to deciding *where* transaction boundaries should be placed rather than *how* to make it all work.

6.5   Server pages and scripting

Web servers are a standard building block in most e-commerce systems. Originally, the main responsibility of a Web server was to deliver pages of HTML to a remote browser. It soon became obvious that services could be much enhanced if the page content could be made dynamic, using data obtained from sources other than the static HTML that formed the basic structure of the page.

We'll focus here on the server end of the activity because it's there that we need to interact with the business logic. Most Web servers provide an ability to create page content on the fly, under the banner of Active Server Pages (ASP) in the Microsoft world, or Java Server Pages (JSP) for those of a different persuasion. In both cases, the pages designer is able to insert into Web pages *scripting* commands that are executed on demand. The scripting language can vary: Java (obviously!) in JSP or a selection available for ASP, of which VBScript (Visual Basic Scripting Edition) is probably the most widely used.

There's a great deal of flexibility in the ways that the various elements can interact. For example, Java can be incorporated into JSP pages or built into *servlets* with their own URLs. One servlet can serve several JSP pages or vice versa, and servlets can use other servlets. To access business services provided by other layers of processing, servlets can call on components (Enterprise JavaBeans). A corresponding set of features is available using Microsoft technology, but the terminology varies somewhat among the various approaches and is probably evolving even as you read these words.

The advantage of a scripting approach is that it's fairly easy to adjust, within limits, the functionality that's provided, but there are some negative points. One is that scripts are inherently less efficient than the equivalent functionality built into a business component. Another is that the very flexibility of scripts opens up opportunities for bypassing configuration-management controls, leading to unexpected side effects on the business services that are being provided.

Scripting is not limited to Web servers. In principle, a script capability could be used in most elements of a system. This provides a form of soft coding for features that are difficult to specify in advance or that change quite frequently. Figure 6-8 summarizes the principle. A chunk of business functionality is designed into a component and implemented in a conventional way—coded in C++ or whatever—but with one twist. At a designated point in its operation, the component code makes use of a script, which gives a subroutinelike capability. The difference

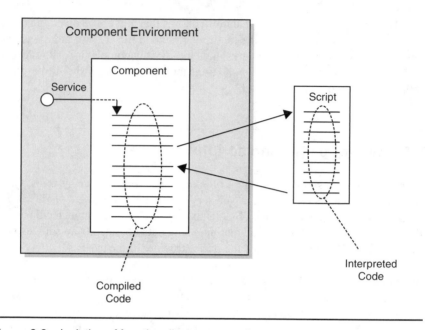

Figure 6-8   Isolation of functionality in separately managed script

is that the script code is managed separately from the remainder of the component. At runtime, the component operates in the normal way until the script is required. The script is then loaded and interpreted, and the result is returned to become available to the remainder of the compiled code in the component.

As an example, say that we want to give our customers a gift token based on their commercial behavior over a given period. This may be a valid business objective even if we have no idea how to calculate the value of the gift token. We could move the algorithm that performs this calculation out into a script. For testing purposes, we could have a simple script: say, a token for a fixed amount if total purchases over the past year exceed a specified threshold value. In production, this script could be changed to one that's more complex with, say, varying reward levels, dependencies on payment record, and other features. Using scripts in this way allows us to change the business behavior without changing the installed component.

6.6   State management

Removing state information from components is an important step toward scalability. But sometimes it's necessary to hold on to information that lasts for a fair period of time. A good example of this is a user session with a Web site. The Web protocols, such as HTTP (HyperText Transfer Protocol), treat each access by a user as individual and separate. From the user's point of view, though, a series of Web pages might form a continuous sequence of activity, with a need to carry information over from one page to the next. Because the protocol has no notion of a "session," it has to be added on top.

Clearly, this involves transferring a record of previous interactions to the user's subsequent activities; the question is, How? Sticking with the Web example for the moment, there are several possibilities. The first step is to embed state information in a *cookie,* a small text file that's returned to the user's browser and stored there for return in a future page access. The cookie can provide an identifier that can be used to look up the records of stages in the session or perhaps even the state information itself.

At the server end, this information has to be recognized. One possibility is to store session information in the Web server. This works for small, single-server, sites, but larger e-commerce systems are likely to have multiple Web servers, where the options become more complicated. If session state is fixed to a particular server, subsequent access attempts by the user have to be directed back to the same server, thus hampering efforts to balance the incoming load over the available servers. It can also be difficult to identify exactly who the user is. The originating address may not be adequate. Some load-balancing mechanisms interpose themselves between browser and server, so all traffic appears to be coming from one address (the load balancer).

A better solution is to maintain a session database that's accessible to all the servers. The cookie returned to the user's browser simply needs to be a unique identifier for the session. On the next access, the Web server—not necessarily the same one—can then retrieve the session information corresponding to the identifier and continue without any apparent interruption to the user.

6.7   Implications for business rules

This has been a very rapid tour around some of the issues involved in building large-scale information systems. All the topics we've looked at could warrant a book or two in their own right, but even at this level, we can start to see some of the implications for business rules. Clearly, realizing the functionality of an e-commerce system in software is not a trivial task. So far in this chapter, we've avoided adding business rules into the mix to avoid any further complication, but the kinds of architectural features we've discussed are certainly going to affect the way that we're able to build rules into the system.

One of the big mistakes made during the development of many existing systems was to bury the rules somewhere in the program code without controlling their implementation. The result is that changing rules often requires a rewrite of the software, and, consequently, changing business functionality is slow and expensive. Understanding the implications of architecture for business rules allows a more positive approach, in which rule implementation is *managed.*

We'll return to the subject of managing rules in a later chapter. For now, it's worth noting some of the most important IT architecture features that are going to have an impact on our realization of business rules. To understand these, it's not necessary to get all the way down to code listings; some features stand out from a higher viewpoint. Ultimately, these will have to be expressed at a lower level as, say, program statements, but it's important not to get bogged down in too much detail at an early stage.

The first thing to come to terms with is the certainty that the rules are going to have to work within a distributed computing environment. This immediately provides a choice of locations where business rules could be implemented. Associating the term *business logic* with a particular architectural tier gives the impression that here is the correct place to put the rules, but this is misleading. There may be excellent reasons, such as efficiency or ease of update, to put rules elsewhere.

It's also a mistake to assume that a rule must be implemented in only one place. An example is shown in Figure 6-9, which shows a service made available through two channels, although it could be more. One channel provides a Web-based service to customers. The other involves data being collected remotely by agents acting on behalf of customers. The remote data is collected at the end of a working day, with the database being updated by a batch process that runs after hours. In contrast, Web-based customers are allowed to update in real time through their browser. This pattern is quite common in such industries as financial services.

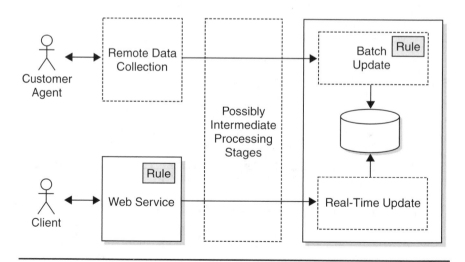

Figure 6-9   Multiple realizations of the same rule

Assume that we have a business rule associated with vetting the data. Where should we put the rule? In the case of the remotely collected data, there may not be much choice. It's clearly sensible to put the rule in the batch process. A mechanism will be necessary to deal with rejected data, such as sending it back to the agent for correction and, presumably, reentry in a subsequent batch.

For the Web-based service, though, the data layer is not the best place to put the rule. Sending bad data to the database will load it with unnecessary activities. Also, the response back to the user with an appropriate rejection message will be slowed down by the need for the wasted round-trip to the data layer. The better answer here is to move the rule closer to the user: in the Web service, as shown in Figure 6-9, or even into the browser via an applet or similar.

The solution to the dilemma is to implement the same rule twice: once for each channel. There's no danger of conflict, because data can flow through only one channel or another, never both. This provides the most efficient implementation in computing terms, at the possible cost of increased management complexity. There's also some degree of correlation between the rule location and the kinds of implementation that might be practical.

6.8   Where rules live

From earlier hints, you're aware that no single place is the natural home for business rules. The places available to you will be constrained by your particular architectures, but here we'll just take the standard *N*-tier architecture as a reference point. From what was said earlier about architectures, it's obvious that rules could pop up in many places. However, sprinkling rules randomly over the system is going to make it difficult to control and to maintain them over a period of time, and it's helpful to have a few more organizing principles to direct our ideas. We'll work through the layers from front to back: the front end being concerned mainly with the interaction of users with the system and the back end containing the core data used to support the system activities.

6.8.1   Client

The client layer represents the device that's being operated by a user of the system. There's plenty of variety among simple terminal screens, Web browsers, and networked personal computers. The rapid expansion of widespread digital communications has added still more: WAP (Wireless Access Protocol) phones, digital TV, and so on.

It's nice to provide a fair amount of functionality at the client end to make the user experience as good as possible, implying that a certain amount of software is running on the client device. For example, it may be possible to check an entry made by the user to see whether it conforms to some constraints. If the client device detects a problem, the user can be alerted immediately and asked to correct the error. This is good for two reasons. First, it minimizes the delay between the entry and the error message, giving a more responsive feel. Second, it avoids wasting communications bandwidth and remote processing on something that has no value.

Unfortunately, there's a downside as well. Large information systems, of the kinds most able to benefit, tend to have a large number of clients spread over a big area. In such an environment, applying the inevitable updates to the client software can cause a serious headache.

A possible compromise is to download the relevant software as and when it's needed—for example, in a script that gets interpreted by the client. This reduces the problems of maintaining widely distributed software, because it can be controlled from a central source. But it raises other problems in turn: For example, the additional time required to download the script, or whatever, can make the system appear sluggish.

A further issue is that the system may have to deal with other information sources that do not have the capability to check and to correct information before entry. The system therefore cannot rely on all error being eliminated by the client software.

With these caveats, the client can be a useful place to put rules when immediate reaction to user input would be valuable, although an additional implementation of the same rules may be necessary to deal with other channels. Typical situations are:

- Checking that input values are in the correct format and within an acceptable range
- Controlling the selection of a workflow path
- Examining a set of data for missing information, inconsistencies, and the like

A useful sanity check is to ask whether the necessary functionality can be captured in a fairly small chunk of scripting code. If not, it's probably best to consider another alternative.

6.8.2 Channel tier

Channels tend to be associated with particular delivery mechanisms, each boasting its own unique set of features. The purpose of the channel tier is to decouple the core systems, which we want to be as standard as possible, from the vagaries of these various mechanisms.

It's important to be clear about the difference between a channel and a client device; for example, digital TV—a potential information channel—is not the same as *a* digital TV—a potential client device. The capability of a channel may not be the same as the capability of a related device. However, particular channels do tend to be associated with particular protocols, and this is often the way in which device capabilities are defined, as in "a WAP-enabled mobile phone."

Channels are also often associated with authentication, for three main reasons.

1. They tend to represent the portals through which the main system is accessed, and so they seem a natural place for a gate-keeping function.

2. The nature of the channel itself—not just the channel tier at the central location—may constrain the kinds of authentication that are possible.

3. Authentication needs may vary from one kind of channel to another. For instance, some may be more exposed to outside access.

Closely related is the potential need to validate the business activity involved. Even if proper authentication is carried out, it may not be appropriate to do some things over some channels. For example, in a head- and branch-office configuration, network limitations may force some functionality out to the branch end. Some effort is again needed to think through the long-term implications of maintaining whatever may be out there, which might not be so amenable to such techniques as script downloading.

The channel tier may be a good place to cache information that's unlikely to change over a short period. An example is a channel-specific Web service, defined by use of HTTP, which could have static page content in HTML held in the channel tier but dynamic content produced from the middle tier. Other channels may use the same dynamic information but have different or no static information. In this case, the channel tier would be the logical place to put rules specific to Web access, leaving the middle tier free to provide a common service to all channels.

6.8.3   Middle tier(s)

This is one of the most popular places to locate rules: so popular, in fact, that the description *business logic* is often indiscriminately applied to all the processing in this layer. Crucially, the middle tier—or tiers in a more complex architecture—occupies a crucial position between data producers and consumers on the one side and the organization's data sources and sinks on the other.

Most businesses expect to compete by offering their customers multiple channels of communication. Along with this goes the capability to suspend an interaction on one channel and to resume it on a different one. For example, a domestic insurance quotation might be requested by e-mail during the day, with queries resolved by telephone while the agent is traveling home, and the deal completed via digital TV in the evening.

In terms of architecture, the ideal situation is for the channel services tier to soak up all the differences in protocols, encoding, timings, and so on, so that the middle tier need be concerned only with providing a consistent, channel-independent set of services. Whereas the channel tier provides much of the look and feel of the business, the middle tier provides most of the *behavior* that's visible to staff, customers, suppliers, and other parties.

This positioning means that a large proportion of the business functionality is likely to reside on the middle tier. The functionality is often tied into *applications,* or collections of software dedicated to a fairly narrow set of business needs. Some applications are built around a purchased software package. Others are developed internally in projects that are closely aligned with the specific application.

Either way, this kind of heritage makes overlap and duplication of business logic among applications quite likely. This is not necessarily a problem: If a business rule is applied in several applications and produces the same logical result in each, the system will still function in the desired way. If the rule changes, though, it may prove more of a challenge to find each of its appearances so that the necessary modifications can be applied consistently.

Unfortunately, the common experience is that each application defines its own logic in isolation. Worse yet, the logic may have been merged into the fabric of the software so that it's not readily available for inspection. This is a typical side effect of development policies that focus exclusively on functionality without considering capability. It's another example of the kind of thinking that led to the stovepipe systems that many organizations still struggle with today.

Given these factors, we can see that the middle tier is the most natural location for rules associated with the dynamic behavior of the core business functions. With workflow, for example, access to electronic work units and schedules may vary by channel, and the channel tier will cover these aspects. Information storage and retrieval will be handled by the data services layer. The remaining functionality—scheduling, allocation of work units, tracking completion, and so on—is likely to be lurking somewhere on a midtier server.

6.8.4   Data services tier

The database is probably the second most popular place to put business rules. Some people go further and claim that the database should be the *only* location, but that seems unnecessarily restrictive in a modern architecture.

It's certainly a good place to put rules that control the validity of the information used by an automation system. Many elements of the database—or databases, if you're ambitious—are easily recognizable from the business model. For example, most kinds of business objects will be represented as tables. To be a little more accurate, the table headers can be derived from the class definitions. Individual instances of business objects will appear as rows in the relevant tables. Relationships among business objects can be represented in the database as foreign keys.

You might want to apply two main kinds of constraints to your data: values and structures. In effect, these constraints control *static* aspects of the database, providing some assurance that the content lines up with the expected norms.

These kinds of constraints are well established in the database world. The important point here is not that business rules offer a new capability but that they offer a way of unifying database practice with other types of constraints.

Constraints on *values* place limits on possible information content, so that other system elements can rely on the data conforming to some general properties. One example is information format: Postal codes, telephone numbers, and currency values may all be laid out in a standardized way. A second example is quantity: Values must lie within a particular range or be selected from a limited list. Another is whether a value is mandatory and must always exist or is merely optional.

Constraints on *structures* control the ways that business objects relate to one another. A class diagram gives an idea of the relationships that exist, with annotations for multiplicity providing additional information. But the class diagram alone does not show more subtle characteristics: These are captured in related business rules. For example, Figure 6-10 shows two sets of relationships that seem structurally identical apart from the names. However, in terms of controlling structure, this is not necessarily so. We would probably want to associate an entry with an account at the time it is created, and so we should never have loose entries floating around without being tied to an account. But in the other case, a shipment may be waiting for some time before a packer becomes available, and so there may be an appreciable period in which the relationship simply doesn't exist.

The database world contains plenty of ideas, such as *referential integrity* and *nullable fields,* that can help to control structure, and most of these notions have been around for a long time. The main value of rules here is, again, the ability to fit all this into a consistent framework.

Rules can also be used to guide information retrieval. A common requirement is to return a collection of rows of data matching some query criteria. Usually, this does not map exactly onto a particular table but represents subsets, possibly from

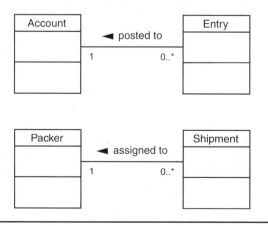

Figure 6-10   Structural similarities can be misleading

multiple tables. Ignoring the communication aspects, you can think of the retrieval operation as logically equivalent to defining a set of objects in terms of the overlap between other, simpler sets. Business rules are an excellent way of capturing this kind of definition. See the appendix for more details on logical relationships.

Putting rules into the data services layer has two big advantages. First, it's an efficient place to be for rules on data integrity. Second, you can make it difficult or perhaps impossible for any application using the database to bypass the rules that are in place. You can therefore be sure that the relevant constraints are being properly applied across the board.

6.8.5   Legacy systems

It may seem strange to be considering legacy systems. Why would we be thinking of putting rules there? The reason is that if you have a legacy system, you already have, embedded within it, a set of business rules. Unfortunately, they are likely to have been so well embedded that locating their individual instances would prove a pretty tough job. Following are a few strategies you can consider to handle your legacy system rules.

- Do nothing. If the system works and there are no plans to redevelop it, reimplement it, or interface any new systems to it, this may be the best option. Finding the rules won't be easy, and there's no point in expending the effort if you have no plans to use the results.

- Identify the rules implemented by the system as a whole but without trying to track down exactly where or how the individual rules are implemented internally. The rule descriptions can be couched in exactly the same terms as we've seen in earlier chapters. What you'll miss out on is the full capability to trace forward from the rule definition to its realization(s); the trace will stop at the boundary of the legacy system. You may be able to soften this a little by defining the legacy rules without analyzing the entrails of the system. Specifications, manuals, and other kinds of documentation may provide enough information to be able to define what the system does, perhaps aided by a little judicious testing.

  This option may be sufficient if you want to get a clear definition of what the legacy system does but aren't interested in exactly how it does it. Two scenarios come to mind. First, you may have developed a business model and may want to assure yourself that you do indeed have coverage of the things that matter. Second, you may want to reimplement some or all the functionality of the legacy system but using newer technology.

- Reverse engineer the rules from the legacy code. This was what many organizations had to do in the late 1990s to make sure that they were not exposed to risks from the millennium date change. It is a slow and expensive process. Some tools are available that analyze code written in, say, COBOL to identify potential rules, but they still require a degree of manual effort and are not guaranteed to identify everything. For example, some important business characteristics may arise from the way that widely separated code modules interact.

The difficulty of ensuring that all the subtleties have been fully captured has led to many legacy systems remaining in operation way past their original expected lifetimes, not because they are so good but because of the difficulty of replacing them. The systems have become so business critical that a failure to replicate part of their functionality could prove disastrous. Organizations in these positions have had to resort to rehosting their systems on replacement hardware that emulates the older systems, but that tactic can't go on forever.

It's doubtful whether legacy systems will ever go away. More likely, over time, we'll just change the definition of what the term signifies, so that it always means "old stuff that we would like to get rid of but can't afford to at present." Defining the system logic in a more portable form, such as business rules, helps to avoid becoming trapped in such situations.

6.9   Summarizing the technology environment

Distributed computing is here to stay. On balance, the advantages of such environments outweigh the additional complexities they bring. The biggest potential headache is controlling transactions when the contributing elements are physically dispersed, but this is being eased as component frameworks take over more of the detail of transaction coordination.

In the near future, the majority of new software, whether purchased or developed locally, will be deployed in the form of components. Rules will exist within components, and they will have to interoperate with other components to perform their specified functions.

The decentralized nature of the technology environment provides a selection of possible rule locations.

- Rules at the client end of the system are best placed to give a rapid reaction to users.
- Rules in the channel tier can deal with any differences between alternative channels for the delivery of services.
- Rules in the middle tier stand at the crossroads between users and data, and it's here that most of the application logic will be concentrated.
- Rules in the data services tier can provide efficient control over data structure and consistency.
- Rules may be located in other areas, such as legacy systems, over which there may be less opportunity for control.

7

Realizing Business Rules

7.1 Taking stock

By now, you undoubtedly have a reasonably good picture of how rules can be expressed. We know how to produce a series of logical statements that will direct or constrain the operation of an information system. These statements are rooted in a business description, so we can take them as being a true representation of what the business wants to do. We've seen how rules can be grouped into rule sets and how rules can be validated, to check that they are self-consistent and that they can produce the intended results.

We also have a broad view of the kinds of structures that frame modern information systems. The next step is to see how we can map the rule definitions onto a practical implementation structure. Small-scale programs, such as spreadsheets, may be adequate for checking out the rule logic, but they're unlikely to scale to a real operational environment.

The good news is that there are many ways of implementing rules. Unfortunately, having so many ways can lead to confusion. Let's lay down a few principles that might help in narrowing the possibilities.

- You will certainly need a way of tracking what's been done with the rules. If a rule definition changes, you will probably need to make a corresponding change in its implementation. Managing rules is covered in more detail in the next chapter, so for now, we'll just assume that a tracking capability exists.

- Any implementation must preserve the inherent logic defined by the rule. You should not add to or subtract from the definition. If a rule is deficient, the right way to deal with it is to go back and change its definition, not patch it in the implementation.

- You should strive to be as neutral as possible toward particular choices of software tools: not just such things as commercial rules engines but also development systems, programming languages, and so on. What looks neat today may become a millstone around your neck in a year or two. If you are considering a technique that's going to lock you into a limited situation, it might be wise to think about possible exit strategies before you become committed.

- You should be sensitive to where the rules fit most naturally. There's always a temptation to try to force all the rules into a single implementation box because it cuts down the amount of thinking you might need to do. The price to be paid is the possible loss of flexibility, efficiency, and control.

- You'll have to trade off advantages and disadvantages across several dimensions in order to get the best fit to your particular environment. Among these dimensions are performance—responsiveness and throughput—scalability, and maintainability. There are no absolutes here: The relative priorities of the various factors will be determined by your local conditions.

We'll add to these principles as we progress though this chapter and delve into more of the details of rule realization.

The potential complexity can be tamed somewhat by looking at things from two points of view: *where* rules should be placed within the constraints of technical and component architectures and *how* rules should be built, using the kind of technology available. These two views inevitably overlap; a particular technology may be more strongly associated with some locations than with others. However, it's a good way to start thinking about realizations.

7.2 Distributing rules

For many years, the industry has been moving more and more toward systems built from networks of midsized computers. It's not uncommon to find systems using several hundred servers over the whole range of applications. These distributed environments introduce some extra complications for the rule implementer, some of which we looked at in Chapter 6. As with many other facets of the system, life would be much easier with just a single thread of operation, a single process space, local data storage, and so on.

The most intense applications of rules were probably the expert systems that became common during the 1980s. These were systems usually created by using an *expert system shell,* a complete environment for building and deploying rule-based systems. These shells usually operated on a very limited choice of hardware and provided their own filing systems and even their own user interfaces. This made it virtually impossible to integrate the resulting system into mainstream operations, and most such systems fell by the wayside.

Physically putting all the rules into one box has some obvious attractions. For example, if all the rules are in the same place, you would expect it to be much easier to locate a particular rule. Nice idea, but, unfortunately, it doesn't work, at least not in this simplistic way.

Let's think about how we would access a rule in a centralized box. At some point in a process somewhere in our distributed system, a rule is invoked. Because we've put all the rules in a single box, the place where the rule is invoked has to communicate with the place where the rule is realized. The rule will need some values in order to do its work, but these values aren't local to it: The rule will have to get them from the place where the rule was invoked. The resulting communication across process and machine boundaries will be horribly slow, several orders of magnitude slower than if the rule realization had been local to the invoker.

We might be able to improve things a little by prepackaging all the data values needed by the rule and sending them all in one lump as part of the invocation request. But this brings another set of problems. First, the invoker has no way of knowing what information is relevant, so it has to send everything that might conceivably be needed. Most of this won't be used, and so the invoker will have wasted a lot of cycles marshaling information that ends up being discarded. Second, it ties the invoker's implementation closely to the current rule definition. Over time, the rule could change: For instance, an extra parameter may be needed. This would mean finding all the places where the rule is used and changing their implementations to marshal the additional parameter.

Let's take the alternative view and assume that the rule is realized close to where it is invoked, perhaps within the same process space. If the rule uses the values of some attributes of a business object, we no longer have to extract them and transmit them to the rule. We simply give the rule the context within which it is being invoked, which in this case would include the associated business object. The rule can decide which values to pick out. A change to the rule requiring the use of another attribute would no longer need a change to the invocation.

Realistically, we have no choice but to accept at least some degree of distribution of our rule realizations. This is not altogether a bad thing. As well as improving performance, we can also choose a realization that's suited to the locality. Next, we'll look at the advantages and disadvantages of a range of implementation techniques. The big, outstanding problem—managing a large population of rules in a distributed environment—we'll leave for the next chapter.

7.3 Realizing rules

We've seen how to create business rule statements and check them for logical consistency. For anything useful to happen, though, the intentions expressed by the rule statements will have to be realized in operational form. There's no single best way to do this. You might instinctively prefer a particular approach, but you're bound to find situations in which an alternative works better. As always, the key to making the right decisions is to have a reasonable understanding of the issues involved.

In this section, we run through a range of possibilities and show various ways of mapping rules from the world of business to the world of technology. It's likely that your own strategy will contain a combination of several of the approaches we discuss. In considering the options, you'll need to bear many factors in mind. As a minimum, you'll need to think about

- The long-term viability of your strategy. (Are you confident that you can maintain it into the future?)
- Runtime performance. (Will your system provide the right level of response under load?)
- The degree of rule enforcement. (Are there any back doors through which the rules could be evaded?)
- Flexibility. (Will you be able to react to business changes in the time scales needed?)
- The ability to sustain business operations. (Will your system cope with failures and unexpected peaks in demand?)

7.3.1   Program statements

Incorporating rules into program code is probably the most common implementation route. It's possible to use the standard features of a programming language to implement a fully working rule. The minimal requirement is to have a way of selecting between alternative code branches, based on a given condition. This is pretty easy to satisfy in any programming language, although the details may vary from one to another. IF-THEN, DO WHILE, DO UNTIL, CASE, and other such constructs can all be used.

Although it's easy to see that a rule can be a program statement, the reverse is not necessarily true. Programs typically use many branching statements that have no particular relationship to any business rule.

So what's different about code that implements a business rule? If we think only in terms of writing a procedural instruction for a computer to carry out, nothing special seems to be going on. But from a broader perspective, just writing a line of code doesn't seem enough. How would we know that the particular rule had been implemented? What would stop another programmer from changing the code to contravene the original intention? If the original rule were to change, how would we ever find the piece of code that implemented it?

Clearly, we need something that identifies a program statement or a group of statements as implementing a business rule or rule set and links it back to its original definition. Changing the structure of the programming language is usually not a practical option. Nor is switching to a specialized rule language, because then we would be compromising our ability to handle the nonrule aspects. All we can do is work within the capabilities that a language provides.

One approach is to encapsulate the rule or rule set in a function call, using whatever syntax the language offers. In Visual Basic, for example, you could define a rule set intended for use within a module something like this:

```
Private Function brValidateEntry (ParamArray aDataBlock)_
   As Boolean
      '...
      'code to implement rules goes here
      '...
End Function
```

The clearly specified start and end of the function also identify a boundary around the rule set. There is a small performance penalty, owing to the overhead of the function call. For a complex rule set that's invoked comparatively rarely, this may be negligible, and the gain in modularity may be worthwhile. More important, there's also the danger of the use of specific parameters, making changes more difficult. Using flexible data containers and weakening type checking—for instance, using the `Variant` type in Visual Basic—can help to reduce this problem but is less satisfactory from the software engineering perspective. It's less efficient, too.

For maximum performance, we need to remove any overhead, implying that code implementing a rule must be in line with other code. To define boundaries around rules, you can make use of whatever comment features are provided by your favorite programming language. For example, let's say that you wanted to implement a business rule defined as follows:

R701   An applicant for an account must be at least 16 years old.

A simple Visual Basic structure to wrap the implementation of the rule could look something like this:

```
' <Rule R701--Minimum age check>
      If applicant.age < 16 Then _
      'code to do something about it goes here
      '...
' <End Rule>
```

It's worth putting a little thought into defining a standard style of decoration, such as angle brackets, to mark out your rules. This makes no difference to the code, because the comment text won't be executed, but it does make it easier to design a filter to pull out rule definitions embedded in the program text. Additional descriptive material, such as `Minimum age check` in the opening comment, is optional but might be helpful to somebody picking up the code in the future.

In compiled languages, comments are not passed through to the object code from the source code, so including them has no impact on runtime behavior. Code that implements a rule will therefore run as fast as any other code in the system. This gives you the best possible performance while retaining the ability to keep tabs on what happened to the rule realization.

Whichever way you decide to implement rules in program statements, you will need to make sure that your local coding standards specify how rules should be handled, so that it's done consistently. You'll also need to give some thought to naming conventions and cross-referencing. It's important that you always handle rules in a standardized way. If you do, it's straightforward to create simple utility programs that identify where rules appear in a code listing. These programs can provide input to a management function that ties the rule implementations back to the original rule statements, as explained in more detail in the next chapter.

The big advantages of putting rules directly into your code are straightforwardness and performance. If you have only a few simple rules to implement, putting them directly into the program code is probably the lowest rung on the complexity ladder. If you want to include some rules in a frequently performed activity or one that has to be performed within tight time constraints, direct coding of the rules may be the more attractive option.

The downside of this approach is that a change to a rule requires a corresponding change to the code. Good management can make it easy to locate the right code module, but testing, integration, and all the other activities that are required could turn even a small change into an expensive, lengthy piece of work.

7.3.2   Scripts

A step up in the manageability of rules is to separate them into scripts. The use of scripting has become fairly familiar through its use in Web pages, with such languages as VBScript and JavaScript in common use.

The choice of language is less important than the core idea: embedding a variable behavior into a relatively fixed structure. This isn't just for Web pages; it's an idea that can be applied anywhere. Library functions, such as Windows Scripting Host, are readily available to add scripting functionality to a program. Scripts are commonly interpreted after loading, but that may change over time if such techniques as just-in-time (JIT) compilation are introduced. (We discussed the general concept of scripts in the previous chapter; see Figure 6-8.)

Here's a simple example. The scenario here is that we want to provide various levels of service to customers ranked in three bands—gold, silver, or bronze—depending on their perceived worth. A cunning algorithm evaluates customers and gives them a rating on a scale of 0 to 100. From time to time, we might want to change the boundaries between the categories but without altering the rating algorithm. All this, including the rating algorithm, can be described by a set of rules, which we won't detail here.

The important idea is that we can pull the ranking decision out of the code and put it into a small piece of script. At the appropriate point, the script is invoked and the ranking evaluated. The main body of the code does not need to know how the ranking was obtained; it simply does the appropriate thing for whatever band it's given. Now, if we want to change the boundaries, we merely need to change the script. We don't have to change, test, and rerelease any of the major software modules. Changing and testing the script is a much easier and faster process, so we can be a lot more reactive to evolving business needs.

Here's how the ranking rules might look in VBScript.

```
'<Rule R702, R703, R704>
'<Gold, Silver, Bronze customer rankings>
Rating = ResultBOS.ReadByRowNumAndColumnNameFromTable _
        (0, "Party2.Party.Rating")
If Not IsNull(Rating) Then
        Rating = CInt(Rating)
        If Rating >= 1 And Rating <= 40 Then _
            Ranktxt = "Bronze"
                Else If Rating <= 70 Then _
                    Ranktxt = "Silver"
                        Else If Rating <= 100 Then _
                            Ranktxt =    "Gold"
                        EndIf
                EndIf
        EndIf
Else Ranktxt = "Not Available"
EndIf
' <End Rule>
```

Again, if you take the scripting route, you'll want to set up some local standards to control the way that scripts are written and used, so that you can manage them effectively.

As always, nothing's for free. In this case, the price to be paid boils down mostly to performance. Loading the script when required is a comparatively slow operation; if the language is interpreted, it will also run fairly sluggishly. Whether this matters depends on your situation. For example, the preceding customer-ranking rules might be run every time there is contact with a customer. If this happens only tens of times per hour, the performance gained by moving the script into in-line code, say, might not be worth bothering about.

The big bonus of scripting is the ease with which rule-based decisions can be clearly separated from drudge code. If you want to be able to do this in a low-throughput situation, scripting may be a good choice.

7.3.3   Rule components

A rule component is dedicated to implementing one or more specific rule sets. It's a half-way house between in-line code and the more generic rules engines that we'll look at shortly. The code within the rule component is written to satisfy a limited set of objectives, and it's not really intended to be reused for other rule sets. This allows the rule component to privately use whatever coding tricks are necessary, without worrying about their general applicability. The internal implementation is hidden from clients of the rule component, and the functionality is available only through its published interfaces. This makes it easy to change the implementation, providing that the original interfaces are preserved. Figure 7-1 shows the general idea.

Rule components have two advantages over a more general-purpose rules engine. First, the internal processing can be made problem specific, allowing higher performance. Second, using rule components may avoid the need to make an investment in or a commitment to any particular rules engine. There's no clear dividing line, though. More elaborate rule components may split internal functionality into modules to allow more flexibility and reuse. Taken to the extreme, the result is a home-made rules engine, so the difference becomes more pragmatic than technical.

The need to manage all interactions through clearly specified interfaces also raises other dangers. The definition of what gets passed across the interface needs careful thought to avoid loss of flexibility. The need to marshal the relevant data and to communicate with the rule component increases the cost for an application wanting to use the rules. In designing rule components, you'll need to take these factors into account, along with the implementation of the rules themselves.

The main characteristics of a rule component are therefore a relatively high cost of invocation but very efficient local interactions thereafter. This makes rule components well suited to situations in which some specialized and complex rule processing has to be done efficiently but not too frequently.

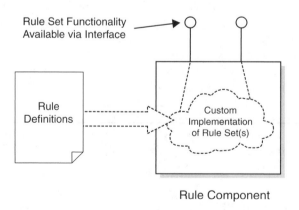

Figure 7-1   Rule component

7.3.4   Rules engines

A rules engine, sometimes also known as a logic server, is a specialized component that's designed for the sole purpose of handling rules. Unlike a rule component, a rules engine is not built to solve any particular problem but instead provides a generic set of capabilities for defining, storing, and applying rules. Some rules engines sit in the data services tier. More frequently, they are positioned in the middle tier, where they form part of an application services platform.

Application servers are a comparatively recent phenomenon, brought about by the growing complexity of the middleware arena. In addition to handling business logic, application servers provide a number of other useful functions, making the life of the developer easier by providing the glue to hold applications together. Typical functions are

- Resilience features to increase system availability
- Caching of data to reduce response times
- Additional security features to protect core systems in a global user environment
- Various techniques, such as resource pooling, to increase application scalability
- Ready-made connectors to interact with specific data sources
- Transactional features and record locking

Most rules engines are commercial products with all kinds of strengths and weaknesses. It's in the vendors' interests to make their appeal as broad as possible, so they often provide a number of features that are more to do with general middleware issues. Here, we concentrate on the business rule aspects and look at some ways in which a generic logic service can be provided.

We'll start with a high-level view. Figure 7-2 shows the main elements of a general-purpose rules engine. The *source rules* are defined offline, using an appropriate rule language and, usually, compiled into an efficient internal representation, although sometimes they are interpreted on the fly. The *compiled rules* are stored in a private data structure, available for use by an *inference mechanism,* which understands the structure and is able to apply the rules at runtime.

The action of a rule affects the *working memory,* a private data area that keeps track of internal computations. In theory, this could be the system database, but it's usually kept sealed off for performance reasons. Some rules engines provide facilities to allow developers to peek at what's going on, mainly for debugging purposes, but it usually has no direct connection with the outside world.

The pivotal role is played by a *control mechanism* responsible for coordinating the actions of the other elements. Two of its functions are particularly important.

- It mediates between internal activity and the outside world. The users of the rules engine are likely to be external processes rather than humans. Incoming messages may be instructions for the rules engine or information

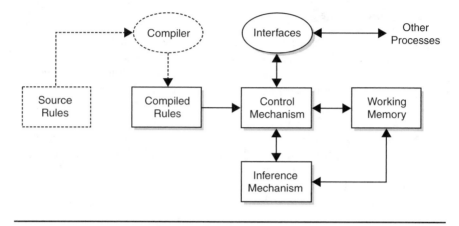

Figure 7-2 Main elements of a typical rules engine

required by the rules in order to reach their conclusions. There's frequently an application program interface (API) that allows external code to partake in various kinds of interactions with the rules engine. In some cases, the rules engine also controls the user interface: efficient, maybe, but perhaps putting unwelcome restrictions on what can be done.

- It determines which rules will be applied and in which order. This usually works in a cyclic way and uses an *agenda* (not shown in Figure 7-2). The current content of the working memory indicates which rules might be able to do something useful, and these rules are listed on the agenda. The rules are ordered according to an internal scoring system, and the highest-ranking rule is applied. This may change the contents of the working memory, and so some rules may be removed from the agenda's list and new ones added. These rules are ranked again, and the cycle repeats until all the rules have been applied. Something similar goes on behind the scenes in a spreadsheet: After you enter a new value into a cell, an internal algorithm decides which other cells need to be updated and fires off the appropriate calculations.

A crucial step that's taken in most rules engines is to compile the rules into an internal structure, which can be used much more efficiently than the rule statements. These statements are often based around the RETE algorithm (Latin for *net*), first defined in the early 1980s (Forgy 1982). This algorithm avoids having the step of matching the conditions of the rules to the contents of the working memory by precompiling a network of associations from the rule definitions. Given such a network, it's then simply a matter of detecting when any piece of information in it changes.

Obviously, there's lots of room for ingenuity here, and plenty of variations exist around this basic scheme. Rules engines can be distinguished in several ways, and we'll take a look at some of the major ones.

Rule expressions   One of the most obvious differences among competing rules engines is the way that rules are expressed. The first main approach uses a specialized language, similar in form to a programming language but with some important differences.

- Rule statements are *declarative,* not *procedural;* they define relationships between facts, not how to do something.
- There's no predetermined flow of control; rules are activated depending on the current state of the problem.

Here's an example of what these languages look like. Let's say that we have the following business rule:

R705   Express shipments may only be made to approved
         customers.

Expressed in a rule language, this might look like:

```
(defrule express-shipment "R705"
;; Assumes facts already set up
      ((customer ?c)
      (order ?o)
      (ordered ?c ?o)
      (approved ?c))
=>
(assert (expressOK ?o)))
```

The *facts* referred to are the ties between the rules engine and the remainder of the system. This is the implementation equivalent of the link between the business rule statements and the supporting fact model, discussed in earlier chapters.

In this case, we might expect the working memory to contain facts such as: (customer Acme), (order O123), (ordered Acme ON123), and (approved Acme). The query sign indicates a variable that will get *bound* to a particular instance, so the pattern (customer ?c) matches the pattern (customer Acme) if ?c is bound to Acme. This *binding* is retained throughout the rest of the rule; similarly, for the order variable ?o.

What's nice about this is that we can abstract away from any particular customer and any particular order. *Any* combination of customer and order matching the given patterns will result in the working memory's containing a new fact indicating that express shipment is OK for this particular order.

A particularly strong candidate for rule-based programming of this sort is Prolog, which is a full-fledged programming language in its own right. Just for fun, here's how the same rule might look in Prolog.

```
/* <R705 -- express shipment> */
/* Assumes ground terms already set up */
expressOK(O) :- order(O), customer(C), ordered(C,O),
    approved(C).
```

You may or may not like the syntax of a particular language, but if you take on a particular rules engine, you have to take it all. In the words of a prominent authority in another field, "That's the way it is" (Presley 1970). It's certainly a factor to be taken into account in choosing a rules engine.

Moving away from programmatic approaches, the alternative way of constructing rules uses a point-and-click visual interface that a designer can use to construct the rules interactively. If you have a copy of Microsoft Access, you'll find something similar in the Expression Builder wizard, and corresponding features can be found in several other products.

The two approaches need not be completely exclusive; an interactive interface can be used as a front end to build rule language statements. But in both cases, the rule expressions are linked internally to their implementation, and there's little or no opportunity to mix and match rule locations and realizations.

Inference mechanisms   One of the most powerful features of rules is the way they can be used in combination. As we've seen, a rule on its own is trivial to hack in any old programming language. Their real power emerges when they work in combination.

As you know by now, a rule is a tiny fragment of business knowledge. A collection of these fragments works together in a coordinated way to achieve the overall aims of the business. We've already seen how rules can be grouped into rule sets to focus on finding a solution to a specific problem. A rules engine provides a particularly comfortable arena for rules to work together, where they can share a common environment and a common means of expression. They also share a common inference mechanism, which is likely to be either data driven or goal driven.

Data-driven inference basically says, "I know X: What rules can make use of this information?" It's a matter of assessing the relevance of a new piece of information and deciding what to do with it. In contrast, goal-driven inference asks, "I want to know Y; which rules will help me?" Here, it's more a question of identifying the rule(s) that will reduce the distance between what we know and what we want to know.

Both of these modes of reasoning can come into play in an information system, although, in a particular rules engine, one or the other will probably dominate. Fortunately, it's possible to emulate goal-driven inference in a data-driven system and vice versa, so it's more a question of convenience, efficiency, and, probably most important, mindset. As well as illustrating differences in syntax, our two language examples are also backed by different inference styles.

In the data-driven case, the mere existence of the right kinds of patterns in memory makes the rule eligible, although it may not become activated immediately if other eligible rules take precedence. Full coverage of how precedence is decided is a bit outside our scope here, but, among other things, it can be influenced by giving the rule a *salience* value—in essence, an idea of its own self-importance.

Sooner or later, then, the conclusion of the rule will become available as a consequence of the input data's becoming available, not because we needed the result at that time. For instance, as it stands, our data-driven rule would tell us about eligibility for express shipping, whether or not the customer had asked for it to be expressed. In complex cases, control over inference can become a major concern, to make sure that only useful information is produced and that it is made available in a timely way.

The alternative, goal-driven approach is often more efficient because rules are invoked only as needed, to resolve something that's unknown at the time. For instance, in our example, we would probably evaluate eligibility for express shipping only if the customer had explicitly requested it.

If a factor in the rule is not known, we can solve it by using exactly the same mechanism; we simply make it a new subgoal. A goal can be followed to as many levels of subgoal as needed to produce a result. The main difficulty in the context of a typical business information system is that there isn't a single problem—many need to be solved simultaneously, and they don't all fit into a nice hierarchy of goals and subgoals.

Deployment   When it comes to building rules engine technology into your operational system, you'll be faced with yet more choices. The most obvious way to go would appear to be to put all the rule machinery into a single box, so that all the parts can cooperate efficiently. In practice, this simplistic approach doesn't work out very well. Having a single server to handle rules raises a number of questions.

- It's a single point of failure, so resilience is suspect.
- It's a potential bottleneck, so scalability is suspect.
- It requires a great deal of cross-platform traffic, which makes performance suspect.

Commercial products of the logic server type therefore use a number of clever strategies to address the potential problems. These strategies include cloning the logic onto multiple servers, with automatic load balancing of traffic and redirection in the event of failure, and caching of values to reduce latency. The details vary from one product to the next, but as we've seen, these are the same general concerns that afflict all the other apparatus that exists in the middle tier.

Another approach gets around these issues in a slightly different way. Instead of releasing the software that implements the rules engine as a package, the rules engine can be made available as a set of library functions. This relieves you of the pain of writing your own rule-handling functions but allows you to build some generic rule machinery into whichever applications you desire. Of course, you still have to deal with resilience, scalability, and so on, but you would still have had to cope with these problems, anyway.

Rules engines and expert systems   Business rule systems are sometimes equated with the expert systems that became common in the early 1980s. But despite the family resemblance and carryover of technology, they aren't quite the same thing. We've already looked at several of the issues, so we can just summarize the main differences here.

- Expert systems tend to be directed at solving a single complex problem. Business systems contain large numbers of relatively simple problems.

- Expert systems usually reach a conclusion at some point, whereupon the problem can be considered finished. Business systems operate continuously, with most organizations aiming for a full 24/7 capability, so they never reach a particular end point.

- Expert system rules generally represent the narrow and deep specialist knowledge of just a few people. Business rules represent the shallow and wide general knowledge of a large number of people.

You therefore shouldn't take a traditional expert system shell and expect it to thrive in a general business environment, although it might be useful for isolated problems.

Pros and cons of rules engines   Rules engines operate at the wholesale level. You would not want to go to the trouble and expense of using one if your situation could be described in just a few rules. If you have a significant amount of business logic to implement—and this describes most medium to large organizations—it's worth considering the use of a rules engine. Here are some of the factors you'll need to weigh, starting with the positive side.

- You'll get a number of complex technical mechanisms provided, which will spare you the time and trouble of brewing your own. This may free up effort to focus more on problems at the business level and will allow you to handle large and complex rule sets.

- You're likely to get a centralized repository: a management facility that allows you to look after your rules in an organized way. (This topic is discussed further in the next chapter.)

- The rules engine will impose a preferred style for expressing your business logic at a technical level. Your staff can learn to use this in a consistent way, cutting down on the scope for misunderstandings and simplifying maintenance.

- Some additional, nonrule middleware functionality may be provided that you can use to make your applications more resilient, more scalable, and so on.

Against these benefits are a few potential disadvantages to consider.

- Adopting a rules engine requires a significant investment. Apart from the initial license and ongoing maintenance fees, you'll also have to consider the cost of training and any adaptation required for interoperability with other systems.
- You will probably become locked into a particular vendor, so you're making your business somewhat dependent on its ability to respond to bug reports, release new functionality, provide ad hoc support, and so on.
- The rules may tend to be pulled into one place, usually the middle tier but sometimes the data services tier. This may make it difficult for you to impose rules in the way that you would ideally want. Also, if the rule implementation has to be remote from the code that needs the rule result, efficiency may suffer.
- It may not be easy to link the rules engine back to your business analysis results, which ideally will be in the form of a business model. If this is the case, it introduces a very dangerous crack into the overall process, seriously degrading your ability to deliver accurately against business needs.

7.3.5   Database mechanisms

Datacentric rules are likely to fit most naturally inside the appropriate database where they can have the most direct contact with the data. The type of database technology you're most likely to encounter is the *relational* model, as represented by such products as Oracle and SQL Server, so we'll frame the discussion around that. The examples here are based on SQL Server 2000, but other relational database products have broadly similar capabilities. For instance, as its name suggests, SQL Server can be programmed in a dialect of SQL called Transact-SQL, or T-SQL for short.

However, approximation to a standard doesn't mean that you can directly export the realization of a rule from one database system to another. It's the rule definitions in the business model that are portable; if you want to implement the same business rule in different database products, you'll simply have to do it over again.

Like all such products, SQL Server does more than storing and retrieving information; it also provides mechanisms for controlling the characteristics of your data. The ones you're most likely to want to use in relation to business rules are those that revolve around the basic CRUD (create, read, update, and delete) functionality. These mechanisms are common to all data services, although relational databases tend to talk about inserting a row into a table rather than creating an object.

For simplicity, we'll assume that the business model and the database structure have a reasonably good correspondence. You shouldn't expect this to always be the case, though. There may be good reasons, such as performance, why the logical view of the business model may look somewhat different when it's translated to a physical database design. For this reason, two sets of models are frequently used: one containing the analysis results and one with the translation of those results into a practical design. We'll look at three kinds of database features that can be used to implement rules: constraints, stored procedures, and triggers.

Constraints   *Constraint* is a generic term for features that act to restrict data values in order to maintain the integrity of the database. The first feature is *referential integrity*. As an example, we'll take the packer and shipment relationship from Figure 6-10. Here, we're interested in seeing how it appears at the database end. Because the relationship is simple and the numbers of instances fairly small, the database structure will likely follow the analysis model quite closely.

That may not be the case for the other relationship in Figure 6-10, between accounts and entries. Although the analysis model may be logically accurate, a direct implementation of it could mean an account table with tens of millions of rows and an entry table with billions of rows: probably not a realistic proposition. This is one of the cases in which a certain level of physical design would be needed to translate the logical relationships into practical reality. Some attention to detail will be needed in such cases to make sure that the intentions of the rules expressed in the logical model are properly preserved.

We'll assume that the packer and the shipment tables both have a primary key defined; it's going to be pretty difficult to control a relationship unless we can identify it! Associations of this kind between business objects will generally map onto foreign keys, where a field in one table will contain a value that's a primary key in another table, as shown in Figure 7-3. The figure shows that making an association between a shipment and a packer corresponds to adding the packer's primary key value in the Packer column for the shipment. A simple way of forcing this to happen when a shipment is entered into the database is to specify the property NOT NULL for the Packer column. This means that a value has to be supplied for Packer in order to be able to create the relevant row in the shipment table.

The alternative is to allow NULL values for references. This would make it possible to create an unassociated object but add the association later. Either is a plausible scenario: The relevant rules will specify which is correct in a particular case. Here, we might expect it to be a while before a shipment is assigned to a packer, so it's reasonable to allow NULL values in the Packer column of the shipment table. A typical rule might look like the following:

R706   A shipment must be assigned to a packer when it becomes fillable.

Model

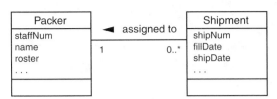

Database

Packer Table

staffNum#	name	roster	etc.
7123			
7456			
7789			

Shipment Table

shipNum#	packer	fillDate	shipDate	etc.
	7456			

Figure 7-3 Packer and shipment tables

Database systems provide additional mechanisms to protect relationships. For example, once a relationship has been set up between a packer and one or more shipments, we should not delete the packer unless we also delete the related shipments; otherwise, they would remain dangling in the database, with no obvious owner. SQL Server provides *cascading* updates and deletes to handle such situations.

Controlling values within a table can be done quite efficiently by using *Check* constraints. (SQL Server also has *Rules*—not the same as business rules—and *Defaults* that offer similar capabilities, but these are provided mainly for historical reasons we won't go into.) You can check to ensure that values fall within a specific numeric range, are one of a limited list of possibilities, or conform to a defined format, such as a social security number. You can also check relationships between columns in the same table. Here are a couple of examples for the simple database in Figure 7-3.

R707 A staff number in the packing department is defined as a four-digit numeric code starting with '7'.

We could add this to a Packer table, using something like:

```
ALTER TABLE Packer
       ADD CONSTRAINT CN_R707_StaffNumberFormat
       CHECK
       (staffNum LIKE '7 [0-9] [0-9] [0-9]')
```

Here is another example:

R708   The 'shipped' date for a shipment must not be earlier
than the 'filled' date.

Adding this to the Shipment table would look something like:

```
ALTER TABLE Shipment
    ADD CONSTRAINT CN_R708_ShipDate
    CHECK
    (shipDate >= fillDate)
```

Incorporating the checks into the database will prevent any actions that would
contravene the rule: not just when the item is created but also if any attempt is
made to change it in the future through a path that we can't even predict at present.

Constraints of this kind are a useful way of controlling the attributes of business objects: Recall that an association is a special kind of attribute. Similar kinds
of constraints can be used for other purposes, such as defining whether an attribute
is mandatory or optional, or is a default value to be used if an attribute value is
not supplied when the object is created. The main disadvantage of these simple
constraints is that they can't be used for more complicated conditions that involve
several objects, equating roughly to multiple tables in a relational database system.

As with other kinds of realizations, you shouldn't forget that you will need a
way of recording what you did with the rule. For example, you could adopt a naming convention, as in our examples, that could be postprocessed to generate the
correct kind of linking information.

Stored procedures   As the name suggests, stored procedures are modules
of procedural code stored in the database. You can treat such modules pretty
much like another kind of script, although they are especially useful in certain
situations.

First, because they are snuggled up so closely to the data, they can be a lot
more efficient if you need to do something that's particularly datacentric. For
example, you might want to carry out a transaction in a high-throughput situation
that involved checking some input against existing data held in several tables, as
defined by some business rules, and then carrying out the update or not, depending on the results. A good strategy in this case might be to ship the necessary input
data down to the database and to use a stored procedure to unpick it, apply any
rules that are needed, and commit or roll back the transaction. This avoids the
round-trip delays that would occur if the data had to be sent back for the go/no go
decision to be made in a middle-tier process.

If efficiency is the main goal, you may need to take some care over the implementation. SQL Server caches compiled versions of procedures, for speedy access,
but by default they are optimized on first use. If subsequent uses follow a different

pattern, the procedure may not be optimized correctly, and performance will suffer. There are ways to tackle this, but they're a bit outside our main concern.

In another scenario, you want to be very sure that some controls are always applied consistently when several applications are using the data. Trusting each application to apply the same checks in the same way would be a bit naïve and also difficult to police. You also wouldn't want to rely on future applications, as yet unwritten, being so kind as to include your constraints. Providing access to the data via a stored procedure makes sure that the same rules are applied to everyone.

Stored procedures are simply code: The fact that the language is a dialect of SQL doesn't change the nature of the beast. The comments made earlier about the need to identify business rule implementations in code therefore apply equally here. Let's look at an example rule.

R709   The credit period allowed to a casual customer must not exceed 60 days.

We'll assume that there's a Customers table with columns called customerType holding the customer type and creditDays holding the number of days credit allowed. A T-SQL code fragment to implement this rule in a stored procedure might look something like the following:

```
CREAT PROC sp_UpdateCreditPeriod
        @CustomerID                           varchar(5),
        @CreditDaysWanted                     int
AS


/* Define local parameters, useful for debugging */
DECLARE
        @Days                                 int,
        @CustomerType                         varchar(10)


SELECT @CustomerType = customerType FROM Customers
        WHERE customerId = @CustomerID


/* <Rule R709   -- Limit credit days to 60 for casual
   customers> */
SELECT @Days = @CreditDaysWanted
IF @CustomerType = 'casual' AND @CreditDaysWanted > 60
        SELECT @Days = 60
/* <End Rule>


UPDATE Customers
SET creditDays = @Days
WHERE customerId = @CustomerID
```

Implementing the same logic in the middle tier would require a read operation to get the customer type before the write operation to do the update. Moving the logic into the database is more efficient because it avoids the need for this round-trip.

This example is slightly artificial; we would probably want a procedure to update several customer parameters in a single hit, not just a single one in isolation. As it stands, it would also be simpler to implement as a straightforward constraint on the column. Additionally, we might want to do a little more work if the condition is detected: for example, raise a warning so that the reason for the attempt to extend the period could be investigated. Even so, this simple procedure does prevent anyone using it from setting an undesirable business condition.

To make this sort of control watertight, you will also need to think through all the possible paths through which the data could be accessed. There's no point in putting a rule into a stored procedure if other routes modify the data. One way of tying this kind of procedural control to a particular action is to use a *trigger*.

Triggers   A trigger is a special kind of stored procedure. A stored procedure is explicitly invoked, but a trigger runs automatically whenever a particular condition is detected. Triggers are attached to an event on a specific table. The event can be any combination of insert, delete, or update actions on the table.

Although it is fired up by something happening on a specific table, a trigger is not limited to controlling the features of that table alone. Unlike the simpler constraints we looked at earlier, a trigger can be used to apply constraints within a table, across tables, across databases, and even across servers. In SQL Server, triggers can be used in very sophisticated ways. An INSTEAD OF variant lets you intercept a would-be insertion, say, and tinker with it before carrying out the action. You can do similar things with deletes and updates.

Of course, all this capability comes at a price. Triggers are slower than other approaches like simple constraints. You also need to take into account the cost of the intellectual energy required and the danger that inexperienced users of power tools could hurt themselves. For example, some database operations won't cause a delete trigger to fire, even though you believe that you have removed rows from a table. You need someone who has a good understanding of your database system before you try to use this kind of feature.

7.3.6   Workflow systems

One of the most important elements of a business model is the definition of the business processes that will operate within the organization. In Chapter 2, we looked at how these could be defined and how they complemented other model elements. One reason business process definitions are so popular is that they can be implemented directly by an automated support tool. Automation of business processes usually goes under the name workflow, and a large number of workflow products are now on the market.

Workflow tools generally provide the following kinds of facilities:

- Interactive editing of process definitions, using a graphical presentation of a flow diagram
- Instantiating defined processes into a control structure that can monitor relevant activity in close to real time
- Tracking the activities of the various participants in the process
- Routing information between participants and other resources, including queuing at appropriate points where there may be resource limitations
- Recognizing external events, and the progress of internal actions, so as to maintain an accurate view of the process state
- Invoking external software units to introduce their capabilities at the appropriate points
- Providing reports and displays to support the management and the supervision of processes

Needless to say, rules have an important part to play in the definition and the control of workflow. In an earlier chapter, we discussed how rules could be used to provide logical definitions and to apply constraints to the structure of the information. In a workflow context, though, rules are most strongly associated with the control of behavior. This is typically associated with branching points in the process, where alternative paths may be taken, depending on the conditions that apply. Figure 7-4 shows how this could be defined on a process flow diagram.

The conditions on the branches are sometimes called *guards*, or *gatekeepers*, because of their role in controlling the entry and exit conditions for various stages in the process. In straightforward cases, like the one shown in the diagram, the workflow engine is likely to implement the rule directly. To deal with more complex cases, most engines have the capability to call out to another component, and so they could potentially also make use of any of the other mechanisms described in this chapter.

Rules that are implemented internally are likely to be in a proprietary format that's part of the workflow product. However, like the other kinds of realizations in this chapter, they still need to be tied back into a larger set of definitions of the business, and they must be coordinated with other rules that can't be implemented within the workflow system. We'll return to the theme of rule management in the next chapter.

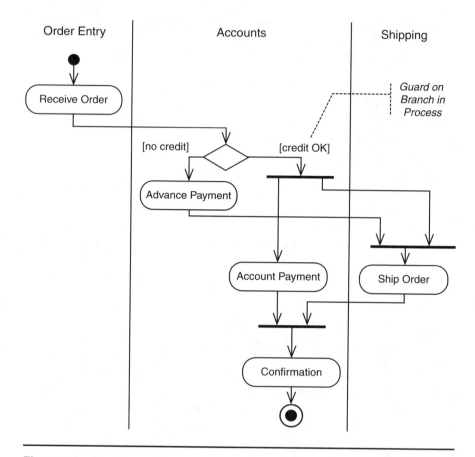

Figure 7-4 Simple workflow process

7.3.7 Look-up tables

A look-up table can be used to express business logic in a form that's easier to use than the original rules. The implications of one or more business rules are encoded into a table so that an application can simply read the relevant result, still applying the rules, but in an indirect way. In effect, the rules are compiled offline by an arbitrary process that reduces them to a simpler structure. Although tables can be convenient, their overuse can make the system difficult to maintain, as we'll see shortly.

A look-up table won't necessarily appear as a table in a relational database system. There might be very good performance reasons why it would be better to hold the table in memory. In such cases, there's also a need for a mechanism to build the table in memory, either by reading it from persistent storage, in which case it might also be a database table, or by creating it from a program.

To make things clearer, we'll take a simple example. Assume that we have defined a set of business events. When one of these events occurs, it may impact a business process, causing it to stop, change direction, or whatever. One way of defining which kind of event will impact which process is to cover all the possible combinations in a table (see Table 7-1). It's now very simple for an application to find out about event impacts. For example, deciding what processes might be impacted by an event is just a question of retrieving all the rows with the relevant event name and Yes in the Impacts? column.

Table 7-1   All event impact results

Event	Process	Impacts?
Event 1	Process A	Yes
Event 1	Process B	No
Event 1	Process C	No
Event 2	Process A	Yes
and so on . . .		

The number of rows in this table will be equal to the product of the number of events and the number of processes. We can cut this by at least half by including only rows for which the impact is Yes or, if it produces a smaller table, only rows for which the impact is No. Assuming that Yes is smaller, we'll get a table like Table 7-2. Because the Yes is implicit, we don't need a column for it. We can still effectively get the missing rows, because for any event/process combination not in the table, we can assume that the impact is No.

Table 7-2   Event impacts

Event	Process
Event 1	Process A
Event 2	Process A
Event 2	Process C
Event 3	Process B
and so on . . .	

This is all very convenient for an application program that needs a quick decision, but tables of this kind hide a couple of lurking dangers. The first is the opaqueness of the underlying logic. From the table, we can't readily answer such questions as, Why does event 1 impact process A but not process B? This opaqueness need not be a problem if the table has been generated from some business rules, because we could always go back to the rule statements if we needed to understand the basis for the table. The danger is that the analyst may produce the table directly, with no supporting rule statements. Over time, such tables become very difficult to maintain. The analyst originally responsible may no longer be available, and the rationale for the entries may not be at all obvious. If we define a new event, what should we do to be consistent with the way that previous events were treated?

The second danger is the possibility of combinatorial explosion. The total number of rows to be considered is the product of all the possible values in all the columns. For example, say that we wanted to relate event impacts to actors, with 20 actors, 30 events, and 40 processes. That's only $20 + 30 + 40 = 90$ entities in total, but $20 * 30 * 40 = 24,000$ combinations we have to think about. Things rapidly get worse if the number of entities grows. For example, adding one actor doesn't sound like much but, for the example numbers above, it would also throw another 1,200 combinations into the pot.

Look-up tables are a good way of showing simple factual relationships when there is no underlying logic or the rationale is of no interest: for example, the relationship between the name of a country and its international dialing code prefix. When tables are being used to implement rule statements, the right way to produce the table is to use an automated tool to generate it from the original logic statements. This will reduce the danger of accidentally introducing errors that might be difficult to spot when the system is in service.

7.3.8   Flags and magic codes

Something in the human psyche is irresistibly attracted to the idea of inventing codes for common situations. The basic idea is that you can build meaning into a short identifier that's also a kind of name for the situation you're describing. These might be called transaction types or process codes or something similar, but the basic idea is much the same.

Typically, such codes have meanings loaded onto the values of characters in particular positions. A relatively innocent example might be, "Retail customers have account numbers starting with 2; wholesale account numbers start with 3." The problem, as with most other things in this universe, is entropy. Over time, the nice, neat coding system starts to fall into disorder as the world moves on. You can imagine the kinds of things that happen.

- "We thought that things could be categorized into distinct groups, but now we find that some things fit into more than one group."
- "We specified just one decimal digit to discriminate between these categories, but now we have more than ten of them."
- "Two departments of the company ended up using this digit of the code for different purposes."
- "These codes seem to mean the same thing; I don't know why they're different."

And so on. You end up with a situation in which the interpretation of code XYZ depends on not just the code itself but all kinds of other factors, some of which might be quite bizarre. As far as business rules are concerned, this is a fragile situation. Rules may be come to be defined in terms of these magic codes instead of what's really intended. Warning bells should ring if you see any rule of this sort:

> R710X   Transaction codes of the form x5xx or x6xx must not be
>   applied to retail accounts.

It may be that you're stuck with data built around assumptions about codes of this sort. If you find yourself in this situation, the best thing to do is to translate the code as early as possible. Expand the intended meaning into explicit attributes of an object as soon as it enters the system, and have no truck with the code thereafter. Use the real attributes that the code was meant to imply. You may need to revisit the business model to make sure that all the nuances of the coding system are properly represented. (If not, make it so!)

If you're tempted to introduce a new coding scheme of this sort, your choices are much more straightforward. Don't do it!

There's a close cousin of this, though, that does not pose the same sorts of problems. It's the use of symbolic flags, which get packed into bit values in order to save memory or communications bandwidth. Say that we want to describe a property that may have various characteristics. Let's assume that we represent *has* by a binary 1 and *has not* by a binary 0. We could represent the characteristics in a binary form:

> property has characteristic 1 = 00000001
>
> property has characteristic 2 = 00000010
>
> property has characteristic 3 = 00000100
>
> property has characteristic 4 = 00001000

The value of the property is the logical OR of all the characteristics. So, for example, 00000101 would mean that the property has characteristics 1 and 3 but none of the others.

Why is this different from a magic code? The property is always described in terms of its characteristics, never its code. The coding is something to be hidden; we might want to change it for a reason that we couldn't anticipate when the code was set up. Programming languages use symbolic constants for this kind of thing, driven by the same sort of motivation. If you want to use this for your rules implementation, it need not pose a problem, providing you observe a few simple hygiene rules.

- Never allow coding of this sort to percolate to the business level.
- Thoroughly document the rationale behind the coding, but make it available only to the few sad people who have to know about such things.

- Hide the coding scheme from everyone else, in a way that would allow you to change it internally without their knowing.
- Make sure that all public information talks only about the characteristics, never the codes.

7.4   System rules

Up to now, we've focused exclusively on rules that have been driven directly by the needs of the business. But another class of rules arises only in an indirect way. These rules are concerned with the operation of technical artifacts that aren't visible at the business level. Such items include a wide range of hardware, including servers, storage systems, and network equipment, and an even wider range of software, from operating systems upward.

The approach to business modeling recommended in earlier chapters deliberately avoids the specification of these things, in order to avoid a premature fixation that could hamper implementation. Although not directly stated as a requirement, these items still form part of the system and have to be specified, designed, implemented, and operated. A general set of development and operation activities dealing with these items are mostly similar, regardless of whether a business rules approach is taken to the functional requirements.

There's one qualification to this, though. Some of the issues that arise in technical implementation can be resolved in much the same way that we tackled the business issues: through the use of rules. In a way, these rules still arise from an underlying business need, but the link is so indirect that it's not really very helpful. We'll call these *system rules,* in contrast to business rules, and look briefly at how they stand in relation to the approach we've discussed so far.

Here's an example of a technology problem that might call for a rule-based solution. Let's say that our organization has an information system that forms the basis of a real-time e-commerce operation. In order to maintain the necessary level of availability, the system is to be hosted on clustered servers, arranged so that activity can fail over to a second server if the first stops working. Configuring such a system is not a trivial job, requiring in-depth technical knowledge and experience. Nevertheless, once it's set up and tested, such systems can preserve some level of operation under failure conditions.

But there's an even better scenario. Instead of waiting for a failure to occur, it may be possible to detect early signs that all is not well. Clues that might indicate this are shrinking system resources, such as free memory, unexpectedly high processor utilization, and rapid consumption of free disk space. If these trends cannot be correlated with load, they may point to the possibility of failure in the near future.

If impending failure is detected early, it may be possible to take action before the problem becomes an emergency. For example, if a memory leak is suspected, it may be possible to transfer the load to a second processor, close the application on the first processor, restart it, and then transfer the load back. This doesn't fix the underlying problem, but it does provide continuity of service while investigations are carried out.

The same kind of thinking is applied on a wider scale in many system management activities. Not surprisingly, rules are frequently used to define the conditions to be monitored and the resulting actions to be taken. It's reasonable to ask how these system rules might differ from business rules.

The answer is: hardly at all. The broad approach is almost exactly the same, which is why we've deferred discussion of this topic until now. Rules need to be defined, documented, reviewed, and realized in a very similar way, whether the influence of the business requirements is direct or very indirect.

There are a few small differences.

- System rule definition will be undertaken by technologists, not business analysts.
- System rules will be rooted in a design model, not a business model.
- The terminology used for system rules will be "closer to the metal," and some specialized templates may be appropriate.
- System rules can't distance themselves from the technology; they're part of it.
- Implementation choices may be tightly constrained, because of the very nature of the problem.

However, these are really only minor variations on the theme, and, in general, system rules can adopt the same approach that's discussed throughout the rest of this book.

7.5   Implementation summary

Distributed systems provide many niches that can accommodate business rules. In some cases, the choice of location will also determine the options available for realization. In others, the designer will have to weigh the alternatives before selecting the way that a particular rule will be implemented.

Some of the main options are

- Program code through in-line code, through scripting, or as a specialized rule component
- Rules engines, which usually come in the form of a logic server with a proprietary rule language and style of operation
- Databases, which offer several ways of implementing rules close to where the information is stored
- Workflow systems with an internal engine and custom styles for encoding rules

- Look-up tables, which contain precompiled knowledge in a form that's fast and convenient to access

In addition to rules that can be traced back to business requirements, there are also rules concerned with the control of technology that have no direct business linkage. These system rules are common in such areas as systems management, but all can be handled by using a standardized, consistent approach.

8

Managing Business Rules and Models

8.1 Life-cycle costs

Like many other complex artifacts, an information system follows a life cycle. The system will be conceived, built, operated, and, eventually, pass into history. There's always a strong temptation to focus on the early stages of the life cycle, when the system is being defined and created, because it's here that the system takes on its fundamental characteristics. However, most of the cost of ownership of the system is incurred during its operational life.

Over this extended period, which can span decades, the system will be subject to various modifications—either to add new functionality or to fix problems—and go through technology updates to the underlying hardware, operating system, network, and so on. The system will also require continual housekeeping support with such activities as data backup. When we talk about life-cycle models, we're therefore talking about something that's a bit wider than the models that you'll find in a context that's pure development.

Experience with previous systems gives some rough guidelines to the sort of cost profile that you might expect. Most medium to large organizations spend around 25 percent of their IT budgets on new systems and 75 percent on maintaining existing systems. Typically, you could expect the cost of development to represent about one third of the total cost of ownership for a system that's in service over a reasonable period of time. This takes into account some skew in the figures caused by systems that aren't successful and end up either getting canceled before commissioning or being withdrawn after only a short period.

E-commerce systems haven't been around long enough for us to know what their typical life cycle would look like, although there are some early indications. Time frames appear to be more compressed, with systems being discarded and replaced after a relatively short operational life but with correspondingly accelerated development times. Overall, though, it looks as though the 2:1 ratio of operational to development costs is likely to remain a reasonable guideline for the near future.

Within the lifetime of a system, bursts of activity tend to be interleaved with periods of comparative calm. Obviously, activity is at its most intense while the system is being created, but the lesser peaks during what is theoretically maintenance of the system will eventually add up to more. Given the dominance of non-development costs, it's obvious good sense to make sure that we do everything possible to minimize them.

8.2   Managing evolution

8.2.1   Coping with changes

It's possible to feel positive or negative about the need for change. If we successfully react to a new business opportunity, we can feel good that our organization is moving forward into a more competitive position. On the other hand, a lot of change is associated with the need to correct a problem, and it can seem that we're running fast but getting nowhere.

One thing's for sure: Change is normal. The world will evolve, and our information systems will have to evolve with it. Unfortunately, the way that most IT development projects are organized encourages denial. Defining and producing an information system is frequently set up as a one-shot exercise, with the need to be reactive seen as Somebody Else's Problem. Taking a broader view, though, the inevitability of change means that any truly useful approach must accommodate change in an organized way, and this has to apply to business rules and business models.

Tracking changes   Let's start with the most basic requirement of all. You can't control something if you can't identify it. You need to be able to look at two versions of the same thing and say, "Aha, they're different!" Because the things we're dealing with are somewhat abstract, you will need labeling to indicate that a change has taken place.

This labeling usually comes as a *version number:* a value that increases in a predictable way with each successive change. Actually, labeling doesn't need to be purely numeric; anything that has a defined order can be used, such as the letters of the alphabet. It's quite common to use a multipart version number, with each part giving a rough indication of the significance of the change; so a change from version 1.1 to version 2.0 might be a major change, whereas going from version 1.1 to version 1.2 would be a minor change. Schemes using two-, three-, or even four-part version numbers abound but not consistent rules about when to update which part, especially at the least significant end of the number. All you can do is demand that at least some part of the version number change *monotonically*—always increasing—so that you can immediately see which version is the latest.

You will need to decide a couple of things in relation to models and rules. The first is the granularity of control you want. If we assume a hierarchical relationship for rules, whereby a rule can appear in one or more rule sets, and a rule set can appear in one or more models, the main choices are

- Control by rule. (Updating a rule updates the version number of the rule, its rule sets, and its models.)
- Control by rule set. (Updating a rule updates the version number of its rule sets and its models.)
- Control by model. (Updating a rule updates the version number of its model.)

A small grain size—by rule, in this case—means that you have more things to control, but changes can be accurately located. A large grain size—by model, in this case—gives you fewer things to control but less precision about what has changed. Extending this approach to models in general brings in more complications, in the form of processes, objects, events, and so on. You've heard it before, but there's no standard answer: It's your call.

The other thing to mull over is whether you need a change history. In some cases, it's enough just to note that A is not compatible with B. In other cases, you may need to know that A used to work with B. If so, you will need to create a historical trail of which change happened when. Similar comments apply to recording who is responsible for each change. You may be happy just to know who fouled up last time, not the whole dynasty.

Maintaining consistency   Of course, simply being able to identify changes is not of much use on its own. We can't even be sure that we've chosen the right level of granularity until we appreciate the real goal: being confident that we can identify a consistent set of independent entities. We need to worry about two main kinds of consistency:

- Getting the right set of peer components that fit together to make up an assembly that we want to treat as a single unit
- Preserving the correspondence between intrinsically different kinds of things that nonetheless have an important relationship

An example of the first type is a software module that's built from several source files. When building the module, we need to be sure that we're using the right version of each of the source files. An example of the second type might be the relationship between the same software module and a business model. Which version of the module goes with which version of the model?

Something to be aware of here is the need to differentiate between *versions* and *variants*. A new version replaces the previous version. The replacement may not happen immediately: If you've got some oldies around, it may not be convenient to slot a newcomer into their place right away. It might even be reasonable to skip an update and wait for a later version. But any new usage should take on the latest version, not try to pick up something that's known to be out of date.

In contrast, a variant is an alternative to what exists. It's a different flavor of something that's already familiar. A variant might arise because of the need to provide the same functionality in a different environment or a slightly different range of functionality in the same environment. Either way, it's not a replacement, and a new variant will exist happily alongside other existing variants.

The essential difference is summarized in Figure 8-1. The diagram shows a time sequence from left to right. We start with thing A at an initial version: 1.0 in this case. Then stuff happens. There's a request to improve the performance of A in some situations. We can do it, but it will make A more expensive. To avoid loading the cost increase onto all the users of A who don't need it all, we make a variant, B, along with a small change to A. We now have a new version of A, along with a new variant, B, both of which can lead independent lives. Later, we need another variant of A, so a new branch, C, starts up. At the point in time corresponding to the right-hand end of the diagram, we can pick from variants A (at version 2.0), B (at version 1.2), or C (at version 1.0), depending on the situation.

This may all seem pedantic and picky, but just ask anyone who's had to grapple with "DLL hell" in Windows about the practical implications. Releases of Windows prior to Windows 2000 made the innocent assumption that a DLL

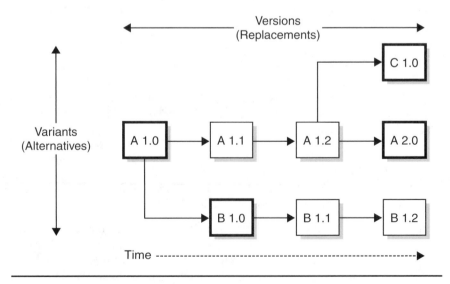

Figure 8-1   Versions and variants

(dynamic link library) could be replaced by a later version without breaking any program's dependence on the earlier version. Like all fairy stories, this is a charming idea but, regrettably, not a good match to the real world. More recent releases of Windows have had to allow for "side-by-side versioning," which is another term for what we're calling variants.

This is something that more mature industries, like manufacturing, understand and work with as a matter of course. With so much hype and so many conflicting agendas in IT, simple truths get buried under this year's new language, this month's conference, or this week's press release. It's really not too difficult to create a manifest for any assembly that details the set of compatible *configuration items* that go together. In fact, the emerging Microsoft .NET framework takes exactly this approach. The unit of deployment is an *assembly,* which contains one or more *modules*. Exactly one module in an assembly contains a manifest, detailing the full contents of the assembly.

You won't be able to solve all the problems of the IT industry. But you can make your own life a lot easier by observing some straightforward principles.

- Make a conscious decision about what you consider to be a configuration item.
- Have a watertight method for tracking changes to those items.
- Make configuration information part of any deliverable.

Managing multiple models   For simplicity, most of the earlier discussion in this book talked in terms of a single model. In reality, you will have to cope with multiple models that need to coexist. For several reasons, you will end up with more than one model, and each will have to be a configuration item in its own right.

- Models may be limited in extent for reasons of practicality or to meet the aims of a particular project. The most common boundaries are defined by the extents of organizational units or geographical locations or both. Over time, models covering several extents of the same sort may be produced, and these will need to be consistent. For example, you might start with a model of the eastern region of the organization and then progress to the central and western regions later.
- Models may be produced to cover different viewpoints on the same area. Especially common in this context is the use of separate models to cover analysis—a logical view of an information system—and design—an implementation-oriented view of the same system. Obviously, these will need to be kept in step, and we'll look at some ideas shortly.
- Models may relate to different points in time. The most obvious examples are models of the situation as it exists at present and as it's intended to be in the future. You may have more than one future model: For instance, there may be a corporate 3-year planning horizon, and you may be required to maintain a model of how things might be in that sort of time frame.

The current state of the art offers little in the way of tool support for coordinating various models of this kind. Some kind of process will be required to keep your models in step. Taking a more specific example, Figure 8-2 shows two ways of coping with the need for both analysis and design models. In both cases, we'll assume that the first steps are going to be an initial version of an analysis model, which becomes the basis for the first version of a design model. If things could end there, life would be great. Life being what it is, though, both models will need to evolve.

The sequential approach tries to achieve consistency through alternating hand-over of the same model from analysis to design and back. Another spin on this is to treat both analysis and design aspects as different areas of the same model. Only one group—analysts or designers—is permitted to edit the model at one time. This helps to prevent analysis and design from getting out of step but only at the price of slowing the work down. Designers have to wait for the analysts to finish their latest round of changes before they can get on, and vice versa. There's also the danger that one group will change a feature introduced by the other group, which then gets reinstated by the first group, and so on.

The parallel approach is probably a more realistic alternative. Now, both teams can progress their respective models at their own pace but at the risk of introducing incompatibilities between the two viewpoints. To check for these,

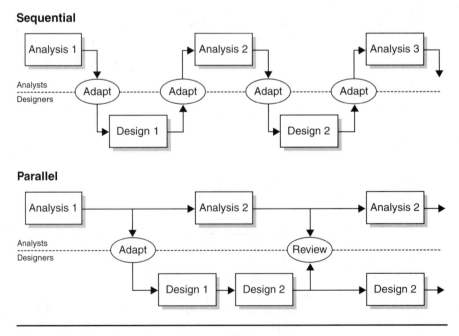

Figure 8-2 Synchronizing analysis and design models

and to decide how to handle modifications proposed by the other team, it will be necessary to set up joint review meetings at appropriate points. These sessions are costly in time and energy and require careful management. The big danger is that an us-versus-them mindset will build up, with each group effectively ignoring the input of the other, so each ends up going its own way.

There's no perfect answer to managing multiple models. But if you at least recognize the potential problems, you can start to think about possible solutions.

8.2.2   Automating housekeeping

Keeping the housekeeping information up to date can become a bit of a chore. If it's not an attractive job to do, the chances are it won't get done well, and some parts may not get done at all. One solution is to automate key steps in the process. Automation can not only make sure that the job is done in the approved manner but also close off various back routes, so that the right way is the *only* way of doing things.

It's fashionable to disapprove of Microsoft's dominance of the desktop, but one of the benefits of the widespread use of Microsoft Office is the emergence of a clear automation standard for other applications. Office applications are *automation enabled,* which means that they expose the internal structure of their constituent parts along with mechanisms that permit external applications to access and to modify them. If a vendor of application X enables automation in the same sort of way, it opens up such possibilities as extracting information from X to create a report in Word, importing data into X from an original source in Excel, or even hooking X up to another, custom-built application.

Many of the products you will want to use for managing analysis, design, and other development stages now have this sort of capability built in. Checking on the availability of automation features should certainly be on your vendor-selection checklist. Microsoft provides a dialect of Visual Basic, VBA (Visual Basic for Applications) as a macro programming language for its products, but you're not limited to using that for automation. In practice, most automation glue seems to be built using Visual Basic.

A pseudocode algorithm for a typical piece of automation will look something like this:

```
When triggered
Begin
        While there is something useful to do
                Get some data from application A
                Fiddle with it
                Write some data to application B, or to file
        End While
End
```

To make this a little clearer, we'll look at an example of the kind of automation you might want to introduce. Here's the scenario. You have a business model containing business processes, business objects, organizational units, actors, and all the rest. You want to catalog some of these elements and make that catalog widely available for training, configuration management, future development of new applications, and so on. For instance, easy access to a catalog of process steps could be a great help to someone trying to engineer new business processes.

Unfortunately, your modeling tool does modeling, period. Therefore, you decide to create entries in another tool, a repository, for the elements you care about. The repository has all the facilities for navigation and presentation that your users need. It's clearly where your catalog belongs. But how to do it? You could always ask Joe. "Joe, whenever the analysts change the model, I want you to update the repository to show the latest set of business processes." "Sure," says Joe, "be glad to."

Problem solved? What happens if Joe is sick, forgets to do it, or does it wrong or the analysts change the model and don't tell Joe, or any of a number of other ways in which a manual process can come off the rails? To prevent these ills, you may end up designing a little business process of your own to ensure that the repository content can be trusted. But this itself will require management.

Fortunately, there is a better way. The crucial step, in this case, is to intercept the release of a new model at the moment of its publication. Figure 8-3 shows the basic structure. Once the analysts are happy with the new version of their model, they can check it into the local version-management tool. Automation is used to introduce a new step, although it's not visible to the analysts. In parallel with the check-in of the new model version, a tool adapter is invoked to compare the new model with the current repository content and to generate a simple data file—in this case, using a *.CSV (comma-separated value) format—containing the delta:

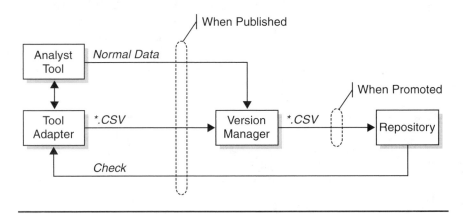

Figure 8-3   Automating repository updates

the differences between new and old. This file is also checked into the version-management tool as part of the new model release.

Review of the new model will result one of two things. The model may be referred back for change. In this case, it will be checked out from the version-control tool, the associated *.CSV file will be automatically deleted, and the cycle will repeat. If the model is approved, it will be "promoted" in the version-management tool, thus changing its status. Once this happens, the associated *.CSV file will be automatically forwarded to update the repository, so that its contents are guaranteed to agree with the latest approved model.

8.3   Deploying rules

8.3.1   Testing a new system

In Chapter 5, we looked at how to check the validity of business rules. At that stage, we weren't testing a system but instead were interested only in seeing that the logic statements properly captured the intentions of the business. Once the rules have been incorporated into a deliverable unit, though, we can do proper testing.

Testing can happen at several levels. Unless you're building something tiny, you will have at least three levels of testing.

- Unit testing, the lowest of these levels, is where the realizations of the rules meet up with other bits of the machinery in a state to do some real work. It's up to you to define what you mean by a unit: In Windows, for example, it might be a COM component encapsulated in a DLL. Before you do anything else with a unit, you'll want to get some confidence that it appears to do what it should. This requires a test harness to cover for the other parts of the system that aren't there yet and a supply of suitable test data.

- The next step up is integration testing. Here, you're progressively adding together the already tested units to make larger and larger chunks of the final system. In the context of a particular system, it should be obvious which units go together to make meaningful chunks. As the functionality included gets more complete, it should be possible to use test data with a closer resemblance to the kind of thing that will be encountered in practice.

- The final level is acceptance testing, so called because it's usually an essential step in the system's being accepted as fit for the business owner's purpose. By this stage, all the units will have been integrated to form a fully working system. Now the test data can look exactly like the real thing, and real users can try the system out, possibly for the first time. It may also be the first opportunity to try out some of the nonfunctional aspects, such as response time.

These levels also form the rough chronological sequence in which tests are applied. It may be possible to overlap unit testing and integration testing to some extent if early modules from the unit test can be integrated while others are being completed. Acceptance testing, though, has to wait until all the integration and integration testing have been completed, so it definitely comes last. Depending on your local situation, you might need to modify this scheme somewhat to introduce additional levels or to make a partial delivery of something less than the full system.

Although business rules are unlikely to be exposed directly at any of these levels, they can provide a very valuable input to the testers and help them to define the test cases that should be applied. For example, a unit might incorporate a rule that says something like:

R801X   An applicant of age 18 or less must . . .

The tester might decide to test the unit, using age values of –1, 0, 17, 18, 19, and 999, with the values 17 to 19 being used because of the existence of the rule and the other values chosen because they represent interesting boundary conditions. These same values may also need to be included in subsequent tests at other levels to make sure that something else hasn't hexed a previously good unit.

At the level of acceptance testing, other parts of the business model can also be used to define what to look for. In particular, it should be possible to run through all the business narratives to show that they all behave as would be expected, especially in the way that they cope with alternative scenarios.

All the materials—test specifications, test harnesses, test data, and test results—should be treated as configuration items in their own right. It should be possible for you to identify exactly what tests have been carried out and to be able to repeat any of the tests, if necessary, in the future.

8.3.2   Rollout

Prior to rollout, you can do a few things to reduce the risks that always accompany new systems. If this is your first attempt at a system relying heavily on business rules, you might consider introducing a proof-of-concept (POC) milestone into your project plan. This should provide assurance that you can manage the technology and gives an early opportunity to check out such features as the ability to scale under load before investing too much effort.

If the new system introduces changes to working practices, it's also worth considering a pilot implementation. This allows you to shake down the rollout procedures on a smaller stage, where problems are easier and less embarrassing to resolve. It gives an opportunity to check the effectiveness of various support functions, as well as the system itself. For example, you can see whether training courses have covered the right areas, the help desk is set up to give the right kind of response, and so on.

One of the intended effects of introducing a rule-centered system is the improved ability to respond to change. This shortens the distance between the system and the business analysts and, ultimately, the business owner. Having more immediate links from rule statements to their implementations allows people to work in a different way, but uncertainties and errors are inevitable during the early days. A pilot implementation can help here by increasing familiarity with the system and revealing any unexpected problems.

Some care might be needed in the choice of area to pilot. For example, it's probably a bad idea to pick something that could seriously harm the business if it goes wrong. If the new system is a replacement for an existing one, this can also be achieved through a period of parallel operation, where new and old ways of working coexist through a transition period.

One final point to bear in mind when planning the system rollout is the need for fallback policies to deal with problems encountered. These policies are not intended to cover the same ground as any business continuity mechanisms that will be in place to support normal operations. The fallback measures will be required for only a short period and will be removed once the system enters live operation. There's no reason why a rule-centered system should be particularly vulnerable to problems during rollout, but anything incorporating new and comparatively unknown technology could have some unexpected side effects, which, of course, are bound to become apparent at the most awkward possible time.

8.3.3   Supporting a live system

Managing problems   Ideally, the system will have been adequately instrumented, so that it's possible to get a clear view of how well—or not, as the case may be—it's working. Even if you don't have a sophisticated system management tool in place, it's pretty straightforward to set alerts for possible danger signs and to examine log files for histories of system behavior.

In addition, you can augment this by creating small processes that can be invoked at regular intervals to probe the system to make sure that it performs in the expected way. For example, you may have a Web-based application that gets data from a back-end database and uses rules to produce dynamic page content. To probe the operation of this service, you could create a simple script providing HTML messages that simulate a typical user interaction. It's important that this follow the same path as an ordinary user, so, in this case, the probing messages would have to go out onto the Internet and reenter the system through the standard portal. You will also want to make sure that any specialized apparatus, such as a rules engine, will be exercised by your probing message. Such proactive problem management can locate deficiencies lurking within the system and head them off before they have a major impact.

You will also need to react to incidents that may indicate undetected problems. The most urgent aim here is to identify the underlying problem causing the incident and to find a workaround to restore service as soon as possible.

Again, there's nothing particularly error prone about rules. It should be straightforward to accommodate a new rule-centered system within your existing problem-management procedures.

Introducing changes   You must have seen the marketing demo: The salesperson enters some data and shows how the Wizzo engine applies the business rules needed to place an order for a box of widgets over the Internet. But wait! The business now needs to change the order process! Quickly, the salesperson edits the rules and reenters the data. With a quick flash of the GUI, the Wizzo engine triumphantly displays the new transaction, running exactly as desired. The message? "An unskilled business user can directly change the rules while the system is running."

This may seem really neat to anyone who has no experience of an actual information system, but it bears roughly the same similarity to running a professional operation as a Hollywood drama does to real life. Certainly, it will be much easier to make changes in a rule-centered system, but a little more discipline is needed if the business intends to survive.

First, a quick fix to a rule may solve an immediate problem, but it may also have side effects that should receive a little thought. Here's a scenario. The customer relationship department receives several complaints from customers who are unable to place "urgent" orders. A quick look at their characteristics shows that they are all silver-level customers but that "urgent" shipping is restricted to gold-level customers. The complainants also share a common characteristic that can be used to classify them. To avoid losing orders, the shipping department changes the rules to temporarily raise all such customers to gold status if they need an "urgent" order. But gold-level customers also have other privileges, such as a much higher credit limit. You can imagine what happens next.

Second, changes usually need to be introduced in a coordinated way. A package of changes may need to be made together to maintain the sanity of the system. Also, several groups around the organization may be itching to make changes. Casual rule editing will rapidly lead to chaos, as group B changes a rule that's just been changed by group A, which in turn depends on another rule that's about to be changed by group C. By the time everyone discovers that the system behavior is not quite what they expected, it will have become a nightmare to sort out.

Third, there's the potential impact on system stability. An innocent-looking change to a rule may have unsuspected repercussions on the internal operations of the system. Servers that were happily coping with the processing load now start to buckle under the pressure, whereas other servers stand idle. Disk space runs out. Network segments become overloaded. The operations staff sees that something is going on but has no idea what has caused the problem and so can't fix it.

Without belaboring the point any more, it's pretty obvious that changes have to be introduced in an organized way. This does not negate the convenience of rules, so the Wizzo salesperson was partly correct. We just need to be clear about which piece of the process is being speeded up. Figure 8-4 summarizes the answer.

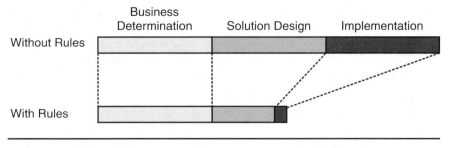

Figure 8-4   Schematic time scales for changing an application

The part that can't be sidestepped is the determination by the business of what it wants to do. If it can't decide, the best strategy is to do nothing. If a coherent business policy can be established, it should be a lot more straightforward to redefine the rules than to redesign some procedural code, assuming that you can find the relevant code. Even better, the transfer of the design to implementation can happen much, much faster than the code-test-crash-recode cycle that most software goes through.

Most information systems of any significance already have change-management procedures in place. In truth, very little should need to be changed in these procedures to accommodate rules. The pragmatic systems manager can just think of rules as being another kind of development process. What really matters to operations is that a package of changes has been defined, implemented, and tested and has been scheduled to go live at a specific time.

Other management processes   Apart from the processes we've already mentioned, several others should already be in place to support your information systems. The names given to these processes may vary from place to place. They may be combined or split out to a finer granularity. But the need for the underlying activities will always be there, whatever they're called.

Because rules don't raise any special issues for these processes, we'll briefly summarize some of them to give a flavor of what they're about, although each of them could warrant a chapter in its own right.

- *Business continuity* refers to the ability of the organization to provide a defined, not necessarily a full, level of service after an unplanned event causes an interruption to normal operations. This includes a range of measures to provide resilience and to permit recovery to acceptable levels.
- *Capacity management* is concerned with maintaining the right level of service and performance against a background of continual change. This

process includes planning for future anticipated loads and making sure that enough capacity is available to deal with unexpected peaks in demand.

- *Service-level management* is the process of coordinating and monitoring service-level agreements (SLAs) to make sure that the service being provided by a supplier is maintained to the appropriate standard of quality.

- *Availability management* deals with the measures needed to ensure continuity of the services provided by the organization's information systems. It includes measurement of system availability, prevention of avoidable causes of unplanned downtime, and steps to restore service as quickly as possible in the event of failure.

8.4   Tools to support rule management

In earlier chapters, we hinted at some of the kinds of capabilities that are required from development tools. "Development" is a slightly misleading term because it implies a one-time usage in the early days of a system. In practice, rules are continually defined and refined during the whole life of an information system. The period called development just happens to be a phase in which a whole load of rule definition takes place within a fairly short period of time.

Here are the most important things you should have in your toolkit in relation to business rules:

- *Modeling tool.* Business rules are rooted in business models, so you're going to need an efficient way of modeling your requirements. Some level of UML compatibility is essential, but don't expect UML alone to be the answer. Separation of structure from presentation; the ability to import and to export a range of formats, including XML; and automation capabilities are much more important than are colored icons.

- *Rule definer.* You can produce perfectly good rule statements by using nothing more than a simple text editor, but it can become hard work, and it's easy for errors to creep in. A better option is a tool that's specialized for defining rules. In earlier chapters, we saw some of the basic principles that could be used: controlling rule structures through templates, enforcing references to the fact model, and so on.

- *Logic simulator.* It's virtually impossible to check even a moderately complex rule set by eye. We looked at a typical scenario in Chapter 5 and saw how using even a simple spreadsheet could reveal unsuspected features lurking in our rules. Little is available on the market in this specialized area, so you may decide to use something that you already have lying around, even though it's not perfect.

- *Repository.* In a large organization, rule populations can run into the thousands, and controlling them with a paper system alone would be well nigh impossible. A good repository is probably the key tool in rule management. It will contain not only the definitions of every rule but also a number of cross-references and other supporting information.
- *Other management tools.* Most of the other tools you'll need will probably already be around because they're a feature of most IT shops. On the development side, these tools include a decent configuration-management tool, or version-control system. On the operations side, such tools as alert detection and log analysis should already be in place.

If you've adopted a particular rules engine, it may bundle in some tools, and these are the ones you'll probably end up using, however far from ideal they may be. When you're evaluating rules engines, don't forget to include the management tools as part of the assessment.

Most organizations will always prefer to buy a product to do a job rather than go to all the trouble and effort of building one themselves. This is usually the right decision because of one simple factor: support. It can sometimes seem strange that you need to go outside to get support for something that's crucial to your organization, but it reflects the economies of scale.

Taking a cold-blooded mathematical view of the world, it's obvious. If the cost of supporting a tool is x, then:

$$\text{Support cost for home-brew tool} = x * 100\%$$

$$\text{Support cost for purchased tool} = x * i/n * 100\%$$

where i is an inefficiency factor, taking into account that the vendor needs to make a profit, and n is the number of customers supported. For an in-house tool, $i = 1$, and $n = 1$, so they cancel out.

For a purchased tool, i is generally much smaller than n, so it's clear that the economics are likely to be better. There's also a simpler existence proof. If doing it in-house were really cheaper, there wouldn't be any products around.

The one area that might be an exception is a rule repository. This is so important that it deserves a separate section.

8.5 Rule repository

8.5.1 Why a repository?

This area is likely to be the main worry about a simplistic buy-before-build strategy because it's the one you will least want to surrender to satisfy someone else's commercial ambitions. The aims of a rule repository, which we'll define in more detail shortly, and some of the capabilities of commercial rules engines overlap, so it's worth taking a little time to understand why you might want to take a special interest in this area.

In earlier chapters, we saw ways of identifying and stating business rules in an implementation-independent way. An information system of any significance will certainly include a fair-sized population of rules. Even if you did not explicitly identify the rules, they would still exist but probably be buried inside the implementation in a way that would make them very difficult to locate and to maintain.

We've also seen how rules can be grouped into rule sets and how the intrinsic logic of a population of rule statements can be checked to confirm that they work together in a coherent way and produce the intended conclusions. Following these principles, we can be very confident that the statements we've captured truly represent the intentions of the business.

Throughout all this analysis activity, we will obviously need a way of tracking what's going on. Jotting a few notes on a piece of scrap paper or exchanging news around the coffee machine won't be enough. We need to take a professional approach to rule management. Here are a few of the things we might want to do.

- List the rules that have been defined, along with their current status.
- Find out all rules contained in a rule set or rules that are related in another way.
- Identify the original author of a rule and the individual who made the last change.
- Locate all the rules that make use of particular terms.
- Pinpoint rules with special conditions that limit their applicability.

In the previous two chapters, we saw something of the technical architectures into which the rules must fit. We looked at the advantages and disadvantages of realizing business rules in a variety of ways and, in particular, how we could mark the rule locations to highlight the rule's presence there. Here are some of the things we might want to know about the rule realizations.

- Find all rules that have multiple realizations (and where).
- Locate the container in which a particular rule is realized.
- List all the rules that are realized within a given container.
- Identify all rules that have a particular type of realization.

These functions aren't meant to be exhaustive, but it's probably already obvious that we need a structured information resource to catalog our rules. In short, we need a rule repository.

8.5.2   Repositories and rules engines

If you have a rules engine, it will already provide at least some of the features just listed, so it's reasonable to ask whether you need a rule repository in addition or whether the rules engine alone is sufficient. The answer hangs on what your rules engine does about external rules: rules that it doesn't implement but that nevertheless exist elsewhere in the system. Most rules engines ignore the existence of any other kind of business logic. Unfortunately, you can't afford to do this.

However wonderful your rules engine, it's not realistic to put absolutely everything in it. The fact that the do-everything expert systems of the 1980s and 1990s are no longer around in their original form is a testament to the failure of this line of thinking. The plain fact is that you're bound to have some rules for which your only alternative is to locate them outside the rules engine: in a fat client, in a database, in a legacy system, in a workflow tool, or in a number of other places.

You can take the attitude that only the rules in the rules engine are proper rules, that all the others can be ignored. But this would be a big mistake. You will lose the ability to check your business logic properly, because chunks of it will be missing. You will not be able to have a rational discussion about whether a rule should be implemented inside the rules engine or outside, if logic outside the rules engine is deemed not to exist. You may be forced into a tortuous realization of a rule or rule set within the rules engine that could have been done in a simpler way outside, just to get some management control.

The other possibility is for a rules engine to introduce a little distance between the definition of a rule and its implementation. In principle, this would allow the rules engine to act as the central control point for all rules and the implementation route for some. For rules not implemented internally, the rules engine could provide a place for the user to add information about how the rule had been realized, along with a modicum of additional housekeeping information. Unfortunately, most current products lean toward the closed-world assumption and aren't very adaptable.

It's more fruitful to think about this in a different way. You would like to have a rule repository that covers all the angles we described, without being boxed in by what a rules engine allows. So treat yourself and have one! It's not as scary as it sounds, and we'll look at the practicalities shortly. Figure 8-5 shows the kind of configuration we want to achieve.

But what to do if you also have a rules engine? Won't they conflict? Not if you manage things correctly. The key point to remember is that most rules engines try to combine rule definition and rule realization. You can treat your rules engine as a kind of container that implements rules in a particular way: a superduper container, for sure, much better than a lump of C++ or Java but ultimately just something that contains some rules. Figure 8-6 shows the concept.

This is not belittling the rules engine; it's enhancing it. You can still use all its facilities, and you'll probably find it a more comfortable way to implement your rules than most alternatives. But you have to make it a member of your family of realizations.

The head of the family is the rule repository, which knows who's related to whom and knows about all the tribal relationships. But not everyone lives with the head of the family; in fact, most members of the family are out living their own lives in their local communities. The wise old repository understands this fact but still keeps lists of addresses and birthdays and a whole load of other things that bind the family members together.

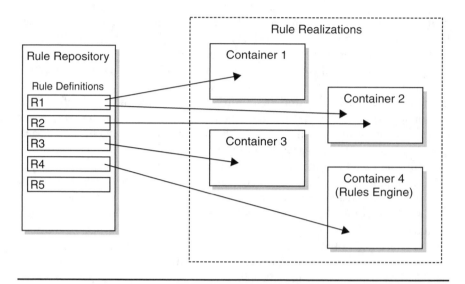

Figure 8-5 Links between rule definitions and realizations

What if you don't have a rules engine? It's not a problem. Contrary to what some vendors will tell you, rules can and do exist without their products. You can think of the repository as a "virtual rules engine," with the implementation aspects federated out to a number of separate resource providers. You can choose the providers and the way that they realize the rules, and you can make a different choice whenever you want to.

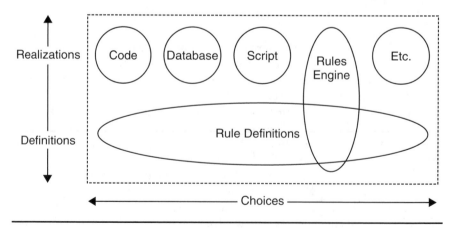

Figure 8-6 Another view of multiple realizations

If you're comfortable with your ability to realize rules outside of a rules engine, this is much the best way to go. You get all the management benefits, but you're not tied down to somebody else's production schedule, resource limitations, commercial ambitions, or any of the other ailments that can afflict vendors. If you want to implement the bulk of your rules in the Wizzo rules engine, it's still a good idea to have a repository to bind everything together. It will allow you to examine whether you want to make something a Wizzo rule or a non-Wizzo rule, while still remaining a valid business rule. It's also good insurance, in case Wizzo goes out of business, is taken over, changes its strategic direction, or fails you in a way you might not anticipate.

8.5.3   An example repository design

Principles versus specifics   In this section, we look at what you might want to see in a rules repository. The information here is enough to allow you to create your own repository, using simple desktop tools. Alternatively, you may prefer to take a commercial offering—for reasons such as support—in which case you can regard this as a list of things to discuss with prospective vendors.

To make some of these concepts a little more concrete, we describe them in terms of a Microsoft Access database. Access is not necessarily an ideal rule repository tool but is something that many people already have on their desktops because it comes as part of the higher-end versions of Microsoft Office. If you don't want to use Access, fine. Just move the concepts into your own preferred framework. Even if you do use Access, you shouldn't see this as a definitive design. It's more of a starter kit, and you can change it to add your own local concerns.

Access is a proprietary database system, and it imposes something of its own shape on the way that information appears. What you need to remember is that what's really important here is the need for an underlying structure, not the specifics of how to do something with a particular product.

Data types   Access allows a field to be one of a limited number of data types. The ones we're going to use are as follows.

AutoNumber	A number assigned by Access whenever a new record is added to a table. Because it can't be updated, this number is guaranteed to be unique for the table.
Number	A numeric value that can be used in mathematical calculations but can also be used to hold a reference to an AutoNumber primary key in another table.
Text	Any textual value but limited to a maximum of 255 characters. Used here primarily for relatively short names and identifiers.

| Memo | Also used for text but capable of holding much larger amounts, up to a maximum of 65,535 characters. |
| Date/Time | A combined date and time value, covering the years 100 through 9999. Used here mainly for timestamps and durations. |

Some conventions   All the Access tables have a primary key that provides a unique identifier for any record in the table. These identifiers are shown in boldface in the figures and are marked with a key symbol in the descriptive tables.

Several of the tables make use of an AutoNumber field to provide the primary key, in preference to an attribute, such as a name, of the object represented by the table. Apart from ensuring uniqueness of the primary key, this convention also gives more flexibility. If a Name field, say, had been put into use as the primary key, changes to the name would not be possible without a lot of grief because the name would have been used as a reference in another table.

The detailed structure of a rule and the corresponding rule template are not explicitly represented in the tables. Instead, the rule is assumed to be encoded in XML, which allows it to be stored as a simple text string. The XML can be processed by external functions to create whatever presentation is required; the important thing is to store the rule or the template in its most structured form.

Despite a fair amount of debate about possible XML schema definitions for rules, no commonly agreed standard has as yet emerged. The penalty for choosing your own schema is fairly light, though. If a standard rule schema does appear, you should be able to translate your rules into the standard form and vice versa, although there may be some information loss in the process.

Design scope   The Access design detailed here covers only the definition of the tables and the relationships between them. You should see this design more as a starter kit for your own repository than an imposed solution. Once you have decided on your own structure, you will also need to design the other features that depend on them: forms, queries, and reports. These features are fairly straightforward to produce in Access, but you need to plan for a certain amount of effort.

Before you get down to details, it's a good idea to get the table definitions clear, and that's where we'll start. For convenience, we split the description into three parts, mainly to avoid overloading the diagrams. However, these are simply different views: They all form part of the same Access database definition.

Intrinsic rule properties   First, we look at things that are mostly intrinsic to the rule, shown in Figure 8-7. This shows the rule itself and several things that are bound closely to it. The tables cover what the rule is, when it applies, and who says it's a rule anyway! Let's start with the rule itself (Table 8-1).

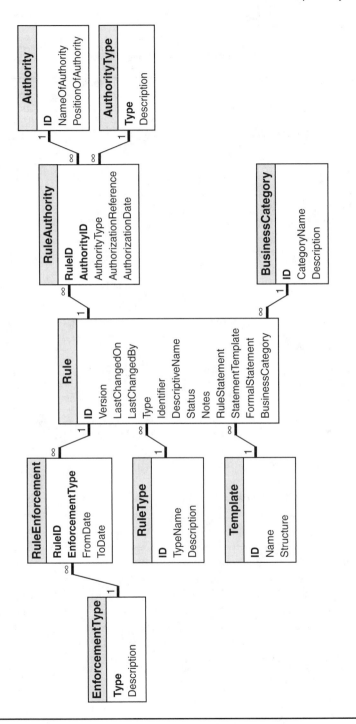

Figure 8-7 Intrinsic rule properties

Table 8-1   Rule

Field Name	Data Type	Description
ID	AutoNumber	Unique ID for the rule
Version	Text	Version number, in whatever format suits
LastChangedOn	Date/Time	When the rule was created or last changed
LastChangedBy	Text	Name of the person responsible
Type	Number	Link to type of rule (see Table 8-4)
Identifier	Text	Application-independent identifier for the rule
DescriptiveName	Text	Longer textual description of rule
Status	Text	Indicator to show the current status of the rule
Notes	Memo	Field for more extensive free-format notes
RuleStatement	Memo	The business rule statement (in XML)
StatementTemplate	Number	Link to template (see Table 8-5)
FormalStatement	Memo	A formal representation of the rule
BusinessCategory	Number	Link to a business category (see Table 8-9)

A few points should be noted here. As the table stands, there's no change history, only a record of the last change. It would be straightforward to add a couple of tables to provide a record of who did what and when. The identifier for the rule is one that stands with the rule itself; we'll see later how the rule can also have aliases in various situations. Rule statements are of the kind we discussed in Chapter 3 and are expressed in the form of an XML string in a memo field to avoid arbitrary size constraints, which preserves the inherent structure but can be processed to provide a straightforward natural language rendition. The status of the rule will have text values such as unreviewed, approved, or retired. If you agree on a fixed set of status values you can keep them in another table, and replace the status text field with a link to the new table.

Table 8-2   RuleEnforcement

	Field Name	Data Type	Description
⊶	RuleID	Number	Link to Rule
⊶	EnforcementType	Text	Link to EnforcementType
	FromDate	Date/Time	Date enforcement starts
	ToDate	Date/Time	Date enforcement ends

Table 8-3   EnforcementType

	Field Name	Data Type	Description
⊶	Type	Text	Name of the type of enforcement
	Description	Memo	Longer description of the nature of the enforcement

Rules may be permanently applicable or may apply for a particular period. Tables 8-2 and 8-3 provide for rules that are in force for specific times or are enforced for particular reasons.

Table 8-4   RuleType

	Field Name	Data Type	Description
⊶	ID	AutoNumber	Unique identifier for the rule type
	TypeName	Text	The textual name of the type
	Description	Memo	Expanded description of the type

Rules can be classified in a taxonomy of types (Table 8-4). In Chapter 4, we discussed a simple top-level breakdown into structural, behavioral, and definitional types. You may want to modify or extend this for your own situation. In Chapter 3, we saw the value of defining rules in accordance with particular patterns, which can be used as templates for the creation and maintenance of rules. Again, we can exploit the structuring capabilities of XML to store the template in a Text field (see Table 8-5).

Table 8-5   Template

Field Name	Data Type	Description
☞ ID	AutoNumber	Unique identifier for the template
Name	Text	Human-readable name of the template
Structure	Memo	The template, expressed in XML

Various kinds of authorities are involved with rules: the expert who was the original source for the definition, the business owner who has to sign off the rule, the project manager who deems it in scope, and so on. All can be accommodated by these tables, along with a link to the documentation that supports their authority and the date that this was effective. See Tables 8-6, 8-7, and 8-8.

Table 8-6   RuleAuthority

Field Name	Data Type	Description
☞ RuleID	Number	Link to Rule
☞ AuthorityID	Number	Link to responsible Authority
AuthorityType	Text	The responsibility assumed by Authority
AuthorizationReference	Text	Reference to supporting documentation
AuthorizationDate	Date/Time	When the responsibility came into force

Table 8-7   Authority

Field Name	Data Type	Description
☞ ID	AutoNumber	Unique identifier for Authority
NameOfAuthority	Text	The person involved
PositionOfAuthority	Text	The person's position in the organization

Table 8-8   AuthorityType

Field Name	Data Type	Description
☞ Type	Text	Name of the type of Authority
Description	Memo	Expanded description of Authority type

Table 8-9   BusinessCategory

	Field Name	Data Type	Description
🔑	ID	AutoNumber	Unique identifier for the category
	CategoryName	Text	Human-readable name of the category
	Structure	Memo	Expanded description

Table 8-9 allows rules to be allocated to one of a number of potential categories with business meaning: core business, legislation, productivity, regulation, and security, for example. If you want to assign the same rule to multiple business categories, you will need to introduce a link table at this point to handle the many-to-many relationship.

Rule cross-references   The next set of tables provides for various ways of cross-referencing rules. You may want to add more references of this sort to meet your own local conditions. Figure 8-8 shows the tables we discuss here. The rule table is the same one that we've already seen, so we'll focus on the other tables in Figure 8-8.

Table 8-10   RuleKeyword

	Field Name	Data Type	Description
🔑	RuleID	Number	Link to Rule
🔑	KeywordID	Number	Link to Keyword

Table 8-11   Keyword

	Field Name	Data Type	Description
🔑	ID	AutoNumber	Unique identifier for the keyword
	KeywordName	Text	Human-readable name of the keyword
	KeywordType	Text	Classification of keyword usage
	KeywordExpansion	Memo	Optional expansion of keyword

Keywords (Tables 8-10 and 8-11) are an ad hoc way of tagging rules with terms that are meaningful to the analysts but don't necessarily fall into any of the stricter classifications provided. In Chapter 4, for example, we saw a rule that prohibited students from receiving a loan from VBB; that rule might be tagged with the keywords "student" and "loan."

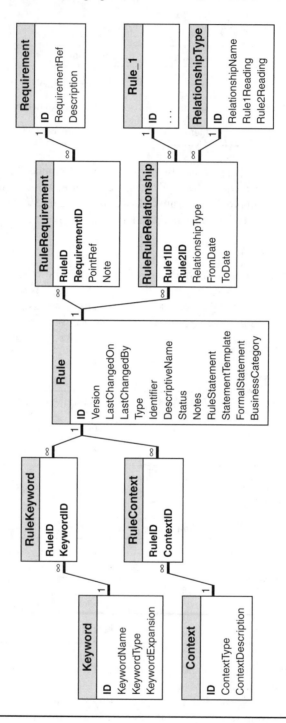

Figure 8-8   Rule cross-references

Table 8-12   RuleContext

Field Name	Data Type	Description
RuleID	Number	Link to Rule
ContextID	Number	Link to Context

Table 8-13   Context

Field Name	Data Type	Description
ID	AutoNumber	Unique identifier for the context
ContextType	Text	Human-readable context type
ContextDescription	Memo	Further detail on the context

It's useful to be able to discuss a group of rules together, perhaps in a review session. The context may be somewhat ad-hoc, such as "the rules associated with the customer service use cases," and a particular rule may be considered in several contexts. See Tables 8-12 and 8-13.

Table 8-14   RuleRequirement

Field Name	Data Type	Description
RuleID	Number	Link to Rule
RequirementID	Number	Link to Requirement
PointRef	Text	Pointer to particular place in the requirement source
Note	Text	Optional note on this reference

Table 8-15   Requirement

Field Name	Data Type	Description
ID	AutoNumber	Unique identifier for the requirement
RequirementRef	Text	Reference to the requirement source
Description	Memo	Description of requirement source

Tables 8-14 and 8-15 allow a rule to be linked back to a specific requirement: a source document, interview notes, workshop results, and so on. All should have a quotable identity: not necessarily a document number but perhaps something as

simple as "notes of a meeting with J. Jones on August 15, 2002." The point reference allows a specific place in the requirement source to be identified, like a
paragraph number.

Table 8-16   RuleRuleRelationship

	Field Name	Data Type	Description
⚷	Rule1ID	Number	Link to rule 1
⚷	Rule2ID	Number	Link to rule 2
	RelationshipType	Number	Link to RelationshipType
	FromDate	Date/Time	When the relationship becomes effective
	ToDate	Date/Time	When the relationship expires

Table 8-17   RelationshipType

	Field Name	Data Type	Description
⚷	ID	AutoNumber	Unique identifier for the relationship type
	RelationshipName	Text	Textual name of the type of relationship
	Rule1Reading	Text	The way the relationship looks from rule 1
	Rule2Reading	Text	The way the relationship looks from rule 2

Rules can relate to one another in several ways, but normally only one at a
time (see Tables 8-16 and 8-17). Examples are rule sets (a rule contains subrules),
similarity or conflict between rules, a rule that covers an exception to another rule,
a rule that supersedes another rule, and so on.

The tables allow these kinds of relationship to be recorded. The Rule table
described in Table 8-1 makes two appearances in Figure 8-8. The tables shown as
Rule and Rule_1 in Figure 8-8 correspond to rule1 and rule2, respectively, in
Tables 8-16 and 8-17. (This slightly confusing numbering is automatically generated by Access.) The two readings of the relationship provide the text to explain
the perspectives of each rule. For example, in an exception relationship, we could
say, "rule1 (has an exception) rule2" and "rule2 (is an exception to) rule1."

The tables as they stand support the linking of only two rules in one single
way. If a need for multiple relationships emerged, the extension would be straightforward.

Models and realizations   The final set of tables we look at focus on the traceability of rules from the business models that support their primary definition to

their realizations in an information system. As before, the rule table is the same one we've already discussed (see Tables 8-18 and 8-19). These two tables provide the link back from the rule to a business model. The same rule could appear in any number of models or none. RefInModel in Table 8-18 allows the rule to take on a reference label that's unique to its appearance in a particular model. This is distinct from Identifier, which is the name it holds independently of any existence in a model.

Table 8-18   RuleModel

	Field Name	Data Type	Description
🔑	RuleID	Number	Link to Rule
🔑	ModelID	Number	Link to Model
	RefInModel	Text	Pointer to location of Rule in Model
	Note	Memo	Optional additional text on the relationship

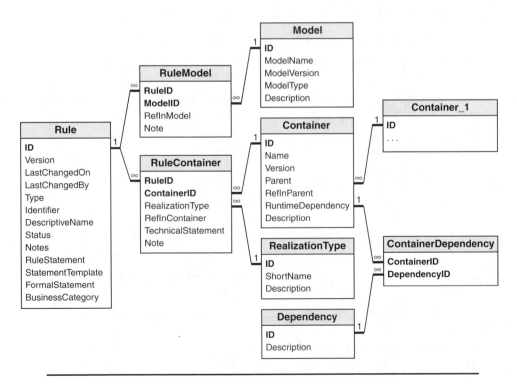

Figure 8-9   Rule model and realization locations

Table 8-19   Model

	Field Name	Data Type	Description
🔑	ID	AutoNumber	Unique identifier for the Model
	ModelName	Text	Textual name of the Model
	ModelVersion	Text	The version number of the Model
	ModelType	Text	The type of Model
	Description	Memo	An optional expanded description of the Model

Table 8-20   RuleContainer

	Field Name	Data Type	Description
🔑	RuleID	Number	Link to Rule
🔑	ContainerID	Number	Link to Container
	RealizationType	Number	Link to RealizationType
	RefInContainer	Text	Pointer to location of the rule in Container
	TechnicalStatement	Memo	Expression of the rule suited to this realization
	Note	Memo	Optional additional text on the relationship

Table 8-21   Container

	Field Name	Data Type	Description
🔑	ID	AutoNumber	Unique identifier for Container
	Name	Text	Textual reference to Container
	Version	Text	The version number of Container
	Parent	Number	Optionally, the parent container of this container
	RefInParent	Text	Name this container is known by in its parent
	RuntimeDependency	Number	Link to runtime dependency for this container
	Description	Memo	An optional expanded description of the container

Table 8-22 RealizationType

Field Name	Data Type	Description
ID	AutoNumber	Unique identifier for the realization type
ShortName	Text	Short descriptive name for the realization type
Description	Memo	Description of the realization type

Tables 8-20 and 8-21 provide a flexible way of relating a rule to any number of realizations; the table Container_1 in Figure 8-9 represents another instance of Container. Each realization is assumed to be located in an identifiable container—which could be a software module, a component, a database, a rules engine, or whatever—which forms identifiable RealizationTypes (Table 8-22). The rule will have a reference within a particular container, but this will be different from its reference in any other realization. A restatement of the rule in technical terms suited to the particular container may also be provided.

Containers can be nested, and the tables support parent/child relationships between different containers but without enforcing the correspondence of rules to any particular level of container. Through their containers, the rules may indirectly depend on a feature or a facility that has to be in place to support their operation. Tables 8-23 and 8-24 allow such dependencies to be identified.

Table 8-23 ContainerDependency

Field Name	Data Type	Description
ContainerID	Number	Link to Container
DependencyID	Number	Link to Dependency

Table 8-24 Dependency

Field Name	Data Type	Description
ID	AutoNumber	Unique identifier for the dependency
Description	Memo	Textual reference to the container

Extending the repository Given this outline, it should be straightforward to extend the basic design to include any additional features that you might need. One particular feature that's missing is any method for relating rules to other elements within the business model. You should seriously consider adding this to make sure that the model ties together nicely.

For example, if a use case description involves rule-based decisions, it's useful to record the relationship between the two. If the use case changes in the future, you can then rapidly identify which rules might be affected. Likewise, if the rules change for another reason, you can easily find any use case that might need to be checked.

A particularly important kind of cross-reference is the relationship between a rule and the terms it uses from the fact model. It's essential that the terms used in the rules are properly defined in the fact model, so this sort of support is useful as the rules are being created. It's also a boon during reviews to check for overlaps, missing rules, and so on. Finally, the cross-referencing comes into play again whenever changes are made to the model, reducing the possibility that errors will creep in.

The intramodel references are not included in the Access repository design, for two reasons.

1. The references will be dependent on the choices you have made in defining your business architecture. Without having these pinned down, the space of possibilities is too large to handle sensibly within the confines of this book.

2. A decent modeling tool should provide a large portion of this functionality. You can then target your effort on any gaps that remain instead of replicating something that's already workable.

If you do want to add intramodel references to your rule repository, you can use the rule realization tables as examples of how it might be done but with business model elements replacing the implementation containers.

8.6   Rule management summary

Caring for your rules and models doesn't end when their definition is complete. They may persist over a very long period, and they need to be managed through their life cycles. Change is normal, and a clear policy to cope with it is essential, particularly as you're likely to have to deal with multiple interrelated elements. A good strategy for reducing the effort involved, and also reducing the possibilities for error, is to automate the housekeeping wherever you can.

Before releasing into service rules or any changes to them, make sure that sensible preparations have been made. Test the implementation properly, and plan ahead to deal with major rollouts. Operational support processes should already be in place, but you should be alert to the need to modify them if necessary.

As with most other pieces of an information system, living with business rules is much easier if you have a decent set of tools. Direct support for rules has not figured largely in previous generations of tools, but this is beginning to change quite rapidly.

Of all the tools you need, the most important is probably some form of rule repository, which can act as the center of your management activities. If you don't have one, it's reasonably straightforward to create one, using common desktop tools.

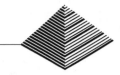

PART IV

THE ROLE OF BUSINESS RULES

9

A Wider View

9.1 Marshaling intellectual resources

In this chapter, we step back a little from the specifics of defining, building, and managing information systems to look at how business rules and models link to a wider set of ideas. All industry sectors have a growing awareness of the need to make better use of the intellectual resources on hand. Such resources are sometimes described as an organization's intellectual capital, partly to emphasize their value alongside more conventional capital resources, such as buildings, plant, and machinery.

We can say the same thing in a more down-to-earth way. What differentiates two companies in the same sector often boils down to the quality and the application of their know-how. Successful companies *know how* to do something better than their competitors: raising financing, bringing products to market, operating efficiently, or perhaps several of these simultaneously.

Unfortunately, the true value of this resource may become apparent only when some know-how that was taken for granted suddenly disappears.

- A company downsizes in pursuit of efficiency, only to find that a key element of its recipe for business success has been lost in the process.
- After outsourcing a major facility, a company discovers that a key differentiator has been replaced by a mundane service that's just the same as that of all its competitors.
- A key staff member retires or resigns, and a rash of acute and unexpected problems start to appear in what seemed to be a routine business function.

The collective knowledge of an organization should be one of its greatest assets. Only fairly recently has it become an explicit business concern, under the general banner of *knowledge management.*

9.1.1   Knowledge management

Knowledge management is a term that's in fashion, and most medium to large organizations have a knowledge-management policy in place. Unfortunately, the term doesn't have clearly defined boundaries or a crisp definition and so is sometimes hijacked by unscrupulous vendors to rename earlier offerings to gain them an additional lease on life. The result is a certain amount of confusion; most people, however, agree that the term includes at least the identification, control, and use of knowledge assets. Following are a few of the factors that make knowledge management attractive.

Maintaining barriers to competition   A number of industries, pharmaceuticals being the most obvious example, have long relied on protecting their specialized knowledge through patents and other forms of legal protection. In some cases, this practice is becoming problematic because of the pace of change and the levels of investment needed to capitalize on the investment. For example, pharmaceutical companies are continually driven to develop new drugs, but the patent may have only a few years left to run by the time the drug reaches the market. Knowledge of how to bring new drugs to market earlier could, potentially, be just as valuable as the drugs themselves.

Seeking market advantage   The appropriate application of knowledge can provide significant market advantage in its own right. Many commercial organizations now have customer relationship management (CRM) efforts under way to improve their retention of valuable customers. Enterprise-wide information systems can make crucial knowledge available rapidly across the whole organization, increasing its responsiveness to customer needs and changing market conditions. Data mining and other techniques can be used to refine raw data first into information and then into knowledge to confer a powerful market edge. For example, it's widely believed that telephone companies are reluctant to release precise details of telephone traffic because that data provides them with a privileged view of a sensitive and accurate economic indicator.

Assessing shareholder value   Understanding how to value themselves correctly is a problem faced by an increasing number of companies. The traditional accounting measures do not always appear to give a true reflection of the worth of the company. For example, Microsoft's market capitalization is appreciably greater than that of many other companies with greater balance sheet assets. The difference stems at least in part from the market perception that the intellectual capital, or knowledge, owned by Microsoft has greater value. Traditionally, this asset does not appear as a balance sheet item, although there are some parallels in the growing valuation of some other intangible assets, such as the value of brands owned by retail companies. The U.S. Internal Revenue Service has issued guidelines on what it believes to be appropriate practices in this field, and many companies can see great advantage in being able to quantify and to demonstrate the growth of value of such assets, even to the extent of including them in their annual reports.

Managing human resources   A continuing trend across many industry sectors is to regard employees not as simple operatives but as knowledge workers, empowered to use their abilities in a variety of ways for the good of the company. Interestingly, this often also has the effect of increasing productivity. This shift in perspective creates a need for better ways of managing employees to allow their knowledge to be used in the most effective way, free from artificial barriers. It also points to the need to maintain the freshness and relevance of that knowledge and to increase it wherever practical. A growth in individual knowledge then also becomes a growth in organizational knowledge.

Capturing know-how   Many companies rely heavily on the know-how they can bring to bear and often make this their sole business rationale. Typical examples are management consultancies, law firms, and consulting engineers. Many of these knowledge-dependent companies, particularly those with the greatest IT awareness, have recognized the need to develop systems to capture experience and to encode it in tangible form. This allows the knowledge to be archived for security and reused to raise the average level of competence in the company. This is especially true in project-based organizations, such as software and aerospace companies.

Interest in knowledge management has been helped by a number of other enabling developments, such as

- The growing use of electronic communications within organizations, including e-mail and corporate intranets
- New approaches to valuing companies, away from exclusive concentration on such tangibles as cash, stock-in-hand, and property, as accountancy practice tries to reflect the growing importance and value of intellectual property
- Technical developments that make it possible to record knowledge in a structured and reusable form

The last item is especially relevant to the concerns of this book, and we'll return to look at more details shortly.

9.1.2   Developing knowledge management

An organization is likely to pass through a number of stages in progressing knowledge management, reflecting its growing maturity and its ability to systematically recognize and apply knowledge. In practice, these stages would overlap and may not progress at the same speed over all parts of the organization. The stages can be roughly summarized as follows:

- *Awareness.* Managers in the organization begin to take notice of the dependency of the organization on key areas of knowledge. This awareness may be triggered by a particular event, such as acute problems caused by the retirement or resignation of a key staff member.

- *Auditing.* The organization takes stock of the knowledge it uses or needs by asking such questions as: What business processes depend on it? How crucial is it? Can it be obtained or replaced easily? How specific is it to the organization or to the sector in which we operate?

- *Policy.* A policy on knowledge management is defined, often in conjunction with the appointment of a manager with specific responsibility for knowledge management.

- *Capture and representation.* Measures are put in place to capture knowledge, including putting tacit knowledge into tangible form and refining low-level data into high-level information.

- *Preservation.* Crucial knowledge is encoded in a structured form and maintained systematically as a standard activity in normal workaday activities.

- *Enhancement.* Knowledge is systematically enriched or extended. Learning, both individual and organizational, is encouraged and acknowledged.

- *Dissemination.* Knowledge is made available for reuse across relevant parts of the organization through such means as training, best-practice guides, workflow, and groupware. In the early days, the main focus is likely to be on providing staff with easy access to internal documents.

For our purposes, the most interesting of these activities is the capture and representation of knowledge. The better we carry this out, the greater the value we can extract. Unfortunately, this activity is typically done in a fairly shallow way, leaving relatively few glimpses of the underlying richness of information that we could exploit in the form of business rules.

9.2   Capturing knowledge

9.2.1   What's the problem?

From the preceding brief outline, we can see that knowledge management promises significant business benefits, even if it's collected, refined, distributed, and reused through traditional means. A low-tech approach, such as writing down your valuable know-how on a piece of paper and using carbons for replication, would still be following the basic principles. However, for the last 30 years or more, it's been easier to type it up and to photocopy the results for distribution. Over the last 10 to 15 years, electronic media have gradually superseded the distribution of photocopied manuals. Indeed, for a brief period in the 1990s, several so-called knowledge-management products did very little more than give people electronic access to documents.

But this misses a crucial piece of the puzzle. In fact, it's exactly the same gap that we find in conventional requirements analysis: a lack of adequate structure. Note the word *adequate* here. A requirements specification—an example of a collection of knowledge—does indeed have a structure, but it's the structure of the document, not of the knowledge. It has sections, pages, paragraphs, and the like, but these concepts have been inherited from the world of publishing as a way of organizing (primarily textual) material.

Imagine that you're a computer. You can navigate a document structure pretty well, at least in one sense. You can easily find that the second word in paragraph 3 on page 128 is "database," as is the fourth word in paragraph 1 on page 256. But how would you know whether these pointed to the same thing or to different things? One might be talking about database systems in general; the other, about a specific database. Poor computer; there's no way you can work this out from the structure of the document.

In fact, you have no reliable way of working it out at all, because the text is coded in a form that's completely opaque (to a computer like you): natural language.

Full natural-language understanding has been a goal of computer science from the time of Alan Turing, more than 50 years ago. Turing laid the mathematical foundations that underpin modern computer science in a seminal paper published in 1936. In the 1940s he was arguably the first person to make serious use of what we now know as a computer. However, decades of subsequent work by thousands of very bright and dedicated people have failed to solve the natural language problem in a completely general way. This might indicate that it's just a tad difficult.

Some successes have been gained by reducing the infinite range of possibilities of unrestricted English or Urdu or Chinese or whatever language you prefer. One way is to restrict the domain of discourse—roughly, the things you're prepared to talk about—to a limited and predefined set of options. Another is to accept only linguistic constructs that fit particular templates with fixed interpretations.

Terms such as *restrict, limit, predefined, templates,* and the like indicate that we're on the trail of structure again. Here's the truth of the matter: If we want to give a machine a chance of interpreting the meaning behind a piece of text or a drawing, we have to be prepared do some work up front, to codify the intended meaning in a regular and predictable way.

Going back to where we started from, it's now clear why knowledge management tends to stick at the level of electronic distribution of documents. Taking matters any further requires a significant step up in complexity in a couple of ways. First, you have to restructure the knowledge in a form that a machine can share. Second, you also have to add in all the missing bits that you assumed human readers of a document could supply from their own experience. This is difficult to do. In fact, it's spawned a whole subfield of computer science, called knowledge representation.

9.2.2 Knowledge representation

The good news is that representing knowledge in machine-readable form can be done in numerous ways. This has been an active area of research in computer science from its earliest days. The bad news is that many of the ideas don't travel well when transplanted from research into a business environment, and we need to be selective about what's likely to work in practice when we come to business modeling.

To show the general flavor of how structure can be imposed, we'll pick out just a few approaches. They're meant to be representative rather than comprehensive. The whole range of ideas, even in summary form, would occupy a very big book indeed. The techniques covered here encapsulate some important ideas that have been around for a while now and that, as we'll see later, have gradually evolved under various guises to become elements of what we now call business models.

The interest in capturing knowledge traces back to the very earliest days of computing, in the 1950s. At that time, attention was directed at getting computers to do things that were regarded as being challenging for human beings: playing chess being a typical example. The assumption was that if computers could do difficult things, it would be trivial to make them do easy things. The reverse has proved to be the case. Chess machines that can beat most human beings are now sold cheaply in supermarkets, but intelligent robots still can't come anywhere near the all-round ability of a three-year-old child.

The reason is not brute-force processing power; it's the breadth of knowledge that's required. To carry out most everyday actions, we unconsciously use a vast array of knowledge that we've acquired, again unconsciously, throughout our lives. In contrast, a lot of tasks that are considered clever rely on a deep but very narrow range of knowledge.

Imagine that you're told that there's gold somewhere in California but are not given any specific reference. Could you set up a profitable mining operation? Probably not: at least, not on the basis of that information alone. On the other hand, if you're told that gold can be found in specific places around rivers near San Francisco, you become part of the Gold Rush. It's similar with knowledge. Within narrow and clearly marked boundaries, it's possible to pan for nuggets of wisdom with a high degree of success. The more general the level of performance required, the wider the range of knowledge that may be needed, and the more difficult it becomes to identify it and to capture it.

The reaction to this, from roughly 1960 to 1990, was to focus on the automation of specialist tasks. Many organizations have individuals with very high degrees of competence in their particular areas. Automation of this expertise has proved valuable in many cases: for consistency of performance, protection against loss of key staff, handling greater workloads, and so on. These so-called expert systems, although useful, were overhyped and limited. The deep and narrow focus of these systems was also at odds with the shallow and wide scope of most business systems, as highlighted in Figure 9-1. However, the activity surrounding them resulted in a number of techniques that are useful in other contexts.

In retrospect, we can always see things that were perhaps not so obvious 10, 20, 30 years ago. The artificial intelligence gold rush of the 1980s represented a small claim that was soon mined out. But to make progress, the miners had to

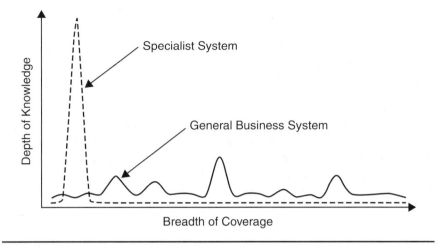

Figure 9-1   Breadth and depth of knowledge

develop a lot of new techniques and concepts, many of which had merits that were not fully appreciated at the time, perhaps because they were focused in a very specific and limited way.

In the remainder of this chapter, we take a more detailed look at some examples of how these ideas have progressed and see how they can be used for business knowledge in a realistic context. For reasons of space, we pick out just a few areas showing different ways in which business knowledge can be used. Some of these ideas have been around for several decades and some are comparatively new, but together they should give a reasonable idea of the wider context surrounding business rules and business models at the present time.

9.2.3   Enriched models

Semantic networks   Semantic networks, a combination of data structure and presentational conventions, are made up of *nodes* to represent concepts and *links* to represent relationships between concepts. The designer of a network is free to select only the concepts and relationships that are immediately relevant. Usually, the concepts will have many other possible relationships, but those not relevant to the problem at hand are omitted to avoid clutter.

One of the good features of semantic networks is that they can be presented so as to be readable in a straightforward way by nontechnicians. To be sure, a pictorial representation can hide a fair amount of computational complexity, but this at least achieves one of our long-standing goals: ease of understanding by the business owner. Figure 9-2 shows a fragment illustrating how relationships in an industrial setting might be modeled. A real network would obviously require a lot more detail to be useful.

Such networks can be encoded as data structures, allowing information about relationships to be used by a set of computer programs to navigate through the network in various ways. It's also possibly to reflect changes in knowledge, perhaps gained through automated learning, by changing the structure.

The basic ideas behind semantic networks have been around for some time. According to the influential *Handbook of Artificial Intelligence*: "Node-and-link structure captures something essential about symbols and pointers in symbolic computation and about association in the psychology of memory" (Barr and Feigenbaum 1981). This statement was already summarizing some 20 years of experience with semantic networks.

Two types of relationships are particularly common.

1. The first of these is the *specialization/generalization* relationship, usually denoted by *ako* (a kind of) or *is-a* (is a). The literature is somewhat inconsistent about the difference between ako and is-a. One interpretation is that ako represents relationships between classes of things (human *ako* → mammal *ako* → animal *ako* → animate object *ako* →, and so on), whereas is-a relates to a particular instance of a thing to its class (Alice *is-a* customer). To avoid confusion, the latter kinds of relationships are shown as instance-of in Figure 9-2.

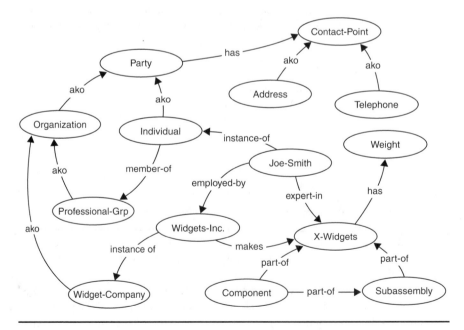

Figure 9-2   Example semantic network

2. The second common relationship is the *whole/part* relationship, which might be denoted by such terms as part-of or has-part, depending on the direction in which the relationship is followed. Such relationships occur when entities form a natural group, such as the employees of a particular company, or when an entity is composed of other entities, such as the engine, chassis, wheels, and other components of an automobile.

The nodes represent concepts, and the complexity or simplicity of what they stand for is entirely at the discretion of the network designer. For example, in trying to capture the essence of the relationship between an online financial business and its customers, it might be important to include such concepts as customer age but to omit others that are not immediately relevant, such as shoe size. However, this would not be true for an online shoe store. Similarly, the model needs to include only those links that provide some value. In short, the success of a semantic network depends to a great extent on the choice of what to put in and what to leave out. You might like to reflect on the similarity of this to business modeling.

Although they were used extensively in quite a few experimental systems, semantic networks never achieved the widespread acceptance that was anticipated in the early 1980s. In retrospect, this probably stemmed from several factors.

- The limited graphical capabilities of low-cost PC platforms at the time made it difficult to design semantic networks in the typical business IT environment of the day.
- The intermingling of theories about human cognition created an impression that semantic networks were aimed primarily at problems in experimental psychology.
- The lack of a widely supported set of conventions for describing semantic networks inhibited the development of good tool support.

In fact, a number of the ideas behind semantic networks were absorbed into the database community and later resurfaced in slightly different forms. Take a look at Figure 9-3. Well, well, it's one of our old friends: a UML class diagram. It's drawn to cover the same ground as the semantic network of Figure 9-2, and the similarities are fairly obvious. Apart from trivial differences, like the shape of the symbols, a few other points are worth noting.

- Concepts (nodes) in the semantic network can be represented as UML classes. The class structure allows both data and behavior to be represented in a consistent way.
- The *ako* links in a semantic network are shown as generalization associations in UML.
- The *part-of* links in the semantic network are shown as aggregation associations in UML, using the diamond symbol on the association line.
- The *instance-of* links in the semantic network are not shown directly in the UML class diagram, because they correspond to instances of the objects.

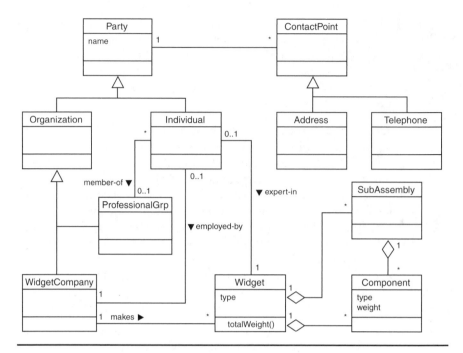

Figure 9-3   A semantic network as a UML class diagram

- Simple properties, indicated by such links as *has* in a semantic network, are modeled as attributes and/or operations.
- Other types of links are modeled as ad hoc associations in UML. These links can be labeled on the UML class diagram to indicate their function, in much the same way as on the diagram of a semantic net.

Probably the biggest difference is the way that individual instances are treated. In UML, classes and objects are separated onto different types of diagram; in the semantic network, they're interleaved.

In spite of the differences, it's clear that we're well able to capture semantic information of this sort within our business model. That semantic information can be used to support more complex applications of the knowledge.

CD, scripts, and MOPs   The notion of conceptual dependency (CD) was developed by Roger Schank and others (Schank and Abelson 1977; Schank 1982) to represent commonplace objects and events, using constructs that reflect how people seem to think about them. Its original application was in representing the mental pictures that might lie behind natural-language statements. Very often, a sentence contains a lot of implicit meaning that's not immediately obvious from the words alone. We rely on underlying assumptions that are shared by both parties in a communication to carry these hidden messages.

For example, the sentence "Earblaster HiFi sold a Dominator system to Alice" indicates a transfer of goods in one direction; Dominator is probably a particularly impressive hi-fi system. But the sentence also implies a transfer of money in the other direction, even though money is not explicitly mentioned.

CD breaks situations, such as the hi-fi deal, into *conceptualizations,* which are built up from particular types of objects linked in ways that are constrained by a set of CD rules. The primitive elements follow:

AA	Action aiders: rarely used modifiers that alter the meaning of an action, such as the speed with which it happens
ACT	Actions: something that's done by an actor to or with an object
LOC	Locations: where the ACT is happening; a source or a destination for an action
PA	Picture aides: object attributes or states that add important details to its description
PP	Picture producers: physical objects that play a role in the conceptualization, such as an object that's being acted on, a recipient of an action, and so on
T	Times: an absolute or relative time point or time interval

ACTs have further specializations, which define the kind of action that's happening. Some examples include the following:

ATRANS	Transfer of an abstract relationship, such as ownership or control
PTRANS	Physical transfer of an object from one location to another
MTRANS	Transfer of mental information from one actor to another or within an actor
PROPEL	Application of physical force to an object, whether or not a movement results
ATTEND	Focusing a specific sensory input of an actor toward a stimulus
MBUILD	Construction of new information from old information

An active conceptualization can be described using terms that define an actor, an action, an object, the direction of the action, and, possibly, an instrument that's effecting the action. A structure for Alices's hi-fi purchase might include something like the following:

Actor	Earblaster HiFi	Actor	Alice
Action	PTRANS	Action	ATRANS
Object	Dominator system	Object	Money
From	Earblaster HiFi	From	Alice
To	Alice	To	Earblaster HiFi

Obviously, some of this text would be replaced by references to business objects in a real e-commerce system; for instance Alice would probably be represented by a customer code, but the general idea should be clear.

This is useful, but we commonly encounter whole sequences of actions that happen over and over again in a very similar way. To accommodate these sequences, we can use the notion of a *script,* which differs from the sense of the word as used in programming and dynamic Web pages. Here, a script is a description of a stereotyped sequence of actions, with blank slots that can be filled in with the values that apply in a specific situation.

For example, we could have a script for the sequence *online purchase,* which might include steps like the following.

1. Customer browses the Web to find a site offering the best deal on the required goods.

2. Customer places an order for the goods on the selected site, giving payment details.

3. Retailer packs the goods, transfers them to a delivery agent, and takes payment.

4. Delivery agent transfers the goods to the customer.

5. Customer accepts and checks the goods.

Again, this is a simplification that omits the full details needed for a real system: What if the goods are out of stock? What if an invalid credit card is offered for payment? What if the goods arrive damaged? Nonetheless, it's clear that a scheme of this sort could have conceptualizations for the various procedures involved and slots for such variables as customer, goods, payment details, delivery agent, and so on. Whenever we want to describe an online purchase situation, we simply need to trot out our predefined script, saving a great deal of time and effort.

Scripts can be a convenient way of packaging sequences together, but we can go even further. A script deals with a fixed scenario, but elements in one script can appear in a very similar form in many others. For example, our earlier Web-based sequence has some similarities with the equivalent set of activities carried out in a store. Maybe we should consider this sequence simply as a special case of retail purchase. But this in turn might just be a special case of commercial transaction.

It would be nice if we could identify reusable pieces of activity that we could combine in flexible ways. One approach to doing this uses units called *memory organization packets* (MOPs). Again, the basic idea has its roots in attempts to describe human cognitive processes.

The most basic element of MOPs is the *scene*. A scene takes place over a fairly short time interval; longer durations require a succession of scenes. The three basic scene types are shown in Table 9-1. Sequences of events are described by a series of scenes linked together physically, socially, or by personal goal. Each event is described by a set of scenes, including at least one of each of the three types in Table 9-1. The MOP structures can be arranged in a flexible way to define stereotyped patterns that correspond to various common situations. For instance, a description of buying and listening to a new disc might include each of the three example scenes in Table 9-1.

Table 9-1   MOP scene types

Scene Type	Usage	Example
Physical	Describes events that take place at a particular location	M-MUSIC-STORE: • Browse CD displays • Select goods • Proceed to checkout
Societal	Describes interactions between actors	M-PURCHASE: • Place order • Check availability • Make payment
Personal	Describes actions in pursuit of an actor's individual goals	M-PLAY-DISC: • Load CD into hi-fi • Select track(s) • Listen with pleasure

How do these ideas relate to our immediate concerns? In Chapter 2, we looked at the various elements that make up a business model. One of the most commonly used elements is a *business narrative,* usually in the form of a use case. We've already bemoaned the fact that use cases often have little in the way of a consistent structure and that what they do have tends to be documentation structure rather than knowledge structure.

What the preceding ideas illustrate is that we don't need to throw away the ease of use of a textual description. Instead, we can find ways of enhancing its value by adding more structure and by marking selected terms and phrases within the narrative to indicate their purpose. Although current tools don't support this, it would be fairly straightforward to add tags so that they could be suppressed for a business user's view—much as HTML tags are hidden on a Web page—but retained for exploitation by subsequent processes. This would allow use cases to be properly linked to the rest of the business model and would dramatically increase their value.

9.2.4   Packaging for reuse

Knowledge-based systems   "Knowledge-based system" roughly equates to "expert system" in describing a way of both recording knowledge and automating its application. In their most popular form, knowledge-based systems rely on *production rules,* defined in a particular format, each of which represents a small unit of knowledge. Several times in this book, we've had cause to sigh over the confusions of terminology, and this is another one. The word *production* does not refer here to industrial production but to the way that the rules produce results.

Production rules do have some degree of overlap with business rules but also have some associated features that don't necessarily carry over. In particular, business rules deliberately decouple rule specification from rule implementation. We've already come across production rules in a previous chapter in the discussion of rules engines. Here we touch on some of the more subtle implications.

Figure 9-4 shows a production system stripped down to its barest essentials. All the data used by or produced by the rules is—conceptually—held in a store called the working memory. When a match is detected between a data pattern and the *if* part of a production rule, a reference to the rule is placed on an agenda. If several rules match patterns in the working memory, a scheduler selects one rule from those waiting on the agenda and activates, or *fires,* it. The rule produces its results and by doing so changes the contents of the working memory. Rules that previously matched may no longer do so, resulting in a new agenda. The cycle of rule selection and firing repeats until a predetermined stopping condition is reached.

One way of thinking about production systems is to imagine the rules as tiny fragments of program swimming in a soup of data. Each rule can ingest a packet of data, perhaps eliminating it in the process, and expel new data. The sequence in which the little program elements are activated is not predefined by a programmer. They activate themselves when they detect a possibility of doing something useful.

The reality is not quite so pure as this. It's necessary to provide some degree of control because the underlying machine can do only one thing at a time. If several rules are eligible to fire at a particular moment, it's a question of deciding which one to pick. In practice, all production rule systems must have a scheduling strategy to resolve this. The simplest is probably lexical order: The rules are prioritized according to their sequence in a source file. But this is suitable only for trivial systems, and it has the disadvantage of hiding knowledge about how to solve a problem in the order that rules are listed in a text file. A more useful technique is

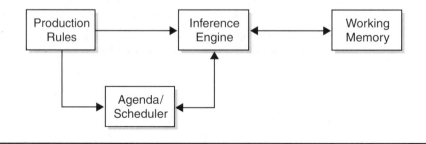

Figure 9-4   Simplified production system

to give the rules a salience value through which they can declare themselves to be important or ever so humble.

Here's a simple example of the need for care. Let's assume that our working memory contains information about Widget parts, looking something like the following:

```
(part-of   X-widget    Baseplate-1)
(part-of   Baseplate-1   Acme-joint)
```

Putting this into a normal sentence, a type of widget called an X-widget contains a part called Baseplate-1, and Baseplate-1 contains an Acme-joint. It's pretty obvious that the hierarchical relationship is as shown in Figure 9-5.

What if we wanted to flatten the hierarchy and find all the components in an X-widget, whether or not they were in a subassembly? We could do it with a rule.

```
(defrule  get-parts  "Finds all the subparts of an assembly"
        (part-of    ?a   ?b)
        (part-of    ?b   ?c)
 =>
        (assert  (part-of  ?a   ?c)))
```

Basically, this says that if *c* is part of *b* and *b* is part of *a, c* is part of *a.* Given these two facts, this rule would add the following new fact to the working memory:

```
(part-of   X-widget    Acme-joint)
```

Just what we wanted! Unfortunately, there are some side effects. As well as giving us the required information for X-widgets, the rule also produces it for Y-widgets and anything else that happens to be present, flooding the working

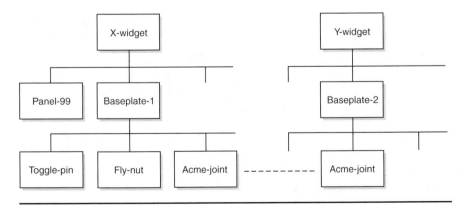

Figure 9-5   Widget hierarchy

memory with loads of facts that we aren't interested in. Also, the rule will pounce on any matching patterns as soon as they appear and make the production, even if we're not interested in a parts breakdown at that time.

Here's another issue. A claim made for production systems is that applications are easier to modify than is a corresponding procedural program. Merely adding extra rules to an existing system is all that's required to incorporate new knowledge. Unfortunately, such optimism is not borne out in practice. Although rules appear to be independent, they interact in subtle ways through the traces they leave in working memory. These interactions can be difficult to predict: Differences in the patterns produced by one rule can ripple through many others and finally cause an unexpected result in an area that appeared to be entirely separate.

These kinds of issues often surface in *forward-chaining* systems of this type. The problems are fixable but at the cost of increasingly complex rules and control structures. In the extreme, deciding how to solve the problem can become as difficult as doing it, and orchestrating the application of knowledge is raised to an important task in its own right.

A useful technique for more complex problems is the approach taken in *blackboard systems,* which segment the rules into groups called *knowledge sources* (KSs), each representing a particular area of expertise. The working memory is also segmented into areas with different types of structures. Figure 9-6 shows a simplified general scheme.

Each KS can be regarded as a small production system in its own right, implementing a small and well-defined area of knowledge. In fact, because of the isolation of one KS from another, they need not have the same internal mechanisms; some could contain rules; some, look-up tables; and some, procedural code. The combined effect of the KSs working in concert is like a group of human experts collaborating by chalking their thoughts onto a shared blackboard, which was the original inspiration for the approach, as well as the name.

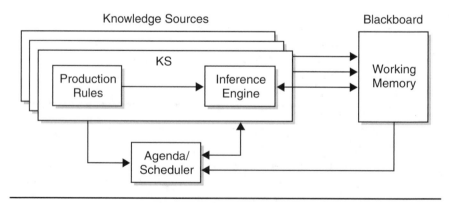

Figure 9-6   Simplified blackboard system

Knowledge-based systems have achieved some notable successes, particularly in automating the application of a narrow area of specialist knowledge. But they also have some limitations, most of which stem from the jumbling together of knowledge representation and automation. Although a useful shortcut for research systems, this mixing is a positive disadvantage in commercial operations, for the following reasons.

- It's difficult to find and to retain staff with expertise in the specialized languages used. Also, analysts need to have significant programming skills and vice versa for programmers, compounding the staffing difficulties.
- The supporting technology is difficult to integrate into mainstream business software and systems. Tracking natural evolution in hardware, operating systems, architectures, and so on, is already a big enough headache.
- It's virtually impossible for a nonspecialist, such as the business owner, to read the rules and to sign them off as a correct representation of the business expertise required.

In addition, some technical features may hinder some types of business operation. For instance, many production systems are built around a consultative model, whereby a specific problem is posed and the system works toward its conclusion. In contrast, most business systems operate continuously, although there may be isolated instances of individual problems. Under the consultative assumption, the contents of the working memory can be always be cleared out once the conclusion has been reached, ready for the next problem. Business systems are much more likely to require continuous operations, which never reach a final conclusion, and so some simplifying assumptions of this sort no longer hold true.

Analysis and design patterns   As used in relation to information systems, a *pattern* is a collection of model elements relating to a particular situation. For a pattern to be useful, the situation it describes should be one that's encountered reasonably often: a one-time experience can hardly be considered a pattern. You can think of a pattern as being a fragment of a model that's already available, ready for you to incorporate—either as it stands or with modifications—into your own complete model.

Patterns have started to attract more attention in the software world, and several influential books have been published. See for example (Gamma et al 1995; Buschmann et al 1996; Fowler 1997). The origin of the idea of patterns is often credited to the Californian architect Christopher Alexander, following his book (1977) that laid out a way of describing architectural patterns in bricks-and-mortar architecture, not software. Some similar ideas had already been circulating in the software world, and in the mid-1990s, these thoughts coalesced into the first expression of the way we use the term in IT today.

Despite some quibbling over whether *patterns* should refer to analysis or to design, at the end of the day, it doesn't seem to matter too much, as long as the intended meaning is clear. For what it's worth, this book has taken the line that *analysis* covers business descriptions with minimal implementation content and that *design* is an expression of the business needs as a description of a specific information system. It's certainly possible to have patterns in either area, and, broadly speaking, the pros and cons are much the same for both.

What you will find in a pattern depends to some extent on the style that its author has adopted, but you could reasonably expect it to contain at least the following:

- A description of the problem the pattern addresses
- A discussion of the influences that bear on shaping the nature of the solution
- One or more solutions to the problem
- An outline of the context in which both the problem and the solution are defined

Some pattern authors prefer one of a few highly stylized formats, even to the extent of claiming that anything in a different format cannot possibly be A True Pattern. There doesn't seem to be much value in going to such extremes, though, as long as the intended meaning is clear. You'll find other kinds of variation, too. Some authors are data oriented, and their patterns fit comfortably into a relational database background. Other authors prefer to couch their descriptions in terms of objects. In the running battles of the notation wars, UML seems to be gaining favor as the preferred style.

The various forms of pattern description are less important than they might appear at first glance, because you will almost certainly have to adapt the pattern to fit your own circumstances. A pattern is more of a starter kit of ideas than a plug-and-play solution. What you'll take from the pattern are its essential characteristics, not the literal text or the diagrams used to define it. Even then, you're likely to want to extend or to modify the original elements. As you blend the relevant features into your model, you will inevitably adjust the expression of the pattern to fit your own modeling style.

One thing it's important not to skip over is the context of the pattern. The original source will, ideally, have resulted from some real-life experience. The pattern author is saying, "I found this useful; maybe you will too." But this experience may have been gained in circumstances that are different from the ones you now find yourself in. The author will probably have tried to generalize to some extent, but there are limits on how far this can be taken before generalization becomes wild extrapolation.

For example, think about updating accounts in a banking environment. Most long-established banks have a rich set of patterns describing, say, the posting of an entry to an account. But the context for these patterns may have been a batched style of operations, whereby all the entries for the preceding day are consolidated and taken into an overnight update run. If the bank moves to real-time account posting, many of the existing patterns will no longer be valid in the new context.

Individual patterns are fairly small, and their benefit is difficult to establish until you understand them. But once you understand a pattern, you already have its essential value. For this reason, it's difficult to imagine a commercial market in patterns. You wouldn't buy one unless you knew what it did. But if you knew what it did, why would you buy it? It's more likely that patterns will continue to appear collected in books or shared by fellow enthusiasts through such media as newsgroups.

Business ontologies   *Ontology,* a long-standing branch of philosophy concerned with the nature of being, is the study of things and the relationship between things. More recently, the term has been adopted in the computing arena and used to describe a collection of information about things and the relationship between things. Of course, this makes an ontology a thing in its own right!

From a business point of view, we can make this a little more definite by taking *things* to mean *business things,* in other words, they might be examples of business objects, processes, actors, and so on. A business ontology is therefore a form of business description. Whether it describes any business, a particular type of business, or an individual business depends on its scope, and that's a matter of choice.

This sounds suspiciously similar to the business model concept we examined in Chapter 2. The significant difference is that the ontology movement has as its explicit ambition the delivery of *semantic* information. It's unfortunate that this phrase has a slightly esoteric ring to it, because additional semantic information can provide very down-to-earth benefits.

The true value emerges when separate organizational units, maybe in different organizations, need to use compatible terminology. This has obvious implications in e-commerce. If I send you a waybill or an invoice, does it mean the same to you as it meant to me? It's not a trivial question. Even within the same organization, it's by no means unusual to find individuals or groups with differing views on how common business terms, such as *customer,* should be interpreted.

The same problem occurs when you put a few appropriate terms into a search engine to try to find Web pages that match your specific interest. The hits that come back are mostly not relevant to what you were looking for, and you have to plough through loads of boring pages that happen to contain the same search words. With the increasing expansion of the Internet, finding the information you need is becoming a major issue. Moves are afoot to develop second-generation Web technologies, based on semantic content that can be processed by machine instead of relying on human interpretation.

One of the intentions of a business ontology is to make the underlying meanings explicit, to eliminate a potential source of uncertainty and error. In this sense, an ontology provides a consistent vocabulary that can be shared by everyone working in a particular area. But the terms in the vocabulary represent meanings, not words. The terms should represent a truth that stands independent of any expression of them in English or Spanish or any other human language.

Some of these ideas overlap with concepts from the database community, which has a long tradition of trying to capture the meaning of the terms used and their relationship to the nuts and bolts of data handling, such as type definitions—in the computing sense—and field sizes. These concerns are usually encapsulated in a data dictionary that forms part of the definition of the database.

We've already seen the use of knowledge bases to support expert systems. Because an ontology is also supposed to contain knowledge in some form, it's reasonable to ask what the difference is between a knowledge base and an ontology. After all, they share a number of common features: They both rely on some internal structure, can both be coded in a form that's navigable by a machine, and so on.

The crucial point is that a knowledge base tends to be built to satisfy a particular purpose, whereas an ontology simply represents the structure of the knowledge itself and can stand independent of any application. Of course, some limits have to be set for practical reasons. An ontology can be limited to cover only concepts related to a particular domain and only to a particular level. Within these limitations, though, an ontology should impose minimal restrictions on the use that's made of it. This should make it easier to use an ontology as a basis for building higher-level constructs, while saving the labor of creating the lower-level underpinnings.

Although ontologies are beginning to attract research interest, there are, as yet, no mainstream business applications. The largest single example of an ontology is the one developed by the Cyc project. Originally based at the University of Austin in Texas, this ambitious project had the long-term goal of encoding sufficient knowledge to allow self-learning by a computer. The ontology now contains tens of thousands of terms. It's unrealistic to expect any business system to match this level of complexity; with careful selection of the domain, however, it should be possible to produce something useful but much smaller.

As an example of how ideas about ontologies could find their way into business systems, imagine chunks of business knowledge being packaged in an application-independent way and made available to would-be system builders as a shortcut to defining a specialized area. An example might be an ontology covering corporate accounting, guaranteed to conform to the generally accepted accounting principles (GAAP) and ready to incorporate into a financial system. It remains to be seen whether this kind of thing can become a realistic commercial proposition.

9.2.5   New kinds of services

Software agents   The interest in software agents is comparatively recent, taking off in the mid-1990s, around the same time that the Internet started to become a realistic commercial proposition. For a while, the term *agent* became so popular that it promised to lose all meaning. Almost any old piece of software became "agentified" or was simply renamed to include "agent" in its title, without changing the software at all. Thankfully, the hype has died down somewhat, and we can take a cooler look at what's involved.

Gaining an understanding of what agents are all about is made more difficult by the many flavors that exist. Agents may be labeled as adaptive, autonomous, communicative, cooperative, goal oriented, intelligent, learning, mobile, purposeful, reactive, smart, social, and a few other things as well. Moreover, the terms are also used in combination, so you might be confronted with an "autonomous goal-oriented mobile agent" and many other complicated possibilities.

All these alternatives show that the basic concept can be developed in many ways, each of which emphasizes different properties according to the purpose for which they are intended. However, some properties are more important than others because they represent common features exhibited by most kinds of agents.

- Agents are autonomous. They are able to take actions on their own initiative without being directly commanded. Of course, there's control of an indirect sort, in that the agent will have been requested to carry out a task, but the details of exactly how that should be done are delegated to the agent.

- Agents are sensitive to their environment. They are able to sense various conditions and to react to them in a timely way, perhaps affecting the environment in the process. They can adjust their activities in line with changing conditions, perhaps modifying their goals in the light of what's realistically achievable.

- Agents are goal oriented. They don't simply react to their environment; they also try to achieve a purpose in a proactive way. The actions taken by an agent at any particular time are governed by a strategy that takes into account the need to achieve a goal—or perhaps multiple goals—and the current circumstances.

- Agents persist over an appreciable amount of time. They are temporally continuous, although with some qualifications about the meaning of continuity. For example, an agent that performs a task related to a business process need persist only as long as that process is active. Nevertheless, the intention is that an agent will hang around for a while, unlike a subroutine, which gets called, does its job, and then terminates.

Another qualification probably ought to be a necessary level of complexity; otherwise, these definitions would include trivial objects, such as thermostats, door latches, and mousetraps, which don't deserve to be elevated to agent status.

Agents can be deployed in several ways. Independent agents work in isolation, reacting to their environment and pursuing their goals without regard to any other agents that might be around. Compare this with expert systems. Both pursue goals and react to data, but the expert system is explicitly invoked and has to be fed with the data. The agent gets up off the bench and goes looking for its data. An expert system is like a fixed box with a mail slot, waiting for something to be posted. An agent is more like a furtive presence lurking somewhere in your network, waiting for the right conditions to arise. Thus, use of an agent is well suited to an application that checks for credit card fraud, for example. The agent hangs around the places where data gathers, checking it over to see whether it contains any suspicious characters.

You can also have multiple agents. They can be peers—the same kinds of agent—as might be the case with multiple agents trying to negotiate a suitable time for a meeting to suit their master's constraints. Alternatively, agents can be of different kinds. For example, supplier and consumer agents might act in a kind of commodity market. In any event, multiple agents brings about a need for additional capabilities, such as discovering who's out there, negotiating over a deal, and concluding a contract. By analogy with the expert system case just discussed, you can think of multiple agents as being something like a blackboard system turned inside out.

Agents haven't yet entered the mainstream of business computing, but why would we think of using them instead of simply writing another subroutine? It probably boils down to two things. First, their autonomous nature makes them a fire-and-forget approach. You don't need to remember to invoke them explicitly at the right point; they are able to react for themselves if they have access to the right data. Second, they are more robust than conventional software. If conditions are less than ideal, they should be able to degrade in a graceful way rather than just failing and perhaps bringing down another process.

Web services   We've already discussed software components in a fairly general kind of way, primarily as containers for an assortment of software functionality. They're now pretty well established as a common software ingredient, so we don't need to dwell on them here, except to remember the importance of the component interface definitions. In Chapter 7, we saw how components can be used as a mechanism for the delivery of business knowledge, either as a specialized rule component or as a unit of deployment for software containing embedded rules. With the growth of the Internet, an alternative has recently appeared in the form of Web services.

Web services build on an infrastructure that's now widespread and well proven. The Web protocol layer—HTTP—can be used to support a wide range of communications between information producers and consumers. Messages use a conceptually simple markup language (HTML) onto which additional facilities can be layered. Messages can be passed securely if desired and are about the only practical means for interprocess communication across firewalls.

A Web service is a relatively simple unit of functionality that makes use of all this existing technology. The service is published on the Internet and, in theory, becomes available for use by anyone needing that function. In practice, some Web services may be offered on a commercial basis, and so access may not be free and easy.

The most widely quoted example of a Web service is Microsoft Passport, a generally available authentication service that can be used by not only Microsoft but also anyone else requiring user authentication. At present, the Passport service is free, so it offers a convenient way of avoiding the time and trouble of creating an in-house equivalent. All that's needed is some appropriate linkage to a known URL.

More proposed examples of this kind of service are various calendar-related activities, language translations, currency conversions, credit checking, and stock quotations. These are not intended as complete business applications in their own right but are simply useful building blocks that can be aggregated together with other services to provide higher-level functions. It's possible to imagine virtual businesses that have no premises or staff to speak of, existing only as a set of Web pages that stitch together a bunch of Web services offered by other people.

From the point of view of the service supplier, offering some existing capability as a Web service doesn't involve much more than providing a suitable front-end adapter in the position we've identified as the channel tier of an N-tier architecture. From the point of view of the provider, anyone using the service is a client: whether an end user at a browser window or another automation system. From the point of view of the client, the service is accessible from any point that needs it through its known URL.

Apart from the widespread availability of Internet access and the universal acceptance of HTTP, the other crucial enabling factor for Web services is the general adoption of XML as a universal message format. Several other new or emerging standards are SOAP (Simple Object Access Protocol), WSDL (Web Services Description Language), and UDDI (Universal Discovery Description and Integration), which extend this basic technology set, but a full discussion of the protocol aspects is a little outside our scope in this book.

Even at its simplest, the technology offers several advantages over using a locally installed software component connected via middleware.

- Interoperability problems are greatly reduced; the Web technology is neutral to such issues as COM versus CORBA (common object request broker architecture) or Java versus .NET.
- The Web service technology is straightforward to understand and to apply, so the barriers to acceptance are low.
- Although agreement on standards is still incomplete, multivendor support for the key elements provides some assurance that the value of investments in Web services will be preserved in the future.
- Maintenance of the service is much easier for the provider. Updating a large number of installed components presents a considerable headache, but a Web service needs to be updated only once at a central point.

It's likely that a range of Web services will emerge, ranging from a simple look-up of facts to higher-value smart services. The latter are ideal candidates for rule-based applications, hosted by the service provider. Anyone possessing useful know-how could potentially make it available to a much larger audience through Web services than any other possible route.

Against these advantages are a few things to bear in mind.

- Although Internet bandwidth is increasing all the time, an inevitable latency exists between a service request and the corresponding response. Also, as noted in earlier chapters, the possible inefficiencies in data marshaling can seriously hamper performance. These factors may make Web services unsuitable for some high-volume or fast-response applications.
- It's not feasible to include a Web service inside a transaction, as would be possible with local functionality, so that problems can be handled through standard operations to abort or complete. Instead, it will be necessary to define an "untransact" operation that can undo the effect of a Web service when required.
- Because the business rules involved are likely to be bundled into the Web service, they probably won't be open to inspection, so you may have to take on trust the nature of the service that's provided. One way of handling this is for you to define the key rules that you believe a Web service incorporates, treating it as another kind of implementation container in your rule repository. This will give you some degree of continuity with your own rules, but you need to check that your understanding is correct.

This last issue is an example of the wider problem of semantic definition, which we'll return to in the next section.

E-commerce workflow   All organizations have a steady stream of incoming and outgoing communications based around a fairly standard range of commercial documents: invoices, purchase orders, quotations, and the like. Conventionally, these documents have been exchanged through the postal system, but there are obvious attractions in doing the same thing electronically. Although electronic data interchange (EDI) has been around for some time, it's been in a form that only large corporations could justify. The ubiquity of the Internet makes it a natural basis for a new wave of electronic business messaging that can inherit from the earlier EDI experiences and make corresponding facilities available more widely.

It goes without saying that XML is again the preferred messaging format, and a number of interests in this area have coalesced into an initiative called ebXML (electronic business XML). The ebXML initiative is sponsored by a number of organizations, including the United Nations; for more details, see www.ebxml.org.

Something more than XML is needed, though. It's easy to define the syntax for an isolated e-commerce document in XML, using a DTD (Document Type Definition) or a schema, but that doesn't mean we've defined any of the underlying meanings. As pointed out earlier, it's difficult enough to get total agreement on a simple term like *customer* within the same organization. Extending this to external parties so that everyone you deal with shares the same set of interpretations is impossible without some extra support.

The reason this is important lies in the scale of the potential savings offered by the automation of commercial transactions. These savings arise from such factors as lower handling costs, reduced errors, and elimination of data reentry. For a large organization, the savings could run into millions or even billions of dollars per year. But these savings can be achieved only if automated processing can be trusted: If all electronic documents require manual intervention, the savings soon disappear.

We need to get a grip on the document semantics. Why? Because otherwise, we can't apply the right business rules. Imagine that I've just sent you an on-demand order. I want 1,000 units but not all at once. We agree on the price per unit, and we agree that I can pull down units at this price as required, ultimately up to a total of 1,000 units. But I assume that the units will be available immediately, on demand, and that I pay on delivery. You assume that units are scheduled in the normal way and become available as and when, after the demand has been raised. Also, I'm expected to pay before shipment. Our two automation systems will be busily applying incompatible business rules, which at some point are bound to collide. That's why we need to have a common understanding of what we mean.

Semantics is one of those slippery words that many people use but few are able to define. Its origins are in the branch of linguistics that deals with meaning. The term is also used to indicate the relationship between symbols and the things they stand for. Taking things further is not easy, and discussions of semantics can decay rapidly into farce:

"What do you mean by semantics?"

"First, you'll have to define what you mean by 'mean.'"

"Depends what *you* mean by 'what.'"

And so on. Fortunately, we don't have to solve the underlying philosophical problems; we simply have to get something that will work in a sensible way. Two approaches are in play at the present time, and it's not clear which is best: one, the other, an amalgam of the two, or some outsider coming up on the rails.

The first line of attack is from the relatively well-understood standpoint of syntax. Crudely speaking, the strategy can be summarized as follows.

- We're all part of industry sector X.
- We all need to do business in a similar way.
- We use a common set of terms but with some variations here and there.
- So, let's agree and publish a common set of terms as an industry standard.
- Then, whenever we use a term, we can all refer to the standard interpretation.

The result is, usually, an XML schema definition. You could imagine that such a schema would form a rallying point for the industry sector concerned. What happens if new concepts emerge? No problem; representatives from the industry get together, agree how to extend the schema, and it becomes a revised standard.

But there is a problem. Let's say that people in the healthcare sector have defined their interpretations of order, contract, customer, and all the other commercial terms that are needed. Meanwhile, so have the people in the financial services sector, and the janitorial supplies sector, and many more.

Unfortunately, health-care providers also need financial services, janitorial supplies, and many other things to function in the real world. So all we've done is to move the debate from one place to another. If a healthcare company needs a financial service, whose set of definitions wins? It might appear that the problem is smaller because the number of industries is less than the number of companies. Sadly, the inertia to change is also greater, by roughly the same ratio, so there's no net gain.

At present, we seem to be awash in all kinds of schemas in various stages of development. Rationalizing all these poses a real problem and, presumably, would be finally sorted out only if every organization in the world agreed to the same definitions of order, contract, customer, and so on. This might prove to be a long job.

The other approach takes a somewhat different line that, roughly, could be presented as follows.

- We may or may not be in the same industry sector.
- We need to do business in a compatible way.
- We may or may not use similar terms for similar things.
- So, I'll define my terms, using a set of syntactic associations as metadata.
- You and your computer can read my metadata and do what you want with it.

The main driving force behind this kind of approach is the World Wide Web Consortium (W3C), which has defined an infrastructure called the resource description framework (RDF). The motivation behind RDF and its relatives has emerged from the growing difficulty of using the Web effectively. Even simple information retrieval is becoming problematic, and attempts at more sophisticated activities quickly get bogged down in a vast swamp of unstructured data. The goal of RDF is to add metadata, or data about data, to Web information in order to allow automated processes to navigate through it in a more meaningful way.

The key notions in RDF are quite simple. *Things* are represented by *resources,* which can be identified using a uniform resource identifier (URI). Resources have *properties,* which can be a value or another resource. Figure 9-7 shows a graphical representation of a simple RDF description. This may look a little bit like the semantic networks we saw earlier in this chapter, and that's exactly what it is! There's also a textual rendering of RDF structures, which is the computer-readable form of the semantic network. We won't go into the details of RDF here, partly for reasons of space, but also because it's still something of a work in progress. It's worth noting, though, that the W3C Web pages describe RDF as "a lightweight ontology system." You can find more up-to-date information on RDF at www.w3.org/RDF.

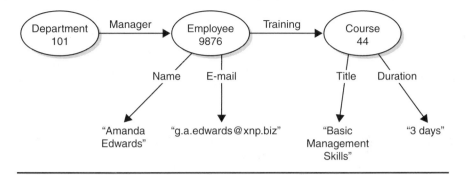

Figure 9-7   Simple RDF example

It's clear that if we want e-commerce to become a matter of routine, we need more than the ability to send XML payloads over the Internet. Automated work-flow—machine processing of electronic commercial documents—will require additional semantic information to make it a reality. Although the dust hasn't yet settled over the standards concerned, the commercial pressures that bear on this area are likely to introduce an aggressive pace into their progress.

9.3   Knowledge summary

Most of the material in this book has focused on the role of business rules in modern information systems. In this chapter, we've seen how much the same ideas are appearing in a number of other contexts. What these ideas share is a quest to find ways of adding meaning to raw data.

Expecting computers to automatically extract meaning from unstructured information is unrealistic at present and perhaps always will be. To make automation of information processing a practical and reliable option, we have to impose structure and enrich data with higher-level constructs that can be exploited in subsequent processing.

This takes us into areas that relate to fundamental philosophical issues, but we need to see these as sources of ideas, not problems to which we have to find the ultimate solution. What we're after are workable notions for deploying knowledge in forms that are accessible by both human and machine users. Let's leave the last word on this subject to R. W. Hamming (1962), one of the fathers of modern information theory: "The purpose of computing is insight, not numbers."

10

Summing Up

10.1 The purpose of this book

The intention of this book has been to provide business and computing professionals with a good understanding of the field of business rules. Armed with this knowledge, you should be able to make informed decisions about the planning and execution of information systems projects, including answering such questions as:

- How do we identify and record business rules?
- Where and how should we implement them?
- Should we build or buy any related technology?
- What management issues are involved?

10.2 Models

Business rules are only one element of modern information systems. To understand how they fit into the big picture, we also have to look at other aspects of a system. The way in which we relate rules to all the other elements is through one or more *models* that describe the system from various perspectives. Even if you're a dyed-in-the-wool technologist, you need to understand business models to a certain extent so that rules can be seen in their proper context.

Within a well-balanced business model, business rules are used to represent the logic that lies behind business decisions. But rules don't stand alone; they must be integrated along with representations of other key business features, such as

- Events, either internal or external, that may impact business activities
- Processes: sequences of tasks that are carried out by the business

- Objects, either real or abstract, that the business needs to deal with and the interrelationships between these objects
- The policies and goals of the business
- Actors and roles: the entities, both human and machine, with which the business wants to interact
- The organizational units that go to make up the business
- Narratives that describe scenes in the life of the business

For both models and rules, the operative word is *business*. Most of the content of this book follows a perspective that's angled more toward the viewpoint of the business owner than the pure technologist. This is deliberate and is simply a reflection of practical experience. Serious problems that emerge in delivered—or perhaps we should say "almost delivered"—systems often stem from a poor appreciation of the underlying business rationale. One way of looking at business rules is to see them as a language for business description that can be understood both by businesspeople and by technologists. Ideally, the contribution made by business rules will be to align systems much more closely to the needs of the business they're intended to serve.

10.3   Trends

If a business rule simply defines a business aspect that we want to build into a system, we could reasonably ask, "What's new? Don't system builders always try to incorporate their understanding of the business?" The answer lies in a new appreciation of the value in separating the definition of the business logic from its implementation. This introduces structure, which in turn allows better control and more opportunities for automation. Most important, it reduces the problems of operating business systems over an extended period of time. This new understanding has been driven from several directions. It's worth reviewing them to get a wider vision of how business rules fit into modern information systems.

10.3.1   Business process reengineering

Business process reengineering (BPR) is an exercise in revamping a business to improve its effectiveness. A clear statement of the as-is and the to-be positions is necessary to ensure that the health of the business will be improved as a result of the BPR exercise. Some of the BPR exercises that were carried out so enthusiastically in the 1980s proved to be disasters for the companies concerned, perhaps because they failed to appreciate the fragile nature of the business knowledge they were dependent on. Making knowledge explicit, in the form of business rules, provides a much better understanding of how the business really works.

10.3.2   Quality management

Achieving and maintaining a controlled level of quality—for example, to ISO 9000 standards—within a business requires a clear definition of the way in which the business operates. Unfortunately, in some companies, a quality system results in a dead weight of bureaucracy that stifles the business instead of invigorating it. This is clearly wrong; a quality program should support, not oppose, business effectiveness. Many of these problems arise because the quality system is applied as a set of clerical procedures laid on top of normal business operations. Business rules offer an attractive supplement—or even an alternative—to this traditional approach: a living, breathing, and readily maintained definition of what the business is really about. In short, it's a way of using business definitions actively instead of consigning them to a set of dusty manuals.

10.3.3   Reducing the maintenance burden

The computer systems that support the business clearly need to reflect the business logic used, but this has often been opaquely coded and buried deep within complex functions, with consequently high maintenance costs. Reports from many companies indicate that they typically spend something like 75 percent of their IT budgets on maintaining existing systems, which doesn't leave much for responding to urgent demands, such as e-commerce. Obviously, business rules won't magically reduce the need for maintenance to zero, but isolating points of flexibility and providing good traceability between the definition of the business logic and its realization can significantly reduce future support costs.

10.3.4   Better specification

Businesses are continually searching for better ways to specify and to develop information systems. A requirements-definition phase is usually the recommended first step in a project of this sort. Although a clear definition of business requirements is undoubtedly essential, defining it as a phase can create the impression that it's a one-time exercise carried out only at the start of an application project. The reality of business life is that requirements are continually changing, with the changes implying a need to update software that might well have been written several decades ago. The accelerating pace of business change, compounded by the growth in e-commerce, has intensified the demand for a means of expressing the needs of business in a form that can be updated incrementally and continually. Along with this is the need to trace the elements of a business specification through into the implementation, so that it's easy to assess the impact of a business change and to organize the relevant modifications. Business rules offer the kind of expression that can be used equally well by business representatives and by technologists.

10.3.5 Distributed computing

A somewhat related trend is the increased use of distributed computing. In the large, monolithic applications of the past, the issue of where to put a line of code had limited practical significance. Nowadays, when business systems tend to be designed as *N*-tier systems, the precise location of a small data or code element can make a large difference to system response, throughput, maintainability, and a number of other factors. A common recommendation is to locate the business logic in a middle tier of processing, but this advice can look simplistic when the middle tier is itself made up of a fairly complex set of servers. Particular cases might have good reasons to deviate from these guidelines. For example, speed of response may be crucial, so locating some logic in the client layer—to avoid network round-trips—may be more appropriate. Alternatively, the nature of the processing load may mandate implementation of some logic in a back-end data server—for instance, to impose consistency across multiple data streams. As we've seen, these design issues have no single right answer. What we can expect from business rules is a series of statements of business logic that are straightforward for the designer to map onto the chosen architecture.

10.3.6 Soft assets

So-called soft assets are becoming increasingly important. At one time, computer software was considered a possible give-away in order to sell hardware. Now the situation is almost totally reversed. Even outside the information technology field, many companies already acknowledge the worth of intangible assets, such as brand names. There's now a growing and widespread recognition of the potential value of the intellectual capital that exists in most, and arguably all, organizations. For example, many competing companies have similar access to raw materials, equipment, markets, and so on. What differentiates the companies is their unique know-how. Management consultancies are obvious examples of knowledge companies of this type. One of the problems in assessing this kind of intellectual capital is that its value will remain as potential unless a way can be found to give it a tangible existence. Business rules offer a systematic way of capturing knowledge in a form that can be preserved and replicated.

10.4 Business rule characteristics

Next, we can try to pull together the characteristics that make a good business rule. The ins and outs of their practical realization will vary from one organization to another, but some fundamental points don't change. You will need to make sure that these points are properly reflected in your own environment. Business rules are

- *Atomic.* Business rules are atomic, meaning that they can be defined in terms of subunits, but these subunits are not themselves rules. Any attempt to decompose a well-formed business rule into a simpler version will result in loss of information. In some situations, it can be convenient to treat a group of rules as a kind of super-rule that obviously can be broken down into individual rules. You should always refer to groups of this sort as a *rule set* so that its composed nature is clear to any of its users.

- *Business statements.* Business rules are crisp statements about an aspect of the business. Individual rule statements should have a clear business meaning to the terms they use, the facts they define, and the logic they dictate. The clarity is important because the rule statements are subsequently translated into one or more realizations. The small size of the rules is helpful here because it reduces the scope for possible confusion. It's sometimes said that rules should not be technology oriented, but this can be misleading. A company in a technology-related business will certainly have business rules that are technology oriented. What's meant is that the rules should be statements of business logic and should not describe the technology of the rule implementation.

- *Declarative.* Rules should be expressed in a way that describes goals rather than actions. A business rule specifying "in situation A, carry out action B" is unsatisfactory because it hides the business logic. We want to know *what* the business aim is, not *how* we achieve it. There may be several ways of getting the desired result. On a larger scale, many business reengineering projects are all about changing the way in which the business gets from A to B. Separating the *what* from the *how* is a key feature of the business rules approach.

- *Constraining.* In one sense or another, business rules are constraints that must be applied in the context of the business. They limit a dimension of possibility by defining what must or must not be the case. In practice, the number of thing we *don't* want to do in business is very much smaller than the number of thing we *do* want to do, and expressing rules as *constraints* instead of *permissions* is simply the most efficient way to do it.

- *Expressed in natural language.* In spite of attempts to impose various formalisms, the dominant means of describing business is through natural language. The advantages are many: no special training required, no special tools needed, universally available, extremely flexible, and so on. These pressing advantages make natural language an obvious first choice for expressing business logic, although not necessarily just on its own. For example, a natural-language rule statement could be mapped onto a more formal mathematical expression and, in turn, onto statements in a programming language. An ever-present danger is the well-known potential for ambiguity in natural-language expressions. You'll need to be constantly on your guard against poorly framed rules.

- *Traceable.* Business rules are but one part of a complete information system, and we need to be able to understand how they fit into the bigger picture. Starting from a business rule, we're likely to want to trace in two directions: backward toward the source of the rule and forward to the realizations that we've chosen. This traceability is useful at all stages of a rule's life cycle buts pays off most handsomely during maintenance.

- *Structured.* Although we want to make business rules easy to read and to understand, we don't want to allow a completely free format. Restricting the options for rule authors may reduce the poetic appeal of the rule statements but improves the prospects for automation support in the authoring process itself, in the mapping of the rules onto their chosen realization, and in validation of rules in their proper business context. We've seen how rule patterns can be applied to achieve this aim.

10.5 Rule populations

Moving from the characteristics of individual business rules onto a larger scale, we come to *populations* of rules: a large group of rules that are intended to form a coherent business definition within a specified scope. The scope need not be the whole business; it could be based on an organizational unit, a geographical region, or any other subset that makes business sense. The important thing is that the associated rules are intended to behave as a cohesive unit. Rule populations are

- *Consistent.* A population of business rules should be self-consistent. There must be no cases of conflict whereby two or more rules in the population disagree about an aspect of the business. This is a rule! If such a situation existed, it would be impossible to know which of the possible interpretations is to be considered correct without recourse to an external authority. You should not be diverted by such arguments as, "But sometimes we do A, and sometimes we do B." This is simply an indicator that another rule needs to be made explicit. Eliminating conflicts is an important facet of reviewing and testing business rules.

- *Complete.* Even though a population of rules may not represent an entire business, we want the rule population to be a complete representation of whatever subset it's intended to cover. If you have an incomplete coverage, you have no way of knowing whether you've finished defining the rules and no possibility of an operational guarantee that you've covered all the bases. If, for some reason, you find that you can't manage a complete coverage, it's worth changing the definition of the population scope to match what the rules do deal with. That way, you're at least clear about what you don't know.

- *Nonoverlapping.* In the early stages of building a rule population, you're likely to be dealing with rules that have come from a variety of sources. Several rules may seem to be very similar, especially if they're designed to prevent real business showstoppers. It's important to resolve any overlaps so that each piece of business logic has a clear point of definition. There's no voting system in logic, so just because an item, such as, "Don't lend to bad risks," is very important to the business, the item doesn't have to be covered many times. One business rule for each point is enough. If you allow overlaps, you introduce inefficiency at best and at worst, sow the seeds for later inconsistencies and conflicts.

- *Managed.* In order to be a coherent unit, a rule population must be managed. For example, it may be necessary to supersede one group of rules with another group of rules. It's no good expecting rules to organize themselves. They need to be tracked and controlled through discovery, definition, review, realization, testing, and so on, so that the population always exists in a known configuration.

10.6 Other properties

The properties we've looked at so far emerge directly from the rules or rule populations themselves. We could call them intrinsic properties. Other properties, which we could call extrinsic, are *applied* to rules or populations. The distinguishing feature of extrinsic properties is that you can have a perfectly valid business rule or population even if the extrinsic properties are not yet defined. In contrast, the intrinsic properties are not negotiable.

10.6.1 Who?

In principle, a business rule is owned by the individual or group that defines it. Ownership, in this context, implies certain rights, such as

- Being able to change the definition of the rule
- Saying when and where the rule should be applied; for instance, only in a particular region or only from a given date
- Approving nonfunctional aspects of the rule realization; for instance, whether it is fast enough or secure enough

We're also assuming that the owner of a rule has the right level of authority to take responsibility for it. Trying to determine ownership and authority often raises interesting and heated organizational debates, but the resolution of these issues is ultimately healthy for the organization, although perhaps uncomfortable for some of the individuals involved.

Often—but not always—the rule owner is part of the business that's using the rule. For example, the demands of e-commerce, and especially the drive toward customer relationship management (CRM), are likely to require rules that define customer-related aspects. Although the business uses these rules, the content of at least some of them may well be under the control of the customer.

In practice, it would be very awkward if all rule owners exercised their rights in an ad hoc way. Certainly, given current technology, it would be almost impossible to guarantee consistency and correctness across the business. Most rule owners will be preoccupied with their local issues, and it would be expecting too much to assume that the rule owners could appreciate the wider impact of their rules. A few rogue rules could have a disastrous impact on the business, and at least some degree of management is essential.

This implies a business role that's associated with the good stewardship of the business rules over an extended period of time. Such a role fits quite well with the wider concerns of knowledge management, which may provide a pointer to the organizational implications.

10.6.2   Where?

Business rule statements contain no direct indication of where they should be located within an information system. The reason is that we want to have a clear view of the business intent, one that's not colored by the containers available in the current environment at the current time. The local technology base should not constrain what the business wants to do. It's true that future technology evolution may open up additional possibilities, such as new channels for reaching customers, but these possibilities will feed through in the form of new business models with new business rules.

The location of a business rule within an information system is determined during development, when a designer selects the most appropriate realization or perhaps multiple realizations. The choice has to take into account not only the business rule statement but also several other factors including the technical architecture of the system and nonfunctional requirements, such as performance, security, and maintainability. The traceability property of a business rule allows us to record its placement so that it can be maintained over an extended period.

10.6.3   When?

Similarly, a business rule statement does not specify when it should be applied. For example, we might be creating a new customer object that has to conform to certain rules. Should we check the rules as individual data items are entered on-screen? Or when the system tries to instantiate the business object? Or when we attempt to create the database records in persistent storage? Depending on the specific business situation and the system design, we might decide to do any or all these things. Although some additional guidance is likely to be available from other parts of the business model, this is a choice that is best made by the designer during the development of the system.

10.7   Rule programming

Those of you with a technology background may be wondering whether rules can be implemented directly. This is often a source of some confusion, largely because of the overlap of business rules with the use of rules as a programming technique.

Rule-based programming is a very useful means of automating logical decision making, especially if the logic is fairly complicated. Many rule languages exist, often coupled exclusively to a specific software tool. This technology came into prominence in the early 1980s, as research in artificial intelligence (AI) spilled over into the commercial world in the form of expert systems. You need to be aware of some important points that differentiate the programming world.

- A programmer's rule is not necessarily a business rule. For instance, additional rules may need to be introduced in a program to control its operation. For some complex problems, such as analyzing the structure of a protein molecule, controlling the reasoning mechanism turns out to be a key automation problem, and many programmed rules are, quite rightly, dedicated to this purpose.

- On a more mundane level, such constructs as IF and CASE in programs written in common languages such as Visual Basic and C++ aren't necessarily related to business rules and, indeed, may not necessarily equate to anything recognizable in business terms.

- Programmatic rules may be an artifact introduced by a tool or a software package that's being used. Such rules may have no real business basis other than "that's the way it's done in package X."

- Business rules don't necessarily require rule-based programming or the use of specialized programming languages, such as LISP and Prolog, that are often associated with AI. Business rules can be implemented in BASIC, COBOL, C++, FORTRAN, Java, Pascal, PL/1, SQL, VBScript, Perl, C#, or just about anything else that you can imagine.

Although business rules are distinct from rule-based programming, this type of technology can be a very effective realization mechanism. However, it's still important to preserve the distinction between specification and implementation.

10.8 Advantages of business rules

It's probably obvious by now that dealing with business rules is going to involve a certain amount of work. It's reasonable to ask why we should bother. After all, we've been building computer applications for many decades without using business rules. Or have we?

In fact, the rules have always been there, but we've tended to bury them inside methods, subroutines, functions, procedures, and other pieces of software. The case we're arguing here is not the need for more business logic but making explicit the key business definitions that the software should be built around.

The points that follow summarize the benefits you can expect to gain by making business rules part of your approach to building information systems. If you already have experience with system development, you should be able to identify with enough of these points to be convinced that raising the profile of business rules is a good idea.

The value of each individual benefit will vary from one organization to another, so they're not in any particular order. They're also variable in the time at which the benefit is realized. First, we itemize the features and advantages of business rules that emerge from the preceding discussion, and then we try to condense these under a few key headings.

10.8.1 Business rule features

- *Modular.* Rules allow modular definition of business knowledge as fine-grained (individual rules) or coarse-grained (rule sets).
- *Understandable.* A natural-language form of expression for business rules simplifies understanding, review, and sign-off by the business owner.
- *Structured.* Defining an underlying formal structure for rule statements facilitates machine checking and processing.
- *Integrated.* Links to other elements of a comprehensive business model help to make business rules an integral part of information systems.
- *Declarative.* Declarative rule statements avoid imposing unnecessary constraints on subsequent implementation.
- *Unambiguous.* A set of clear and well-structured rule statements greatly reduces the possibility of ambiguity in the definition of business logic.
- *Support BPR.* Separating rules from presentation, process, and data makes business (re)engineering faster and more predictable.
- *Explicit declaration.* Forcing business statements to be explicit instead of leaving them implicit contributes to improved system design and operational quality of service.

- *Functional encapsulation.* The functional encapsulation enabled by business rules reduces long-term maintenance costs by localizing changes to well-defined areas.
- *Rapid adaptation.* Rules identify points of flexibility that can be adapted rapidly to meet new conditions, such as changes in legislation.
- *Handling complexity.* Rules provide a systematic way of expressing some of the more complex functionality required of modern information systems, especially the intricate behavior demanded by such new features as customer relationship management.
- *Tangible knowledge.* Making business knowledge explicit rather than implicit facilitates the process of knowledge management.
- *Future enabling.* A good rule base provides a platform for future technology developments, such as intelligent agents, that are likely to become increasingly important in a networked business environment.
- *Business metrics.* Rules can help to define metrics that allow the business to understand the full implications of its business operations. Does it cost too much to implement? Do our constraints limit commercial opportunity too much?
- *Provide explanation.* Rules can be used as a basis for explaining business decisions. This is useful when it's necessary to demonstrate compliance with regulatory requirements. For example, it may be a requirement that an applicant must be given a reason for rejection of a loan application.
- *Support integration.* Access to explicit rules can ease the understanding and integration of heterogeneous information systems, such as those of customer and supplier or companies that are attempting to merge.
- *Support risk management.* Rules support the organization's risk-management process by clearly stating business rules that can be linked directly to the risks they are meant to address.
- *Promote reuse.* This can be at several levels. For example, a large collection of rules could be packaged as a generic description of the logic underlying a particular business area, such as retail banking, requiring only a small amount of customization to be usable by most businesses in that sector.
- *Force issues.* The process of rule discovery can force issues into the open by insisting on clear definitions of areas that may otherwise be left vague because they're difficult, hot political issues, or have been overlooked.

10.8.2   Categories of benefits

It's useful to think about these benefits under a few broad categories. At a high level, we can group them under the following headings:

- *Control.* What we're after here is the ability to give a reasonably confident prediction of the likely extent of the rules element of a business model and a good view of the instruments and levers that we can use to steer a rulecentric exercise to its desired destination.

- *Quality.* Quality has a multitude of interpretations. The one we should focus on is *fitness for purpose.* We're looking for features that help us to build information systems that do what they're supposed to do, coupled with ways of measuring that this is indeed the case.

- *Cost.* We need to be concerned about both short-term costs during development and long-term costs during maintenance. Business rules can help to contain or even reduce the costs of implementing a given level of functionality.

- *Flexibility.* This is a key area for business rules. We want to open up ways of dealing with externally imposed changes, opportunities for honing our competitive edge, and strategies for reengineering our business to a more effective commercial instrument.

There's obviously a fair amount of overlap between the detailed points and these headings. Table 10-1 summarizes the relevance of each of the features of business rules in this context.

Table 10-1 Business rule benefits

	Category of Benefit			
Feature	**Control**	**Quality**	**Cost**	**Flexibility**
Modular	Crucial	Marginal	Crucial	Crucial
Understandable	Marginal	Valuable	Marginal	Valuable
Structured	Crucial	Valuable	Valuable	Crucial
Integrated	Crucial	Valuable	Marginal	Valuable
Declarative	Valuable	Valuable	Not especially relevant	Crucial
Unambiguous	Marginal	Valuable	Valuable	Valuable
Support BPR	Marginal	Not especially relevant	Valuable	Crucial
Explicit declaration	Crucial	Crucial	Marginal	Marginal
Functional encapsulation	Valuable	Valuable	Crucial	Crucial
Rapid adaptation	Not especially relevant	Marginal	Crucial	Crucial
Handling complexity	Valuable	Marginal	Valuable	Marginal

	Category of Benefit			
Feature	**Control**	**Quality**	**Cost**	**Flexibility**
Tangible knowledge	Crucial	Valuable	Marginal	Valuable
Future enabling	Marginal	Marginal	Not especially relevant	Crucial
Business metrics	Not especially relevant	Crucial	Marginal	Not especially relevant
Provide explanation	Not especially relevant	Crucial	Not especially relevant	Marginal
Support integration	Marginal	Marginal	Valuable	Valuable
Support risk management	Crucial	Valuable	Crucial	Not especially relevant
Promote re-use	Valuable	Marginal	Crucial	Valuable
Force issues	Valuable	Valuable	Marginal	Not especially relevant

APPENDIX

A Little Bit of Logic

A.1 Business Logic

A.1.1 Why logic?

The term business logic is used a lot in e-commerce. In fact, its meaning has become diluted, standing for just about any combination of hardware or software that provides business functionality. Unfortunately, that's much too vague to be a useful foundation for building business rules. To get onto the right track, we need a great deal more clarity and precision. The best way of achieving this is to drill down to some of the basic principles of logic itself, and that's what we do in this appendix. Logic is the foundation that business rules are built on, and, as you'll see, it's reassuringly solid.

If you're short of time, you can skip over this appendix. However, you'll probably find it useful to at least skim through it. If you felt that some of the advice in earlier parts of the book seemed a little bit fussy, the reason is probably the need for logical precision, and the explanation is likely to lie somewhere in this appendix.

The basic principles of logic have been around for more than two thousand years, so by now, people have a pretty good understanding of what does and does not work. The downside is that some of the terminology has also been around for a while and can seem a little old-fashioned, which is probably why some people feel that logic is a remote academic subject with little relevance to the hectic world of e-commerce. Nothing could be further from the truth. The computer systems you use are, quite literally, built from this stuff. All the graphics, animations, audio streams, and other elements of an e-commerce site are produced by the application of exactly the elements we're going to discuss here.

It's difficult to overstate the importance of getting the logic right. One aspect of e-commerce that many large organizations have been slow to understand is that it removes the protective layer of human intervention found in traditional business operations. In e-commerce, business processes are fully exposed to an unforgiving world. Shortcomings in the business logic are quickly exposed, with effects ranging from embarrassment to serious financial loss.

Logic is a big subject. You don't need to be an expert in logic to use business rules successfully. However, it's important that you know at least a little about logic, if only to avoid falling into some well-known and well-marked potholes. We don't attempt a full course in logic here, but we do focus on the key principles that underpin the earlier material in the book. What we're aiming for is a framework that will allow us to make clear business statements that will be straightforward to automate.

For the time being, we'll also put aside any concerns about how this might be implemented: coded in a programming language, integrated into our database, or lots of other how-to-do-it issues. However, we should be concerned to see that we have a clear and consistent description of what our business is trying to achieve. When defining our business logic, we'll be concentrating on *what,* not *how*.

A.1.2   Logic and logics

We focus mainly on *classical,* or *standard, logic* in which the value of a variable must be either true or false. If you're familiar with writing program code, these are the values that are allowed for variables of type Boolean or something similar, such as bool, depending on your programming language. (The name comes from the nineteenth-century logician George Boole, who introduced a lot of the refinements to logic that we use today.) A very well worked out subset of mathematics is based on standard logic, and it has many attractive features. Just as an example, an often-used trick is to find that something is true by showing that it is not false or vice versa.

However, you should be aware that several other logical frameworks attempt to overcome some of the problems in standard logic. For example, the question "Is it raining?" often has a straightforward answer: yes in the Northwest and no in the deserts. But there are other possibilities. In Ireland, many days have a fine, mist-like precipitation without perceptible raindrops, graded by the locals as *soft*. Classical logic demands an absolute true or false view of the "Is it raining?" question, but we would find it difficult to choose between these two on a soft day. It's obviously not dry; nor is it clearly raining buckets. In these sorts of situations, we feel a need to reply to the question with "a bit," "somewhat," or "perhaps it will brighten up later"—thus neatly avoiding a Boolean answer!

To deal with problems of this sort, various attempts have been made to define *nonstandard logics,* sometimes called *deviant logics,* which sounds much more intriguing. Probably the best known of these is *fuzzy logic*. Instead of assuming that we have only true or false, fuzzy logic allows a range of truth values, usually expressed on a numerical scale from 0 (absolutely false) to 1 (absolutely true). This would allow us to answer the "Is it raining?" question with "0.3" on a damp Irish afternoon.

The philosophical merits of fuzzy logic are hotly disputed, as they are for other deviant logics. What's not disputable is how successful fuzzy logic has been when applied to some real-world problems. It's quite likely that the spin cycle in your washing machine, the antilock braking in your car, and the cooking time in your microwave are controlled by fuzzy logic elements. The extent to which this is publicized varies according to local markets. In Japan, fuzzy logic is seen as a positive selling point. Recently, this has also become true in Europe. However, in the United States, "fuzzy" appears to imply confused thinking and so often does not figure in sales literature, even though the product may be fundamentally the same in Japan, Europe, and the United States.

Unfortunately, gaining the ability to describe intermediate truth values also introduces a subjective element into the proceedings and weakens the certainty that we can give to a wholly Boolean logical process. In a few cases, we might be tempted into deviant ways—credit scoring is one example—but they are surprisingly rare. For the majority of cases, we can stick with standard logic and draw on the wealth of solid experience and powerful mechanisms that it provides.

A.1.3   A logical framework

As we observed earlier, the price to be paid for more than two thousand years of experience is a vocabulary that can seem a little dated. For example, some constructions are still known by their traditional Latin names. It's still handy to know about these in case you encounter them. We'll start by laying out a sketch of the main topics that are relevant to business rules.

One of the defining features of standard logic is that we're concerned only with two values: true and false. Everything that we consider must be one of these two values; there's nothing in between true and false: the *Principle,* sometimes *Law,* of *Excluded Middle.* As we've already noted, this corresponds closely to the software concept of a Boolean data type.

For business rules, we're going to be especially interested in what's called *deductive* logic, which is concerned with establishing a conclusion from a given set of facts in a way that we can be sure is logically correct. Another branch, *inductive* logic, is important in such applications as data mining. In a sense, these two branches run in opposite directions: Deduction applies general rules to particular facts to reach a result, whereas induction uses particular facts and results to infer the rules.

Figure A-1 shows a simplified high-level picture of the process we're interested in. From a given set of facts, or *premises,* we can use a logical *argument* to deduce new facts. The results, the *conclusion* of our argument, can be used directly or as premises for another argument. We can make things a little easier by assuming that both inputs and outputs—premises and conclusion—are in the form of statements representing *propositions.* A proposition is a tentative fact that will be either true or false but might be unknown at present if we haven't yet established its truth value.

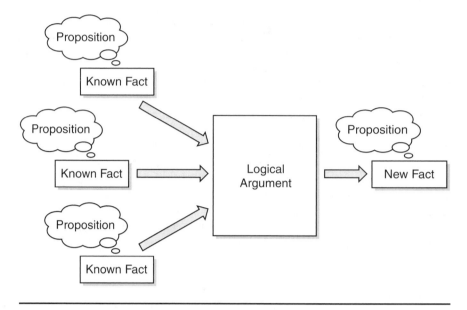

Figure A-1 Propositional logic

So far, this looks very similar to a function in a typical programming language, with the premises as the parameters, the argument as the body, and the conclusion as the result of the function. For simple cases, this is, indeed, a possible way of implementing the logic. However, we're after bigger fish. Manually programming the large number of functions needed for an e-commerce system is slow, expensive, error prone, and difficult to maintain. Instead, we want the system itself to be able to create the equivalent of these functions automatically from our descriptions of the business logic required.

This may seem an ambitious target, but it *is* achievable. To make it possible, we need to be meticulous about setting up the right kind of framework, but this is a small price to pay for the return that we get. To understand what's involved, we need to look at three main things. First, we must be able to make statements about our business in a consistent format that will simplify subsequent automation. To do this, we'll examine propositions in more detail because they are very close to the forms that we use in business rules. Second, we need to know how to combine propositions to reach conclusions. For this, we can draw on some standard logic mechanisms, with full confidence that their properties are well understood and 100 percent reliable. These first two objectives relate to the elements shown in Figure A-1. Finally, because we're dealing with Boolean quantities, it will be useful to know how to handle combinations of true and false values accurately and efficiently.

A.1.4   Forms and symbols

Because logic and mathematics are closely related, it should come as no surprise to find that logic makes use of *symbols* to stand for things that would otherwise be too cumbersome to write out in words. Although the appearance may be less familiar than standard arithmetic, symbolic notation in logic serves much the same purpose. We'll look at symbolic representations in more detail later in this appendix.

Symbolic logic is also said to be *formal,* in the sense that it lays down standard forms, or patterns, for many commonly occurring situations. In principle, this is no different from the use of formal parameters in a method call as used in an object-oriented programming language.

In mathematics, we also make use of symbols to stand for variables in a formula. When we use the formula to calculate a result, we replace the variables with the values that we're interested in. So it is with logic. Using the more clinical symbolic representation also has another advantage. It stops us from reading meaning into the values of the symbols and thereby coming to invalid conclusions. For example, take the following argument:

> All supervisors are on the payroll.
>
> No customers are supervisors.
>
> Therefore, no customers are on the payroll.

Although this sounds plausible, the conclusion is not valid from a logical standpoint. We'll see how to detect problems of this sort a little later.

A.2   Propositions

A.2.1   What's a proposition?

We normally use logic unconsciously. In other words, we do many things that could be described in a formal framework, but we usually don't bother. The exceptions are a few special situations in which the need for precision takes precedence over colloquial ease. Legal documentation is a good example. The wording may not be easy to read, but it is intended to convey a very precise meaning.

In everyday business, we often make loosely worded statements. We unconsciously do this knowing that the listener will make adjustments or fill in the gaps, probably without being aware that he or she is doing so. Unfortunately, if the listener is a computer, it's not able to use the same range of knowledge that human beings use to make these corrections. Instead, we must be consistent and accurate in the statements that we give to the computer so that they can be processed using only the information available to the system.

In logic, we're interested in statements that we can say are either true or false. This eliminates things like inquiries, commands, or exclamations. For example, the following statements can't really be said to be true or false, although in the case of a question, we might be able to phrase it in a way that would bring a true or false response:

> What's the weather like?
>
> Close the account!
>
> Good Golly Miss Molly!

The kind of statement we're after is what's called a *categorical proposition,* or simply proposition. A proposition has two main parts: the *subject* and the *predicate*. Both of these parts represent logically distinct *classes,* and the proposition makes an assertion about the relationship between the two classes. Not surprisingly, the classical approach to handling propositions is called *propositional logic*. It's worth noting that "subject" has a particular meaning in a proposition: It's not necessarily the same as the grammatical subject of a natural-language rendering of the sentence.

We've already come across classes: The term is used in object-oriented programming and in business modeling to indicate a collection of instances of the same kind. This also equates roughly to the heading of a table—the column definitions—in a relational database. For example, we could have a class called Customer, with individual customers represented by object instances or, equivalently, individual rows in a customer table.

However, there is a subtle difference with the way the word class is used in logic. The subject or predicate of a proposition might be a collection that is something less than a complete database table. For example, we might want to talk about customers with a current balance greater than $5,000, which would probably give us a collection that's smaller than the entire list of customers and would correspond to a subset of the rows in a customer table. We can also create collections that don't correspond to any particular object type, by operations such as a join across two tables. Another feature that's sometimes useful is the ability to distinguish between the properties of all instances of a class and the properties of the class itself, as with static methods and fields in Java. In the interests of clarity, we'll therefore depart from the classical terminology and use the word *collection* to indicate a group of objects with similar characteristics, whether or not this corresponds to a class in our business model or a table in our database.

To give a concrete example, let's look at the proposition:

> All supervisors are on the payroll.

If we want to be particularly dainty, we could restate this as:

> All individuals who are supervisors are individuals who are on the payroll.

The collection "individuals who are supervisors" is the subject, and the collection "individuals who are on the payroll" is the predicate of the proposition. This has the general form:

All S are P

where S and P are our two collections.

Obtaining either of the collections is a fairly straightforward operation. Assume that we have in our database an Individuals table that contains, among other things, an ID column with a unique identifier for each individual and Supervisor and Payroll columns, both of which can contain the values Yes or No. We can then find the collections for S and P with SQL statements like the following:

```
S = SELECT Individuals.id FROM Individuals WHERE
    ((Individuals.supervisor)=Yes);
P = SELECT Individuals.id FROM Individuals WHERE
    ((Individuals.payroll)=Yes);
```

So, what our proposition is asserting is that all of the ID values in S will be included among the ID values in P but not, you'll notice, the other way around.

A.2.2   Standard forms of proposition

Traditionally, it was held that all propositions could be put into one of four standard forms, perhaps after tinkering with the wording a little. These forms start with a *quantifier* that defines how much of the subject collection we're interested in—*none, some,* or *all*—followed by the subject, followed by a form of the verb *to be*—usually, *is* or *are* and perhaps accompanied by *not* if we want to deny a relationship—then finally the predicate. The four standard forms are shown in Table A-1. The types A, I, E, and O supposedly come from the Latin AffIrmo "I affirm" and nEgO "I deny." The *quantity—universal* or *particular*—indicates whether we're talking about the entire subject or a particular subset of it; the *quality—affirmative* or *negative*—indicates whether we're asserting or denying something.

Table A-1   Standard forms of proposition

Type	Form	Quantity	Quality
A	All S is P.	Universal	Affirmative
I	Some S is P.	Particular	Affirmative
E	No S is P.	Universal	Negative
O	Some S is not P.	Particular	Negative

We've already come across a use of quantifiers in UML, where associations have a multiplicity marking that might typically look like `1..*`. In logic, the quantifiers have particular interpretations that are quite important. *All* certainly includes all the instances in the S collection, if there are any. However, on its own, *all* does not imply that any instance of S actually exists; in other words, S could be an empty collection. If we know that S exists, we have to say so explicitly, if we want the logic to work correctly. On the other hand, *some* is taken to imply that there must be at least one instance of S, although it doesn't exclude the possibility of all instances. Equating this to UML, we could say that, roughly speaking:

All	is similar to	`0..*`	although it's not obvious that we take * to mean "every instance"
No	is similar to	`0`	which means that it's simply not shown on a UML diagram
Some	is similar to	`1..*`	although it's not obvious that we take * to mean "not necessarily every instance"

The UML-style notation is not used in logic, because there's a better, and clearer, way of saying what we mean, which we'll come to later.

A.2.3   Visualizing propositions

Keeping a clear mental picture of a proposition can be difficult, particularly if complicated wording is involved. A useful technique to show the characteristic pattern of a proposition is to draw it in the form of a *Venn diagram,* first introduced by nineteenth-century mathematician and logician John Venn.

We start with a rectangular frame that represents our *universe of discourse.* As far as we're concerned, that means everything that's relevant to our business model. Inside that, we represent collections that we're interested in by circles, with labels to indicate which collection we mean. Figure A-2 shows a collection called Supervisors. Everything inside the circle is a supervisor. Everything outside the circle is the logical *complement* of supervisor: everything that's not a supervisor, not only other kinds of individuals but potentially *anything* that's not a supervisor, which could include automobiles, Mount Everest, zebras, the Statue of Liberty, and so on.

On its own, a circle makes no statement about whether a supervisor or anything else exists. We can add some additional marking to indicate a statement we want to make about a collection. The convention we'll adopt here is to mark a collection with no instances—an *empty* collection—with Ø and a collection with at least one instance with X. Figure A-2 is therefore showing that

- There are such things as supervisors, and—because of the X—at least one of them exists.

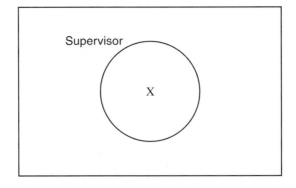

Figure A-2   Venn diagram with one class

- There may also be things that are nonsupervisors, but we're making no statement about whether any exist.

A word of warning about the logical complement. In the heat of the moment, it's easy to use a term that we instinctively feel is being an opposite but that is not really the complement. For example, the complement of *debtor* is not *creditor* but *nondebtor;* the complement of *high* is not *low* but *not high;* the complement of *winner* is not *loser* but *nonwinner.*

Things get more interesting when we have more than one collection. Figure A-3 shows the collections for "all individuals who are supervisors" and "all individuals who are on the payroll." By overlapping the two circles, we break the diagram into four regions corresponding to the four possible combinations of the two collections: supervisor/not a supervisor, on the payroll/not on the payroll.

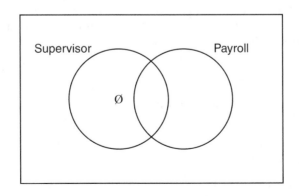

Figure A-3   Venn diagram with two classes

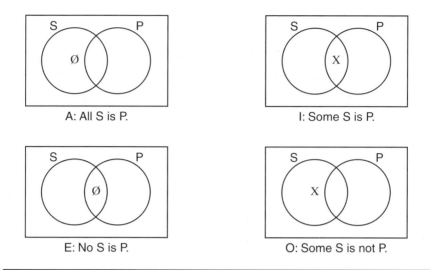

Figure A-4   Venn diagrams for the four standard propositional forms

Now by adding the markings Ø, for no instances, or X, for at least one instance, we can use the diagram to show a proposition. The particular marking in Figure A-3 shows what we mean by the proposition:

> All individuals who are supervisors are individuals who are on the payroll.

In other words, because we're stating that there aren't any supervisors except those on the payroll, we can mark that region of the diagram inside the "Supervisor" circle and outside the "Payroll" circle with Ø. We can produce diagrams for the four standard kinds of proposition in the same way, as shown in Figure A-4. The first of these is the same diagram as the one we produced for "supervisors on the payroll," which reveals it as being a proposition of type A.

A.2.4   Alternative forms of propositions

The standard forms of proposition give us a basic structure, but there are obviously more ways of making statements than just these four. It's useful to know about these other ways.

- It's often possible to make a statement in several ways. One way may seem preferable because it sounds more natural than the others. If we want to rephrase a statement, it's important to be sure that we're not adding to or subtracting from the original meaning.

- It's important to avoid duplication or contradiction in our business rules. At best, this leads to inefficiency; at worst, it can lead to business logic failures that will be very difficult to track down. Understanding the various forms that statements can take will help us to spot the same rule repeated with a different wording or rules that are making contradictory statements.

Rephrasing standard propositions can be done in standard ways without changing their meaning. We've already met one of these, in restating the first sentence with the second one:

> All supervisors are on the payroll.
> All individuals who are supervisors are individuals who are on the payroll.

We introduced "individuals" as an auxiliary term, or *parameter*. The objective here is to make the reference quite clear. We're not really interested in "the payroll" as an object; the proposition is really about the relationship between two collections of individuals. The underlying meaning is probably still understandable in the original statement, but some alternative ways of saying the same thing won't make sense unless the "individuals" parameter is introduced.

We look next at some standard operations to give us alternative forms. The examples given show how the propositions might be phrased in a relatively informal way, but even some of these need a parameter to read sensibly.

Converse   The *converse* is formed by interchanging the subject and predicate terms of a proposition. This operation is valid only for type E and type I propositions. Figure A-4 shows that these patterns are symmetrical for S and P, so swapping the labels makes no difference to the statement. Table A-2 summarizes the structure, using informally worded examples.

Table A-2   Converse of standard propositions

	Original		**Converse**	
Type	**Form**	**Example**	**Form**	**Example**
A	All S is P.	All supervisors are on the payroll.	—	—
I	Some S is P.	Some supervisors are on the payroll.	Some P is S.	Some individuals on the payroll are supervisors.
E	No S is P.	No supervisors are on the payroll.	No P is S.	No individuals on the payroll are supervisors.
O	Some S is not P.	Some supervisors are not on the payroll.	—	—

Obverse   Forming the *obverse* is also a fairly mechanical process. We change the qualifier from affirmative to negative or vice versa and replace the predicate by its complement. This time, the operation is valid for all types of propositions. The results are summarized in Table A-3.

Table A-3   Obverse of standard propositions

	Original		Obverse	
Type	**Form**	**Example**	**Form**	**Example**
A	All S is P.	All supervisors are on the payroll.	No S is non-P.	No supervisors are not on the payroll.
I	Some S is P.	Some supervisors are on the payroll.	Some S is not non-P.	Some supervisors are (not not) on the payroll.
E	No S is P.	No supervisors are on the payroll.	All S is non-P.	All supervisors are not on the payroll.
O	Some S is not P.	Some supervisors are not on the payroll.	Some S is non-P.	Some supervisors are not on the payroll.

Sometimes, following the process blindly produces some awkward wording. For example, we would probably take out the double negative in the obverse of the I proposition to leave it pretty much unchanged from its original form. In other cases, as in the O proposition, the natural wording of the obverse comes out the same.

Contrapositive   The *contrapositive* is, again, found by a fairly mechanical process (Table A-4). First, we find the obverse of the original proposition, then the converse of that, and then, finally the obverse of *that*! The result is to place the subject by the complement of the predicate and predicate by the complement of the subject. Because we know that we can find the converse for only two of the four forms, it's not surprising that the same applies to the contrapositive: only A- and O-type propositions have a valid contrapositive.

Table A-4   Contrapositive of standard propositions

	Original		Contrapositive	
Type	**Form**	**Example**	**Form**	**Example**
A	All S is P.	All supervisors are on the payroll.	All non-P is non-S.	All individuals not on the payroll are not supervisors.
I	Some S is P.	Some supervisors are on the payroll.	—	—

Type	Form	Example	Form	Example
E	No S is P.	No supervisors are on the payroll.	—	—
O	Some S is not P.	Some supervisors are not on the payroll.	Some non-P is non-S.	Some individuals not on the payroll are not supervisors.

A.3   Logical operations

So far, we've been concerned about how to make statements involving facts from our business model. One of the most powerful features of logic is its ability to derive new facts from information that we already have, even if the facts aren't explicitly stated. In this section, we look at how we can derive new facts from old ones.

A.3.1   Syllogisms

A *categorical syllogism,* or simply syllogism, has a standardized structure involving three categorical propositions. Two of the propositions state facts that we already know. The third proposition is something new that we can deduce from the first two propositions. All the propositions have the same structure that we've seen previously. If we represent subjects and predicates by letters of the alphabet, the skeleton of a syllogism might look something like the following:

We know	A–B.
And we know	B–C.
Therefore,	A–C.

The relationships A–B and B–C might be facts that are obvious, trivial even, and openly visible in our business model. But the relationship between A and C may be something that's not explicitly stored in our database. It's a new fact that we've derived by a logical process.

We're not limited to one step; we can carry this on for as long as we have the relevant information. This can build up chains:

We know	A–B.
And we know	B–C.
Therefore,	A–C.
We know	C–D.
Therefore,	A–D.
We know	D–E.
Therefore,	A–E.
We know	and so on

Fortunately, we need to consider only one step at a time, because each has the same structure.

Moods, figures, and frames   Any of the propositions in a categorical syllogism can be any of the standard forms (A, I, E, O), so we can indicate the pattern of propositions by concatenating the appropriate abbreviations. For example, AIO indicates initial propositions of the form A and I and a conclusion of the form O. This is known as the *mood* of the syllogism. Because each of the propositions can be one of four forms, we can have $4 \times 4 \times 4 = 64$ possible moods.

This is not quite enough to pin down a syllogism completely. The extra piece of information we need is the location of the *middle term:* the one that appears in both the original propositions but not in the conclusion. This can be arranged in four ways, called *figures*. Using S and P for the subject and predicate of the conclusion and M for the middle term gives us the four possible figures shown in Table A-5. So now we have to consider all the moods—64 of them—in each of the possible four figures, giving a total of $64 \times 4 = 256$ possible combinations, or *frames,* with a short-form label, such as AIO-2, indicating "the second figure of mood AIO."

Table A-5   The four syllogism figures

1	2	3	4
M–P	P–M	M–P	P–M
S–M	S–M	M–S	M–S
Therefore, S–P.	Therefore, S–P.	Therefore, S–P.	Therefore, S–P.

That's the bad news. The good news is that it's possible to show that most of the 256 combinations are not valid, although we won't go through every single one here. Even better, it doesn't matter what we're saying in S, P, and M! If we've been consistent in our use of terms, a mood/figure combination such as AIO-2 is either valid or it's not, regardless of the textual values that we've plugged in for S, P, and M. Looking ahead to the ways in which we might realize an e-commerce system in the future, we can imagine building standardized pieces of software that recognize logic patterns—arranged in the sorts of ways we've talked about—and generate required data, without piecemeal programming or manual intervention.

Checking validity   How can we check to see whether a syllogism is valid? One approach is to return to the Venn diagram. We need three partially overlapping circles, one each for the subject, predicate, and middle terms, which will divide the diagram into eight regions. Next, we mark the regions to correspond to the statements made by the premises. Finally, we check to see whether the resultant marking agrees with the conclusion. Figure A-5 shows the example we looked at earlier:

All supervisors are on the payroll.

x   <u>No customers are supervisors.</u>

Therefore, no customers are on the payroll.

The syllogism types for the premises are A and E, and the conclusion is also E. The middle term here is "supervisors," which is the first figure, making the structure of this syllogism AEE-1. Again, we can see a possible need to introduce a parameter; "customers" are also "individuals," but we'll stick with the informal statements for now.

When we put together the markings for these premises and compare the result to the conclusion, we can spot a problem, shown by ? in Figure A-5. For the conclusion to be true, this region would have to be marked as Ø, but nothing in the premises allows us to do this. We can therefore conclude that this argument is not valid. In fact, we can go further and say that any argument of the form AEE-1 will be invalid, regardless of the specific values plugged in for each of the terms.

It's worth restating the difference here between validity and truth. In saying that this argument is invalid, we are not saying that the conclusion is false. In fact, in this particular case, it's quite plausible that all the propositions are true. What we are saying is that it's not possible to use this argument to reach that conclusion. There may be another valid way of reaching the conclusion, but not this one!

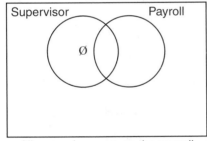
All supervisors are on the payroll.

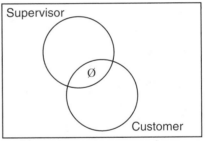
No customers are supervisors.

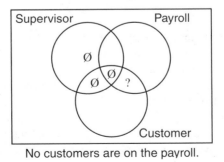
No customers are on the payroll.

Figure A-5   Checking a syllogism with Venn diagrams

Who are these people?   Several rules can be applied to identify the valid syllogisms out of the 256 possibilities. We won't go through all of them here but simply list the valid combinations (Table A-6). Just for interest, the names in the last column were derived by classical teachers of logic as mnemonics, to help their students remember the valid forms. The vowels identify the mood of the syllogism, and the consonants help to indicate possible operations on the syllogisms, which we won't go into here.

Table A-6   Valid forms of syllogisms

Figure	Valid forms	Name
1	AAA-1	Barbara
	AII-1	Darii
	EAE-1	Celarent
	EIO-1	Ferio
2	AEE-2	Camestres
	AOO-2	Baroco
	EAE-2	Cesare
	EIO-2	Festino
3	AII-3	Datisi
	IAI-3	Disamis
	EIO-3	Ferison
	OAO-3	Bocardo
4	AEE-4	Camenes
	IAI-4	Dimaris
	EIO-4	Fresison

Weakening some of the assumptions we made earlier can increase the number of valid syllogisms. For instance, we assumed that "All S . . ." did not necessarily mean the existence of an instance of S. If we allow it to mean that at least one instance of S exists, other forms, such as AEA-1, also become possible. However, we'll stick with the stronger assumptions and the list in Table A-6.

Enthymemes and the sorites   An *enthymeme* is an incompletely stated argument, with the missing component being "understood." An example might be:

Jones is a bad risk.
_____
Therefore, Jones should not be offered a loan.

This is a syllogism with a missing term—presumably, something like "Individuals who are a bad risk should not be offered a loan." Holes of this sort are very common in early attempts to create a set of business rules. The usual reason given is, "But everyone knows that!" Unfortunately, the poor old computer isn't able to share in this pool of common knowledge unless the facts are explicitly stated. Squeezing out such common assumptions, often unconsciously held, and making them explicit is one of the defining skills of a good business analyst.

This kind of thing is especially difficult to spot when it's embedded in a sequence of syllogisms. The special technical name for a chain of syllogisms with only the starting propositions and the conclusions—and lots of enthymemes along the way—is a *sorites*. In these situations, the analyst should play dumb—"Imagine that I'm just a computer"—and clinically check the basis for each argument: "How would I know that?"

Extended arguments of this sort can lead to the *sorites paradox,* also known as the "little-by-little" argument, or "salami-slicing." A commercial version of this might go along the following lines.

> We made a huge profit, so if we spend a dollar on expenses, it'll still be a huge profit.
>
> As that's still a huge profit, it wouldn't matter if we spend one more dollar.
>
> That's still a huge profit, so. . . .
>
> Ultimately, however much we spend on expenses, we still have a huge profit!

This situation can happen when a vaguely expressed quantity is involved: in this case, "huge profit." We might be tempted to use fuzzy logic to avoid the need for an absolute statement about hugeness. However, this is probably not much different from representing the quantity numerically instead of using Boolean variable to represent huge/not huge.

A.3.2   Other kinds of arguments

The arguments we've encountered so far have involved only simple propositions, such as "All S is P." Now we consider a couple of other useful argument forms involving slightly different kinds of propositions.

Transitivity   *Transitive* relationships arise when entities have a natural ordering. Numerical values and ancestor/descendant associations are examples of such ordering relationships. For example:

Brown has been a customer for longer than Jones.

Jones has been a customer for longer than Smith.

Therefore, Brown has been a customer for longer than Smith.

The general form is:

$$A \text{ rel } B$$
$$\underline{B \text{ rel } C}$$

Therefore, A rel C

where "rel" is the particular relationship involved. This obviously has to be used consistently in all the propositions and must be truly transitive for the entities involved. In particular, class membership is not transitive. An example that uses transitivity incorrectly might be:

Smith works for Acme Rulebusters.

x $\underline{\text{Acme Rulebusters works for the government.}}$

Therefore, Smith works for the government.

Disjunction   A *disjunction* has the characteristic form:

Either A or B

This seems deceptively simple, but many mistakes are made about disjunction. The crucial point is whether the disjunction allows something to be A *and* B. In English, the conventional interpretation is that "either A or B" means A or B or *both*. If we want to exclude the possibility of both A and B, we need to say explicitly "either A or B but not both." These two cases are sometimes known as *inclusive or* and *exclusive or,* respectively. Here's one classical world—Latin had different words for the two meanings of the English word 'or': *'vel'* for inclusive-or and *'aut'* for exclusive-or.

Disjunction allows us to have arguments like the following:

Shipping advice must be sent by post or e-mail.

$$\underline{\text{We can't use e-mail in this case.}}$$

Therefore, in this case, the shipping advice must be sent by post.

The characteristic form of a *disjunctive syllogism* looks something like:

A or B   (We know it's A or B or maybe both.)
$$\underline{\text{Not B}}\qquad\text{(It's not B.)}$$
Therefore, A   (So it must be A.)

Similarly, if the second term had been "Not A," then we could have deduced the result "B."

You need to avoid the trap of the following kind of invalid argument:

A or B   (We know it's A or B.)
x $\underline{\text{B}}\qquad\text{(It's B.)}$
Therefore, Not A   (So it can't be A.)

The reason this is wrong lies in the assumption of *inclusive or.* Knowing that B is true doesn't exclude the possibility that A also could be true.

Hypotheticals   Hypothetical or conditional statements express a specific dependency between two terms, so that, roughly speaking, if the first term is true, we can logically assume that the second must be true. For example:

> If interest rates rise, we must reduce our borrowings.

Hypothetical statements can be put into the general form:

> If A then B

The first term (A) is known as the *antecedent;* the second term (B), as the *consequent.* Because we can say that A implies B, this kind of statement is also known as *implication.* Hypothetical statements may be arranged in a more natural-sounding way rather than this exact pattern. For instance, the word *then* is sometimes assumed, as in the preceding example.

We're interested here in hypothetical arguments, in which consequents follow *logically* from their antecedents. However, this form of words is commonly used in other ways. Here are some examples of the "if-then" form that don't express a logical relationship.

If A is a debtor, then A must owe us money.	(From standard definition of "debtor")
If I don't get a bonus, then I'm going to resign.	(Choose to behave in a particular way)
If we lose power, then the supply voltage will be zero.	(Natural cause and effect)

Pinning down the exact logical definition of a hypothetical statement is a little tricky. What we want to know is the truth value for the statement as a whole as the truth values for A and B vary.

If A is true, things fall in pretty much with common sense. The statement is true if B is true and false if B is false.

What if A is false? The statement doesn't seem to give much of a clue about the effect of B; in fact, it doesn't matter whether B is true or false, as the result is the same. The convention adopted is that if A is false, the whole statement is true, regardless of the value of B. This is much more difficult to stack up against common sense. For example:

> If interest rates rise, we must reduce our borrowings.

If interest rates are not rising, this statement is true, whatever we do about our borrowings. To be extra clear: In this situation, it's the *complete* statement that's true.

We are *not* saying that "we must reduce our borrowings" is true; whether it's true or false makes no difference to the statement as a whole if interest rates are not rising.

We'll return to the possible truth values of implication in the next section because it's easier to see the structure of implication when it's in symbolic form. First we'll look at some arguments that we can construct by using hypothetical statements. These arguments are quite powerful, so it's well worth persevering with implication even though it may not seem entirely intuitive.

A *pure hypothetical syllogism* has hypothetical statements as both premises and conclusions. For example:

> If customer defaults payment, then no credit facility is allowed.
>
> If no credit facility is allowed, then immediate shipment is not possible.
> _____
>
> Therefore, If customer defaults payment, then immediate shipment is not possible.

This is like the *transitive* argument we saw earlier. The general form is:

> If A then B.
>
> If B then C.
> _____
>
> Therefore, if A then C.

A *mixed hypothetical syllogism* has a hypothetical statement as one premise and categorical statements for the other premise and the conclusion. Two modes can be used. In the first, usually known as *modus* (mode) *ponens* (to affirm), the categorical premise states that the antecedent of the hypothetical is true. Here's an example:

> If credit check has failed, then order is not fulfilled.
>
> Credit check has failed.
> _____
>
> Therefore, order is not fulfilled.

The general form is:

> If A. then B.
>
> A.
> _____
>
> Therefore, B.

In the other variant, *modus* (mode) *tollens* (to deny), the categorical premise states that the consequent of the hypothetical is false. The general form is:

> If A then B.
>
> Not B.
> _____
>
> Therefore, Not A.

Using the same hypothetical as before, we therefore get:

> If credit check has failed, then order is not fulfilled.
>
> _____ Order is fulfilled. _____
>
> Therefore, credit check has not failed.

Note that the wording of the second premise has been massaged slightly from "Not (order is not fulfilled)" to give a more natural reading.

Given the slippery nature of implication, it's maybe not surprising that mistakes are often made with hypotheticals. These common errors in reasoning, known as _fallacies,_ are so well known that they've been given their own names. One is the Fallacy of Affirming the Consequent. An example might be:

> If credit check has failed, then order is not fulfilled.
>
> x _____ Order is not fulfilled. _____
>
> Therefore, credit check has failed.

This is _not_ valid; check with the preceding patterns to see why. This is an erroneous version of _modus ponens;_ the mistake is to assume that the antecedent is the only reason why the consequent could be true. A failed credit check isn't the only reason why an order might not be fulfilled: There could be many other reasons, such as lack of stock, no shipping address, and so on.

Of course, there's also a mistaken version of _modus tollens,_ known as the Fallacy of Denying the Antecedent, which looks like this:

> If credit check has failed, then order is not fulfilled.
>
> x _____ Credit check has not failed. _____
>
> Therefore, order is fulfilled.

A.4   Handling logical values

A.4.1   Nothing but the truth

So far, we've dealt with individual statements that are relatively simple, with each one having a corresponding Boolean value that can be used in a logical argument. However, any of these statements could, in principle, be replaced by an arbitrarily complex combination of Boolean values. Ultimately, these values will reduce to a single true/false result, but it will be more difficult to see the result than in the simple one-to-one examples we've looked at so far.

We can think of complex statements as being equivalent to a logic function, with a number of input values and a single output value. If the function is particularly tricky, we might also want to examine some intermediate values that can be used to build up the result. This idea is summarized in Figure A-6, which not surprisingly, is quite close to the scheme outlined in Figure A-1. But here, we're trying to reduce the process to a mechanical operation that simply works on the truth value of each variable. To make this practical, we need to abstract away from the statements that we saw earlier and to consider only sets of symbols. Doing so has a number of advantages:

- The inherent structure of the logic is more visible, and it becomes easier to spot standard patterns.

- Complex expressions can be written down in a much more compact way.

- We're looking at the logic in a way that's closer to what the computer will "see," avoiding the distractions of meanings attached to words in a statement.

How do we get to this clinical world, in which only truth values exist, when the real information we handle is made up of text strings, currency amounts, dates, and other nonlogical quantities? The trick is to carry out a test on the real-world value that will deliver a Boolean result. The type of test depends on the kind of value involved. Table A-7 gives some examples.

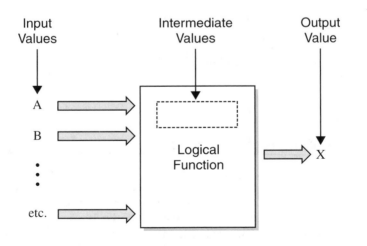

Figure A-6   Arbitrary logical functions

Table A-7   Converting arbitrary values to Booleans

Value type	Typical Tests
Numeric	Greater than, less than, equal, not equal
Date; currency	Use numeric tests but with caution
Enumerated	Equal, not equal
Text string	Equal, not equal, included in
Object	Exists (or not), member-of-collection (or not)

Here, we'll simply assume that such tests can be carried out correctly, although their realization may require some attention to detail. For example, tests on floating-point values need to take possible rounding errors into account.

A.4.2   Combining logical values

Now we can focus exclusively on Boolean values, using such symbols as A and B to represent items of interest. These symbols could stand for any statement that could have a value of true or false. For example:

A = "the account has been opened."

B = "the balance of the account is greater than zero."

We can indicate the value of the statement by using the symbol. So, in this case, "A is true," or just A, can be taken to mean "the account has been opened"; "A is false," or just Not A, to mean "the account has not been opened."

It's important to remember that "true" and "false," too, are symbols. All this would be just as valid if it were to be in a language other than English or if we used another pair of symbols, such as yes and no or T and F. For instance, hardware designers commonly use the binary digits 1 and 0.

Common sense tells us such things as "the balance of an account can't be greater than zero if it's not even been opened." So we can't have a case in which A is false and B is true. Written as an equation, this looks like:

(Not A) And B = False

But what about other possible combinations of A and B? How many combinations could there be? We need a systematic way to write them all down.

Truth tables   A simple but very effective tool to analyze complex functions is the truth table, which is usually arranged with a column for each term that we're interested in. Typically, this table has the input values on the left, intermediate values in the middle, and the final output value on the right. The rows of the table contain a systematic listing of all possible combinations of input values. For our two input values, the truth table would look something like Table A-8. Here, we're using T and F for our truth values to make the table more compact. The question is, What are the possible values for the output value, X? In fact, the column for X could be filled in several ways, depending on the logical function relating A and B.

Table A-8 Truth table layout

A	B	X
T	T	?
T	F	?
F	T	?
F	F	?

Negation Negation produces the opposite logical value, the *complement*, so T becomes F and vice versa. This leads to a very simple truth table (Table A-9).

Table A-9 Truth table for negation

A	X
T	F
F	T

Negation is sometimes indicated by a symbol rather than text, so that you might find

$$X = \text{Not } A$$

written as any of the following:

$$X = {\sim}A$$
$$X = \neg A$$
$$X = \bar{A}$$
$$X = A'$$

Of course, double negation leads us back to the original value, so

$$\text{Not (Not } A) = A$$

Conjunction   Things get more interesting when we consider functions that genuinely depend on more than one variable. The first of these functions is conjunction, which produces a value of true when all its inputs are true; otherwise, false. We'll consider two inputs: A and B. Because its value is true only when both A *and* B are true, it's better known as the And function. The truth table is shown in Table A-10.

Table A-10   Truth table for conjunction

A	B	X
T	T	T
T	F	F
F	T	F
F	F	F

Conjunction is also sometimes indicated symbolically, so that you might find

X = A And B

written as any of the following:

X = A & B

X = A • B

X = A ∧ B

A variant of this is a combination of conjunction and negation, which gives a "Not And" function. This is an important building block in digital electronics, in which the name of the function is usually abbreviated to "Nand."

Disjunction   The second important multi-input function is disjunction, which produces a value of true when at least one of its inputs is true; otherwise, false. Because its value is true only when either of A *or* B is true, it's better known as the Or function. As we saw earlier, the standard assumption is to take this to mean *inclusive or*. The truth table is shown in Table A-11.

Table A-11   Truth table for disjunction

A	B	X
T	T	T
T	F	T
F	T	T
F	F	F

Just as with the And/Nand pair, a negated version corresponds to "Not Or." Again, this is a useful electronic building block and is usually referred to by the abbreviated form "Nor."

Again, symbolically:

X = A Or B

might be written as any of the following:

X = A / B

X = A + B

X = A ∨ B

The "wedge" symbol in the last of these variants is supposed to resemble the letter *v*, the start of the Latin word *vel* (inclusive or).

Equivalence   The equivalence function is true when both inputs have the same value. The truth table is shown in Table A-12.

Table A-12   Truth table for equivalence

A	B	X
T	T	T
T	F	F
F	T	F
F	F	T

This is written symbolically as:

X = A ≡ B

Exclusive or   Because it specifically excludes the case in which both input values are true, "exclusive or" needs to be treated separately from the standard meaning of disjunction. The truth table is shown in Table A-13.

Table A-13   Truth table for exclusive or

A	B	X
T	T	F
T	F	T
F	T	T
F	F	F

This function is sometimes known as "Xor" for short. Interestingly, this function is the complement of the equivalence function. There's no commonly used symbol, but we can use this correspondence with equivalence to write "exclusive or" as:

$$X = \overline{A \equiv B}$$

Implication   We've already seen that implication is less easy to pin down with an everyday meaning. Table A-14 gives the truth table.

Table A-14   Truth table for implication

A	B	X
T	T	T
T	F	F
F	T	T
F	F	T

Unlike the other functions, this one is not symmetrical; changing the order of A and B changes the meaning. The function is indicated by a nonsymmetrical symbol, usually one of:

$$X = A \supset B$$

$$X = A \rightarrow B$$

The sense of it is easier to see from the truth table. What is valid if A is true? This limits us to the first two rows of the table. However, the second row is false, so the only valid inference in this case is the first row; therefore, B must be true. What if we know that B is false? This time, we have to use the second and fourth rows, but because the second row is false, we know that in this case, we have to use the fourth row. Therefore, A must be false. The other cases—if we know that A is false or that B is true—don't allow us to make any judgment about the unknown value.

A.4.3   How many functions?

It's easy to show that we've now considered all the functions needed for two variables. The four rows in the truth table correspond to the four possible combinations of the input values. The output value for the first row could either be T or F, so that cell of the table can be filled in two possible ways. Similarly, each of the other three cells could be filled in exactly two ways. The total number of possible combinations is therefore:

$$2 \times 2 \times 2 \times 2 = 16$$

We can list out all these 16 possible values. Table A-15 is built up by mechanically entering all the possible T/F combinations, so there's no significance to the order in which the functions appear or the numbers that they've been given.

Table A-15   Possible logic functions for two variables

A	B	X_1	X_2	X_3	X_4	X_5	X_6	X_7	X_8	X_9	X_{10}	X_{11}	X_{12}	X_{13}	X_{14}	X_{15}	X_{16}
T	T	T	T	T	T	T	T	T	T	F	F	F	F	F	F	F	F
T	F	T	T	T	T	F	F	F	F	T	T	T	T	F	F	F	F
F	T	T	T	F	F	T	T	F	F	T	T	F	F	T	T	F	F
F	F	T	F	T	F	T	F	T	F	T	F	T	F	T	F	T	F

To see the meaning of each of these functions, we can call on our old friend the Venn diagram. Figure A-7 shows each of the 16 possibilities. As usual, two overlapping circles on each diagram represent the two variables, A and B. The shaded areas represent regions where each function is true; the nonshaded regions, where it is false.

As Figure A-7 shows, there are exactly 16 ways of shading the combinations of the four regions on each Venn diagram, corresponding to the 16 possible functions. Obviously, we've now covered all the basic functions: those that have particular names. Next, we need to think about how to tackle arbitrary and nameless combinations of logical values.

Handling more complex equations   We must be able to cope with more than two variables and with functions that have any possible combination of true and false values. The preceding standard functions appear frequently and often come into play. However, they are, in a sense, overkill. We can define *any* logical function by using just one of the basic forms, which can be either the *Nand* function or the *Nor* function.

To show this, we can use some neat definitions pointed out by Augustus De Morgan, another nineteenth-century logician. Usually known as *De Morgan's theorems,* they can be stated in a combined way as:

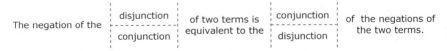

In symbolic form, this looks like the following, as can easily be verified by using truth tables:

$$\overline{A + B} = \overline{A} \cdot \overline{B}$$

$$\overline{A \cdot B} = \overline{A} + \overline{B}$$

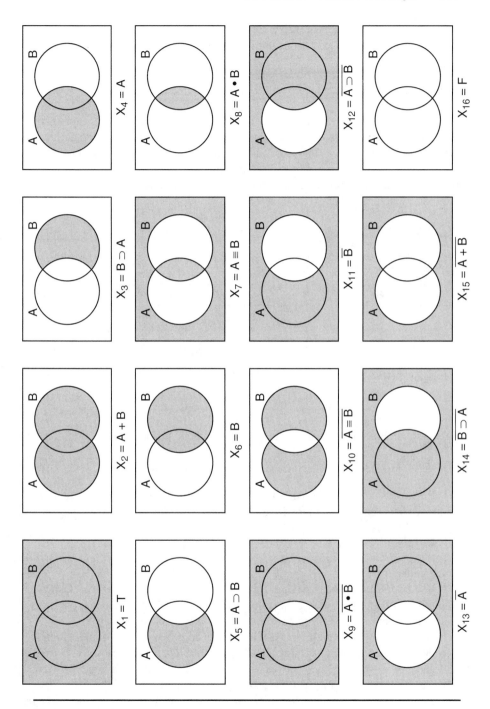

Figure A-7   Venn diagrams for all functions of two variables

As an illustration of this, we'll show how to define *implication* in terms of the *Nor* function alone. To start with, *implication* can be broken down into *Not* and *And* functions:

$$A \supset B = \overline{A \cdot \overline{B}}$$

This is straightforward to show with a truth table. This time, we have some intermediate columns to help build up the values (Table A-16). The last two columns are the same, which shows that the initial breakdown was correct. The penultimate column is a conjunction, but from De Morgan's theorem, we can change this by negating the whole expression, changing conjunction to disjunction, and negating the individual terms, that is:

$$\overline{A \cdot \overline{B}} = \overline{A} + B$$

Table A-16   Breakdown of implication function

A	B	$\overline{B}$	$A \cdot \overline{B}$	$\overline{A \cdot \overline{B}}$	$A \supset B$
T	T	F	F	T	T
T	F	T	T	F	F
F	T	F	F	T	T
F	F	T	F	T	T

Taking the double negation of a value does not change it, so:

$$\overline{A} + B = \overline{\overline{\overline{A} + B}}$$

Because a *Nor* function with a single input simply gives the complement of its input, this is equivalent to the following, using functional notation:

Nor (Nor ((Nor A), B))

Try it with a truth table!

Used a lot in hardware design, this kind of process can be used in business rules to find better and simpler ways of expressing a knotty piece of logic or to check that a set of rule statements really means what it appears to say.

Another useful technique in handling more complex logical relationships is to reduce them to standard patterns, known as *canonical forms*. These use combinations only of *And, Or,* and *Not* functions to express any required logic function. For example, the truth table in Table A-17 has three input values.

There are two variants. The first is an *Or* combination of *And* functions of each input value or its complement. Each of the *And* terms is known as a *minterm*.

Because of its appearance, it's sometimes known as the *sum-of-the-products* form. In this form, the arbitrary function shown in Table A-17 would look like:

$$X = (A \bullet \bar{B} \bullet C) + (A \bullet \bar{B} \bullet \bar{C}) + (\bar{A} \bullet B \bullet C) + (\bar{A} \bullet B \bullet \bar{C})$$

Table A-17   Arbitrary logic function

A	B	C	X
T	T	T	F
T	T	F	F
T	F	T	T
T	F	F	T
F	T	T	T
F	T	F	T
F	F	T	F
F	F	F	F

The second variant is an *And* combination of *Or* functions of each input value or its complement. Each of the *Or* terms is known as a *maxterm*. Because of its appearance, it's sometimes known as the *product-of-the-sums* form. For the example, shown in Table A-17, this would look like:

$$X = (\bar{A} + \bar{B} + \bar{C}) \bullet (\bar{A} + \bar{B} + C) \bullet (A + B + \bar{C}) \bullet (A + B + C)$$

We won't go through the details here. (*Hint:* Write down the minterms, where X is *false,* to get an expression for *Not X;* invert both sides of the equation, and then use De Morgans theorem twice: once on the whole expression and then on each of the minterms.)

The big advantage of using canonical forms is the simplicity of creating an algebraic representation of a function from a scattering of known truth values. It's extremely easy to automate the creation of a canonical expression for a truth table, so this is a good first step in a brute-force approach. As we'll see shortly, it's a crude but effective way to express a function, but being crude may not necessarily matter, as long as we have an expression that we know is accurate. You've probably seen enough by now to realize that the reduction of a logic expression to a more elegant form is also something that can be automated.

An idea similar to the *sum-of-the-products* form is used in many rule-based expert systems as an organizing principle. In these systems, each rule is an *And* combination of selected variables or their complements, although the rules don't attempt to include every term or its complement. All the rules operate, conceptually, in parallel, with each adding its separate contribution to the result, effectively producing an *Or* combination. You may find this approach useful if you have to deal with a complex piece of logic that can be described only by multiple interlocking rules.

The final technique we'll look at in this appendix helps to find the best way of expressing arbitrary logic functions. Known as the Karnaugh (pronounced car-no) Map, this is a bit like a truth table arranged in a grid, where the values of the input variables identify a position in the grid. The number of cells in the grid is the same as the total number of possible values of the function, which will be 2^n for n inputs. The grid is arranged to be as square as possible; it can't be square if n is odd. The vertical and horizontal edges of the grid are labeled with the equivalent input values in such a way that only one changes from T to F or vice versa when moving to the next row or column.

An example shows this more clearly. Figure A-8 shows an empty map for a function of three variables: A, B, and C. The cell marked with a query corresponds to the combination:

$$\bar{A}\ B\ \bar{C}$$

The map wraps around, so the top edge is adjacent to the bottom and the right edge adjacent to the left. To show a function, the map is filled with the true values in the appropriate positions. Figure A-9 shows what the arbitrary function in Table A-17 looks like as a Karnaugh Map.

Now it's easier to see that *true* values can fall in blocks. Depending on the function, you may be able to find blocks of 2, 4, 8 or more cells, up to 2^{n-1}. These blocks can be used to identify the most economical expression for the function. The basic idea is to find the largest blocks possible, define an expression for each block—easy to read off from the axis labeling—and then use *Or* on these terms.

A few simple rules need to be followed in assigning blocks.

- Blocks of T values must be square or rectangular, not diagonal.
- All T values must fall within at least one block.

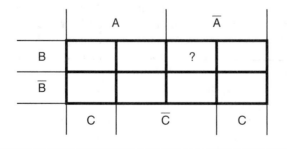

Figure A-8   Empty Karnaugh Map for three variables

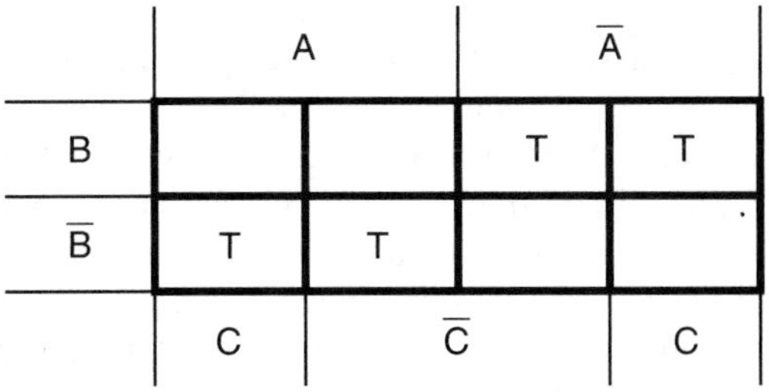

	A		Ā	
B			T	T
B̄	T	T		
	C	C̄	C	

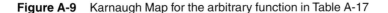

Figure A-9   Karnaugh Map for the arbitrary function in Table A-17

- A block may not contain any F value.
- Blocks can overlap.

Figure A-10 shows a grouping for the preceding example.

Looking at the values associated with each block, we see that they are:

Ā • B (upper right)

A • B̄ (upper left)

A minimal expression for this function is therefore:

$$X = (\bar{A} \bullet B) + (A \bullet \bar{B})$$

What the Karnaugh Map clearly shows in this case is that although we have three input values, *A, B,* and *C,* one of these values (*C*) has no impact on the result. Comparing this with the canonical form representation, which blindly includes *C* and its complement, it's obvious that the Karnaugh Map gives us a better insight. However, it requires eyeballing a graphic representation: something that computers are less good at.

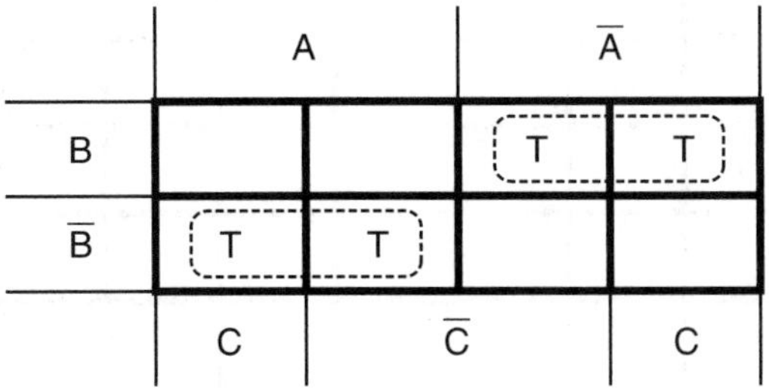

	A		Ā	
B			T	T
B̄	T	T		
	C	C̄	C	

Figure A-10   Minimization in the Karnaugh Map

The Karnaugh Map has some plus and minus points. If we have a logic expression for which we know that some values must be true, some must be false, but others can be either, we can include "don't care" in the map, using another symbol, such as ?, in the related cell. We then have an extra rule, which allows us to include a "don't care" value if it helps us to make bigger blocks but to ignore it otherwise.

On the other hand, the size of the map increases rapidly with the number of variables. Karnaugh Maps aren't feasible above about six variables, involving a map with $2^6 = 64$ cells. Figure A-11 shows an example of a blank map for six variables, denoted A to F. This is not as bad as it may sound. It's very unlikely that you will need a business rule statement involving this many variables. If you do, it's a warning sign that your statements are way too complex, and you're getting into an area that can't be realized by a few simple rules.

In summary, then, you're likely to find the Karnaugh Map most useful in the analysis stage, when you're trying to think through a piece of logic involving two to four variables. Just sketching out a map for the statements you're trying to set down can illuminate possible holes in a specification. More complex situations are best left to the machine.

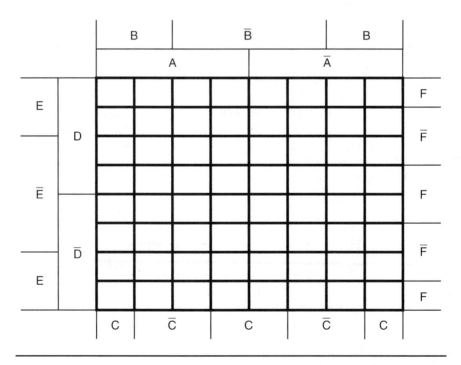

Figure A-11   Empty Karnaugh Map for six variables

A.5   Final words

Lets stop and take stock. We've now found new ways to use information from our business: automatically and with 100 percent accuracy. All we have to do is to take a little care about how we make statements, and the rest is for free! We haven't plumbed the full extent of logic by any means, but it should already be clear that building this kind of stuff into our information systems could give us some pretty powerful capabilities.

If you want to get into logic further, you need to move into what's known as *predicate logic* and on to the *predicate calculus*. The main reason that these additional topics aren't covered in this book is that they are less appropriate for the early analysis stages, which is where we've put most emphasis. Once you can be sure that your business descriptions are in good logical shape, you can use these more powerful mechanisms to gain even more value from your investment, but that's starting to move beyond the scope of this book.

Some of the terminology surrounding logic may seem a little archaic, but that's only because it's just as true today as it has been for hundreds of years. You don't need to remember all the specialized terms that are involved, although that can be useful sometimes. It's more important to appreciate that there's a large body of understanding of the right and wrong ways to combine knowledge about the world.

What's more, this same set of principles underlies the most basic operations of digital computers. It's therefore not surprising that it's fairly straightforward to implement the logic itself. The difficult part is understanding how to describe a sometimes chaotic world with sufficient clarity and precision.

Although we've only skimmed the surface of logic, a few facts are probably already clear.

- Manipulating logic values can be reduced to a fairly mindless mechanical process.
- Machines are better at doing this than people are.
- It all depends on how well we can state the logical relationships for our business. Everything else can be reduced to machinery.

At the start of the book, we laid out a vision of a development process that could be increasingly automated, ultimately to the point of generating a complete information system from a set of models. Ideally, you now have a better understanding of why business rules might have a crucial part to play in this evolution by providing the vital link between the two different worlds of human statements and machine logic.

Selected Bibliography

The literature on business rules has been growing rapidly over the past few years, making an exhaustive bibliography something of a moving target. The entries listed here include both the direct references made in the text and also a selection of other works relevant to the concerns of the book. For additional references, check the Addison-Wesley Web site at www.aw.com/cseng.

Alexander C. (1977) *A Pattern Language: Towns/Buildings/Construction,* Oxford University Press.

Allen P. (2001) *Realizing eBusiness with Components,* Addison-Wesley.

Barr A. and Feigenbaum E.A. (eds) (1981) *The Handbook of Artificial Intelligence,* Vol 1, W. Kaufman.

Booch G., Rumbaugh J. and Jacobsen I. (1999) *The Unified Modeling Language User Guide,* Addison-Wesley.

Britcher R.N. (1999) *The Limits of Software: People, Projects, and Perspectives,* Addison-Wesley.

Buschmann F., *et al.* (1996) *Pattern-Oriented Software Architecture: A System of Patterns,* John Wiley & Sons.

Date C.J. (2000) *What Not How: The Business Rules Approach to Application Development,* Addison-Wesley.

Engelmore R.S. and Morgan A.J. (eds). (1988) *Blackboard Systems,* Addison-Wesley.

Eriksson H-E. and Penker M. (2000) *Business Modeling with UML: Business Patterns at Work,* John Wiley & Sons.

Forgy C.S (1982) RETE: a fast algorithm for the many pattern/many object pattern match problem. *Artificial Intelligence* **19**, 17–37.

Fowler M. (1997) *Analysis Patterns: Reusable Object Models,* Addison-Wesley.

Gamma E., *et al.* (1995) *Design Patterns: Elements of Reusable Object-Oriented Software,* Addison-Wesley.

Haack S. (1996) *Deviant Logic, Fuzzy Logic: Beyond the Formalism,* University of Chicago Press.

Hamming R.W. (1962) *Numerical Methods for Scientists and Engineers,* McGraw-Hill.

Herbst H. (1997) *Business Rule Oriented Conceptual Modeling,* Physica-Verlag.

Lenat D.B. and Guha R.V. (1990) *Building Large Knowledge-Based Systems: Representation and Inference in the Cyc Project,* Addison-Wesley.

Presley E. (1970) *Elvis: That's the Way It Is,* Directed by Denis Sanders. 92 min. Turner Entertainment Co., Digital Video Disc.

Ross R.G. (1997) *The Business Rule Book: Classifying, Defining and Modeling Rules* (2nd edition), Database Research Group Inc.

Ross R.G. (1998) *Business Rule Concepts: The New Mechanics of Business Information Systems,* Business Rule Solutions Inc.

Schank R.C. and Abelson R.P. (1977) *Scripts Plans Goals and Understanding,* Lawrence Erlbaum.

Schank R.C. (1982) *Dynamic Memory: A Theory of Learning in Computers and People,* Cambridge University Press.

Strassman P.A. (1999) *Information Productivity,* The Information Economics Press.

von Halle B. (2001) *Business Rules Applied,* John Wiley & Sons.

Warmer J.B. and Kleppe A.G. (1999) *The Object Constraint Language: Precise Modeling with UML,* Addison-Wesley.

Zachman J.A. (1987) A framework for information systems architecture. *IBM Systems Journal,* Vol. 26, no. 3, pp. 276–292.

Index